Germany and the Next V
By Friedrich von Bernhardı

1912

All the patriotic sections of the German people were greatly excited during the summer and autumn of 1911. The conviction lay heavy on all hearts that in the settlement of the Morocco dispute no mere commercial or colonial question of minor importance was being discussed, but that the honour and future of the German nation were at stake. A deep rift had opened between the feeling of the nation and the diplomatic action of the Government. Public opinion, which was clearly in favour of asserting ourselves, did not understand the dangers of our political position, and the sacrifices which a boldly-outlined policy would have demanded. I cannot say whether the nation, which undoubtedly in an overwhelming majority would have gladly obeyed the call to arms, would have been equally ready to bear permanent and heavy burdens of taxation. Haggling about war contributions is as pronounced a characteristic of the German Reichstag in modern Berlin as it was in medieval Regensburg. These conditions have induced me to publish now the following pages, which were partly written some time ago.

Nobody can fail to see that we have reached a crisis in our national and political development. At such times it is necessary to be absolutely clear on three points: the goals to be aimed at, the difficulties to be surmounted, and the sacrifices to be made.

The task I have set myself is to discuss these matters, stripped of all diplomatic disguise, as clearly and convincingly as possible. It is obvious that this can only be done by taking a national point of view.

Our science, our literature, and the warlike achievements of our past, have made me proudly conscious of belonging to a great civilized nation which, in spite of all the weakness and mistakes of bygone days, must, and assuredly will, win a glorious future; and it is out of the fulness of my German heart that I have recorded my convictions. I believe that thus I shall most effectually rouse the national feeling in my readers' hearts, and strengthen the national purpose.
THE AUTHOR.
October, 1911

GERMANY AND THE NEXT WAR

INTRODUCTION

The value of war for the political and moral development of mankind has been criticized by large sections of the modern civilized world in a way which threatens to weaken the defensive powers of States by undermining the warlike spirit of the people. Such ideas are widely disseminated in Germany, and whole strata of our nation seem to have lost that ideal enthusiasm which constituted the greatness of its history. With the increase of wealth they live for the moment, they are incapable of sacrificing the enjoyment of the hour to the service of great conceptions, and close their eyes complacently to the duties of our future and to the pressing problems of international life which await a solution at the present time.

We have been capable of soaring upwards. Mighty deeds raised Germany from political disruption and feebleness to the forefront of European nations. But we do not seem willing to take up this inheritance, and to advance along the path of development in politics and culture. We tremble at our own greatness, and shirk the sacrifices it demands from us. Yet we do not wish to renounce the claim which we derive from our glorious past. How rightly Fichte once judged his countrymen when he said the German can never wish for a thing by itself; he must always wish for its contrary also.

The Germans were formerly the best fighting men and the most warlike nation of Europe. For a long time they have proved themselves to be the ruling people of the Continent by the power of their arms and the loftiness of their ideas. Germans have bled and conquered on countless battlefields in every part of the world, and in late years have shown that the heroism of their ancestors still lives in the descendants. In striking contrast to this military aptitude they have to-day become a peace-loving—an almost "too" peace-loving—nation. A rude shock is needed to awaken their warlike instincts, and compel them to show their military strength.

This strongly-marked love of peace is due to various causes.

It springs first from the good-natured character of the German people, which finds intense satisfaction in doctrinaire disputations and partisanship, but dislikes pushing things to an extreme. It is connected with another characteristic of the German nature. Our aim is to be just, and we strangely imagine that all other nations with whom we exchange relations share this aim. We are always ready to consider the peaceful assurances of foreign diplomacy and of the foreign Press to be no less genuine and true than our own ideas of peace, and we obstinately resist the view that the political world is only ruled by interests and never from ideal aims of philanthropy. "Justice," Goethe says aptly, "is a quality and a phantom of the Germans." We are always inclined to assume that disputes between States can find a peaceful solution on the basis of justice without clearly realizing what international justice is.

An additional cause of the love of peace, besides those which are rooted in the very soul of the German people, is the wish not to be disturbed in commercial life.

The Germans are born business men, more than any others in the world. Even before the beginning of the Thirty Years' War, Germany was perhaps the greatest trading Power in the world, and in the last forty years Germany's trade has made marvellous progress under the renewed expansion of her political power. Notwithstanding our small stretch of coast-line, we have created in a few years the second largest merchant fleet in the world, and our young industries challenge competition with all the great industrial States of the earth. German trading-houses are established all over the world; German merchants traverse every quarter of the globe;

a part, indeed, of English wholesale trade is in the hands of Germans, who are, of course, mostly lost to their own country. Under these conditions our national wealth has increased with rapid strides.

Our trade and our industries—owners no less than employés—do not want this development to be interrupted. They believe that peace is the essential condition of commerce. They assume that free competition will be conceded to us, and do not reflect that our victorious wars have never disturbed our business life, and that the political power regained by war rendered possible the vast progress of our trade and commerce.

Universal military service, too, contributes to the love of peace, for war in these days does not merely affect, as formerly, definite limited circles, but the whole nation suffers alike. All families and all classes have to pay the same toll of human lives. Finally comes the effect of that universal conception of peace so characteristic of the times—the idea that war in itself is a sign of barbarism unworthy of an aspiring people, and that the finest blossoms of culture can only unfold in peace.

Under the many-sided influence of such views and aspirations, we seem entirely to have forgotten the teaching which once the old German Empire received with "astonishment and indignation" from Frederick the Great, that "the rights of States can only be asserted by the living power"; that what was won in war can only be kept by war; and that we Germans, cramped as we are by political and geographical conditions, require the greatest efforts to hold and to increase what we have won. We regard our warlike preparations as an almost insupportable burden, which it is the special duty of the German Reichstag to lighten so far as possible. We seem to have forgotten that the conscious increase of our armament is not an inevitable evil, but the most necessary precondition of our national health, and the only guarantee of our international prestige. We are accustomed to regard war as a curse, and refuse to recognize it as the greatest factor in the furtherance of culture and power.

Besides this clamorous need of peace, and in spite of its continued justification, other movements, wishes, and efforts, inarticulate and often unconscious, live in the depths of the soul of the German people. The agelong dream of the German nation was realized in the political union of the greater part of the German races and in the founding of the German Empire. Since then there lives in the hearts of all (I would not exclude even the supporters of the anti-national party) a proud consciousness of strength, of regained national unity, and of increased political power. This consciousness is supported by the fixed determination never to abandon these acquisitions. The conviction is universal that every attack upon these conquests will rouse the whole nation with enthusiastic unanimity to arms. We all wish, indeed, to be able to maintain our present position in the world without a conflict, and we live in the belief that the power of our State will steadily increase without our needing to fight for it. We do not at the bottom of our hearts shrink from such a conflict, but we look towards it with a certain calm confidence, and are inwardly resolved never to let ourselves be degraded to an inferior position without striking a blow. Every appeal to force finds a loud response in the hearts of all. Not merely in the North, where a proud, efficient, hard-working race with glorious traditions has grown up under the laurel-crowned banner of Prussia, does this feeling thrive as an unconscious basis of all thought, sentiment, and volition, in the depth of the soul; but in the South also, which has suffered for centuries under the curse of petty nationalities, the haughty pride and ambition of the German stock live in the heart of the people. Here and there, maybe, such emotions slumber in the shade of a jealous particularism, overgrown by the richer and more luxuriant forms of social intercourse; but still they are animated by latent energy; here, too, the germs of mighty national consciousness await their awakening.

Thus the political power of our nation, while fully alive below the surface, is fettered externally by this love of peace. It fritters itself away in fruitless bickerings and doctrinaire disputes. We no longer have a clearly defined political and national aim, which grips the imagination, moves the heart of the people, and forces them to unity of action. Such a goal existed, until our wars of unification, in the yearnings for German unity, for the fulfilment of the Barbarossa legend. A great danger to the healthy, continuous growth of our people seems to me to lie in the lack of it, and the more our political position in the world is threatened by external complications, the greater is this danger.

Extreme tension exists between the Great Powers, notwithstanding all peaceful prospects for the moment, and it is hardly to be assumed that their aspirations, which conflict at so many points and are so often pressed forward with brutal energy, will always find a pacific settlement.

In this struggle of the most powerful nations, which employ peaceful methods at first until the differences between them grow irreconcilable, our German nation is beset on all sides. This is primarily a result of our geographical position in the midst of hostile rivals, but also because we have forced ourselves, though the last-comers, the virtual upstarts, between the States which have earlier gained their place, and now claim our share in the dominion of this world, after we have for centuries been paramount only in the realm of intellect. We have thus injured a thousand interests and roused bitter hostilities. It must be reserved for a subsequent section to explain the political situation thus affected, but one point can be mentioned without further consideration: if a violent solution of existing difficulties is adopted, if the political crisis develops into military action, the Germans would have a dangerous situation in the midst of all the forces brought into play against them. On the other hand, the issue of this struggle will be decisive of Germany's whole future as State and nation. We have the most to win or lose by such a struggle. We shall be beset by the greatest perils, and we can only emerge victoriously from this struggle against a world of hostile elements, and successfully carry through a Seven Years' War for our position as a World Power, if we gain a start on our probable enemy as soldiers; if the army which will fight our battles is supported by all the material and spiritual forces of the nation; if the resolve to conquer lives not only in our troops, but in the entire united people which sends these troops to fight for all their dearest possessions.

These were the considerations which induced me to regard war from the standpoint of civilization, and to study its relation to the great tasks of the present and the future which Providence has set before the German people as the greatest civilized people known to history. From this standpoint I must first of all examine the aspirations for peace, which seem to dominate our age and threaten to poison the soul of the German people, according to their true moral significance. I must try to prove that war is not merely a necessary element in the life of nations, but an indispensable factor of culture, in which a true civilized nation finds the highest expression of strength and vitality. I must endeavour to develop from the history of the German past in its connection with the conditions of the present those aspects of the question which may guide us into the unknown land of the future. The historical past cannot be killed; it exists and works according to inward laws, while the present, too, imposes its own drastic obligations. No one need passively submit to the pressure of circumstances; even States stand, like the Hercules of legend, at the parting of the ways. They can choose the road to progress or to decadence. "A favoured position in the world will only become effective in the life of nations by the conscious human endeavour to use it." It seemed to me, therefore, to be necessary and profitable, at this parting of the ways of our development where we now stand, to throw what light I may on the different paths which are open to our people. A nation must fully realize the probable consequences of its action; then only can it take deliberately the great decisions for its future development, and, looking forward to its destiny with clear gaze, be prepared for any sacrifices which the present or future may demand.

These sacrifices, so far as they lie within the military and financial sphere, depend mainly on the idea of what Germany is called upon to strive for and attain in the present and the future. Only those who share my conception of the duties and obligations of the German people, and my conviction that they cannot be fulfilled without drawing the sword, will be able to estimate correctly my arguments and conclusions in the purely military sphere, and to judge competently the financial demands which spring out of it. It is only in their logical connection with the entire development, political and moral, of the State that the military requirements find their motive and their justification.

CHAPTER I. THE RIGHT TO MAKE WAR

Since 1795, when Immanuel Kant published in his old age his treatise on "Perpetual Peace," many have considered it an established fact that war is the destruction of all good and the origin of all evil. In spite of all that history teaches, no conviction is felt that the struggle between nations is inevitable, and the growth of civilization is credited with a power to which war must yield. But, undisturbed by such human theories and the change of times, war has again and again marched from country to country with the clash of arms, and has proved its destructive as well as creative and purifying power. It has not succeeded in teaching mankind what its real nature is. Long periods of war, far from convincing men of the necessity of war, have, on the contrary, always revived the wish to exclude war, where possible, from the political intercourse of nations. This wish and this hope are widely disseminated even to-day. The maintenance of peace is lauded as the only goal at which statesmanship should aim. This unqualified desire for peace has obtained in our days a quite peculiar power over men's spirits. This aspiration finds its public expression in peace leagues and peace congresses; the Press of every country and of every party opens its columns to it. The current in this direction is, indeed, so strong that the majority of Governments profess—outwardly, at any rate—that the necessity of maintaining peace is the real aim of their policy; while when a war breaks out the aggressor is universally stigmatized, and all Governments exert themselves, partly in reality, partly in pretence, to extinguish the conflagration.

Pacific ideals, to be sure, are seldom the real motive of their action. They usually employ the need of peace as a cloak under which to promote their own political aims. This was the real position of affairs at the Hague Congresses, and this is also the meaning of the action of the United States of America, who in recent times have earnestly tried to conclude treaties for the establishment of Arbitration Courts, first and foremost with England, but also with Japan, France, and Germany. No practical results, it must be said, have so far been achieved.

We can hardly assume that a real love of peace prompts these efforts. This is shown by the fact that precisely those Powers which, as the weaker, are exposed to aggression, and therefore were in the greatest need of international protection, have been completely passed over in the American proposals for Arbitration Courts. It must consequently be assumed that very matter-of-fact political motives led the Americans, with their commercial instincts, to take such steps, and induced "perfidious Albion" to accede to the proposals. We may suppose that England intended to protect her rear in event of a war with Germany, but that America wished to have a free hand in order to follow her policy of sovereignty in Central America without hindrance, and to carry out her plans regarding the Panama Canal in the exclusive interests of America. Both countries certainly entertained the hope of gaining advantage over the other signatory of the treaty, and of winning the lion's share for themselves. Theorists and fanatics imagine that they see in the efforts of President Taft a great step forward on the path to perpetual peace, and enthusiastically agree with him. Even the Minister for Foreign Affairs in England, with well-affected idealism, termed the procedure of the United States an era in the history of mankind.

This desire for peace has rendered most civilized nations anemic, and marks a decay of spirit and political courage such as has often been shown by a race of Epigoni. "It has always been," H. von Treitschke tells us, "the weary, spiritless, and exhausted ages which have played with the dream of perpetual peace."

Everyone will, within certain limits, admit that the endeavours to diminish the dangers of war and to mitigate the sufferings which war entails are justifiable. It is an incontestable fact that war temporarily disturbs industrial life, interrupts quiet economic development, brings widespread misery with it, and emphasizes the primitive brutality of man. It is therefore a most desirable consummation if wars for trivial reasons should be rendered impossible, and if efforts are made to restrict the evils which follow necessarily in the train of war, so far as is compatible with the essential nature of war. All that the Hague Peace Congress has accomplished in this limited sphere deserves, like every permissible humanization of war, universal acknowledgment. But it is quite another matter if the object is to abolish war entirely, and to deny its necessary place in historical development.

This aspiration is directly antagonistic to the great universal laws which rule all life. War is a biological necessity of the first importance, a regulative element in the life of mankind which cannot be dispensed with, since without it an unhealthy development will follow, which excludes every advancement of the race, and therefore all real civilization. "War is the father of all things." [A] The sages of antiquity long before Darwin recognized this.

[Footnote A: (Heraclitus of Ephesus).]

The struggle for existence is, in the life of Nature, the basis of all healthy development. All existing things show themselves to be the result of contesting forces. So in the life of man the struggle is not merely the destructive, but the life-giving principle. "To supplant or to be supplanted is the essence of life," says Goethe, and the strong life gains the upper hand. The law of the stronger holds good everywhere. Those forms survive which are able to procure themselves the most favourable conditions of life, and to assert themselves in the universal economy of Nature. The weaker succumb. This struggle is regulated and restrained by the unconscious sway of biological laws and by the interplay of opposite forces. In the plant world and the animal world this process is worked out in unconscious tragedy. In the human race it is consciously carried out, and regulated by social ordinances. The man of strong will and strong intellect tries by every means to assert himself, the ambitious strive to rise, and in this effort the individual is far from being guided merely by the consciousness of right. The life-work and the life-struggle of many men are determined, doubtless, by unselfish and ideal motives, but to a far greater extent the less noble passions—craving for possessions, enjoyment and honour, envy and the thirst for revenge—determine men's actions. Still more often, perhaps, it is the need to live which brings down even natures of a higher mould into the universal struggle for existence and enjoyment.

There can be no doubt on this point. The nation is made up of individuals, the State of communities. The motive which influences each member is prominent in the whole body. It is a persistent struggle for possessions, power, and sovereignty, which primarily governs the relations of one nation to another, and right is respected so far only as it is compatible with advantage. So long as there are men who have human feelings and aspirations, so long as there are nations who strive for an enlarged sphere of activity, so long will conflicting interests come into being and occasions for making war arise.

"The natural law, to which all laws of Nature can be reduced, is the law of struggle. All intrasocial property, all thoughts, inventions, and institutions, as, indeed, the social system itself, are a result of the intrasocial struggle, in which one survives and another is cast out. The extrasocial, the supersocial, struggle which guides the external development of societies, nations, and races, is war. The internal development, the intrasocial struggle, is man's daily work—the struggle of thoughts, feelings, wishes, sciences, activities. The outward development, the supersocial struggle, is the sanguinary struggle of nations—war. In what does the creative power of this struggle consist? In growth and decay, in the victory of the one factor and in the defeat of the other! This struggle is a creator, since it eliminates." [B]

[Footnote B: Clauss Wagner, "Der Krieg als schaffendes Weltprinzip."]

That social system in which the most efficient personalities possess the greatest influence will show the greatest vitality in the intrasocial struggle. In the extrasocial struggle, in war, that nation will conquer which can throw into the scale the greatest physical, mental, moral, material, and political power, and is therefore the best able to defend itself. War will furnish such a nation with favourable vital conditions, enlarged possibilities of expansion and widened influence, and thus promote the progress of mankind; for it is clear that those intellectual and moral factors which insure superiority in war are also those which render possible a general progressive development. They confer victory because the elements of progress are latent in them. Without war, inferior or decaying races would easily choke the growth of healthy budding elements, and a universal decadence would follow. "War," says A. W. von Schlegel, "is as necessary as the struggle of the elements in Nature."

Now, it is, of course, an obvious fact that a peaceful rivalry may exist between peoples and States, like that between the fellow-members of a society, in all departments of civilized life—a struggle which need not always degenerate Into war. Struggle and war are not identical. This rivalry, however, does not take place under the same conditions as the intrasocial struggle, and therefore cannot lead to the same results. Above the rivalry of individuals and groups within the State stands the law, which takes care that injustice is kept within bounds, and that the right shall prevail. Behind the law stands the State, armed with power, which it employs, and rightly so, not merely to protect, but actively to promote, the moral and spiritual interests of society. But there is no impartial power that stands above the rivalry of States to restrain injustice, and to use that rivalry with conscious purpose to promote the highest ends of mankind. Between States the only check on injustice is force, and in morality and civilization each people must play its own part and promote its own ends and ideals. If in doing so it comes into conflict with the ideals and views of other States, it must either submit and concede the precedence to the rival people or State, or appeal to force, and face the risk of the real struggle—i.e., of war—in order to make its own views prevail. No power exists which can judge between States, and makes its judgments prevail. Nothing, in fact, is left but war to secure to the true elements of progress the ascendancy over the spirits of corruption and decay.

It will, of course, happen that several weak nations unite and form a superior combination in order to defeat a nation which in itself is stronger. This attempt will succeed for a time, but in the end the more intensive vitality will prevail. The allied opponents have the seeds of corruption in them, while the powerful nation gains from a temporary reverse a new strength which procures for it an ultimate victory over numerical superiority. The history of Germany is an eloquent example of this truth.

Struggle is, therefore, a universal law of Nature, and the instinct of self-preservation which leads to struggle is acknowledged to be a natural condition of existence. "Man is a fighter." Self-sacrifice is a renunciation of life, whether in the existence of the individual or in the life of States, which are agglomerations of individuals. The first and paramount law is the assertion of one's own independent existence. By self-assertion alone can the State maintain the conditions of life for its citizens, and insure them the legal protection which each man is entitled to claim from it. This duty of self-assertion is by no means satisfied by the mere repulse of hostile attacks; it includes the obligation to assure the possibility of life and development to the whole body of the nation embraced by the State.

Strong, healthy, and flourishing nations increase in numbers. From a given moment they require a continual expansion of their frontiers, they require new territory for the accommodation of their surplus population. Since almost every part of the globe is inhabited, new territory must, as a rule, be obtained at the cost of its possessors—that is to say, by conquest, which thus becomes a law of necessity.

The right of conquest is universally acknowledged. At first the procedure is pacific. Over-populated countries pour a stream of emigrants into other States and territories. These submit to the legislature of the new country, but try to obtain favourable conditions of existence for themselves at the cost of the original inhabitants, with whom they compete. This amounts to conquest.

The right of colonization is also recognized. Vast territories inhabited by uncivilized masses are occupied by more highly civilized States, and made subject to their rule. Higher civilization and the correspondingly greater power are the foundations of the right to annexation. This right is, it is true, a very indefinite one, and it is impossible to determine what degree of civilization justifies annexation and subjugation. The impossibility of finding a legitimate limit to these international relations has been the cause of many wars. The subjugated nation does not recognize this right of subjugation, and the more powerful civilized nation refuses to admit the claim of the subjugated to independence. This situation becomes peculiarly critical when the conditions of civilization have changed in the course of time. The subject nation has, perhaps, adopted higher methods and conceptions of life, and the difference in civilization has consequently lessened. Such a state of things is growing ripe in British India.

Lastly, in all times the right of conquest by war has been admitted. It may be that a growing people cannot win colonies from uncivilized races, and yet the State wishes to retain the surplus population which the mother-country can no longer feed. Then the only course left is to acquire the necessary territory by war. Thus the instinct of self-preservation leads inevitably to war, and the conquest of foreign soil. It is not the possessor, but the victor, who then has the right. The threatened people will see the point of Goethe's lines:

"That which them didst inherit from thy sires,
In order to possess it, must be won."

The procedure of Italy in Tripoli furnishes an example of such conditions, while Germany in the Morocco question could not rouse herself to a similar resolution.[C]

[Footnote C: This does not imply that Germany could and ought to have occupied part of Morocco. On more than one ground I think that it was imperative to maintain the actual sovereignty of this State on the basis of the Algeçiras Convention. Among other advantages, which need not be discussed here, Germany would have had the country secured to her as a possible sphere of colonization. That would have set up justifiable claims for the future.]

In such cases might gives the right to occupy or to conquer. Might is at once the supreme right, and the dispute as to what is right is decided by the arbitrament of war. War gives a biologically just decision, since its decisions rest on the very nature of things.

Just as increase of population forms under certain circumstances a convincing argument for war, so industrial conditions may compel the same result.

In America, England, Germany, to mention only the chief commercial countries, industries offer remunerative work to great masses of the population. The native population cannot consume all the products of this work. The industries depend, therefore, mainly on exportation. Work and employment are secured so long as they find markets which gladly accept their products, since they are paid for by the foreign country. But this foreign country is intensely interested in liberating itself from such tribute, and in producing itself all that it requires. We find, therefore, a general endeavour to call home industries into existence, and to protect them by tariff barriers; and, on the other hand, the foreign country tries to keep the markets open to itself, to crush or cripple competing industries, and thus to retain the consumer for itself or win fresh ones. It is an embittered struggle which rages in the market of the world. It has already often assumed definite hostile forms in tariff wars, and the future will certainly intensify this struggle. Great commercial countries will, on the one hand, shut their doors more closely to outsiders, and countries hitherto on the down-grade will develop home industries, which, under more favourable conditions of labour and production, will be able to supply goods cheaper than those imported from the old industrial States. These latter will see their position in these world markets endangered, and thus it may well happen that an export country can no longer offer satisfactory conditions of life to its workers. Such a State runs the danger not only of losing a valuable part of its population by emigration, but of also gradually falling from its supremacy in the civilized and political world through diminishing production and lessened profits.

In this respect we stand to-day at the threshold of a development. We cannot reject the possibility that a State, under the necessity of providing remunerative work for its population, may be driven into war. If more valuable advantages than even now is the case had been at stake in Morocco, and had our export trade been seriously menaced, Germany would hardly have conceded to France the most favourable position in the Morocco market without a struggle. England, doubtless, would not shrink from a war to the knife, just as she fought for the ownership of the South African goldfields and diamond-mines, if any attack threatened her Indian market, the control of which is the foundation of her world sovereignty. The knowledge, therefore, that war depends on biological laws leads to the conclusion that every attempt to exclude it from international relations must be demonstrably untenable. But it is not only a biological law, but a moral obligation, and, as such, an indispensable factor in civilization.

The attitude which is adopted towards this idea is closely connected with the view of life generally.

If we regard the life of the individual or of the nation as something purely material, as an incident which terminates in death and outward decay, we must logically consider that the highest goal which man can attain is the enjoyment of the most happy life and the greatest possible diminution of all bodily suffering. The State will be regarded as a sort of assurance office, which guarantees a life of undisturbed possession and enjoyment in the widest meaning of the word. We must endorse the view which Wilhelm von Humboldt professed in his treatise on the limits of the activity of the State.[D] The compulsory functions of the State must be limited to the assurance of property and life. The State will be considered as a law-court, and the

individual will be inclined to shun war as the greatest conceivable evil.
[Footnote D: W. von Humboldt, "Ideen zu einem Versuch, die Grenzen der Wirksamkelt des Staates zu bestimmen."]

If, on the contrary, we consider the life of men and of States as merely a fraction of a collective existence, whose final purpose does not rest on enjoyment, but on the development of intellectual and moral powers, and if we look upon all enjoyment merely as an accessory of the chequered conditions of life, the task of the State will appear in a very different light. The State will not be to us merely a legal and social insurance office, political union will not seem to us to have the one object of bringing the advantages of civilization within the reach of the individual; we shall assign to it the nobler task of raising the intellectual and moral powers of a nation to the highest expansion, and of securing for them that influence on the world which tends to the combined progress of humanity. We shall see in the State, as Fichte taught, an exponent of liberty to the human race, whose task it is to put into practice the moral duty on earth. "The State," says Treitschke, "is a moral community. It is called upon to educate the human race by positive achievement, and its ultimate object is that a nation should develop in it and through it into a real character; that is, alike for nation and individuals, the highest moral task."

This highest expansion can never be realized in pure individualism. Man can only develop his highest capacities when he takes his part in a community, in a social organism, for which he lives and works. He must be in a family, in a society, in the State, which draws the individual out of the narrow circles in which he otherwise would pass his life, and makes him a worker in the great common interests of humanity. The State alone, so Schleiermacher once taught, gives the individual the highest degree of life.[E]

[Footnote E: To expand the idea of the State into that of humanity, and thus to entrust apparently higher duties to the individual, leads to error, since in a human race conceived as a whole struggle and, by Implication, the most essential vital principle would be ruled out. Any action in favour of collective humanity outside the limits of the State and nationality is impossible. Such conceptions belong to the wide domain of Utopias.]

War, from this standpoint, will be regarded as a moral necessity, if it is waged to protect the highest and most valuable interests of a nation. As human life is now constituted, it is political idealism which calls for war, while materialism—in theory, at least—repudiates it.

If we grasp the conception of the State from this higher aspect, we shall soon see that it cannot attain its great moral ends unless its political power increases. The higher object at which it aims is closely correlated to the advancement of its material interests. It is only the State which strives after an enlarged sphere of influence that creates the conditions under which mankind develops into the most splendid perfection. The development of all the best human capabilities and qualities can only find scope on the great stage of action which power creates. But when the State renounces all extension of power, and recoils from every war which is necessary for its expansion; when it is content to exist, and no longer wishes to grow; when "at peace on sluggard's couch it lies," then its citizens become stunted. The efforts of each individual are cramped, and the broad aspect of things is lost. This is sufficiently exemplified by the pitiable existence of all small States, and every great Power that mistrusts itself falls victim to the same curse.

All petty and personal interests force their way to the front during a long period of peace. Selfishness and intrigue run riot, and luxury obliterates idealism. Money acquires an excessive and unjustifiable power, and character does not obtain due respect:

"Man is stunted by peaceful days,

In idle repose his courage decays.
Law is the weakling's game.
Law makes the world the same.
But in war man's strength is seen,
War ennobles all that is mean;
Even the coward belies his name."
SCHILLER: Braut v. Messina.

"Wars are terrible, but necessary, for they save the State from social petrifaction and stagnation. It is well that the transitoriness of the goods of this world is not only preached, but is learnt by experience. War alone teaches this lesson." [F]

[Footnote F: Kuno Fischer, "Hegel," i., p. 737.]

War, in opposition to peace, does more to arouse national life and to expand national power than any other means known to history. It certainly brings much material and mental distress in its train, but at the same time it evokes the noblest activities of the human nature. This is especially so under present-day conditions, when it can be regarded not merely as the affair of Sovereigns and Governments, but as the expression of the united will of a whole nation.

All petty private interests shrink into insignificance before the grave decision which a war involves. The common danger unites all in a common effort, and the man who shirks this duty to the community is deservedly spurned. This union contains a liberating power which produces happy and permanent results in the national life. We need only recall the uniting power of the War of Liberation or the Franco-German War and their historical consequences. The brutal incidents inseparable from every war vanish completely before the idealism of the main result. All the sham reputations which a long spell of peace undoubtedly fosters are unmasked. Great personalities take their proper place; strength, truth, and honour come to the front and are put into play. "A thousand touching traits testify to the sacred power of the love which a righteous war awakes in noble nations." [G]

[Footnote G: Treitschke, "Deutsche Geschichte," i., p. 482.]

Frederick the Great recognized the ennobling effect of war. "War," he said, "opens the most fruitful field to all virtues, for at every moment constancy, pity, magnanimity, heroism, and mercy, shine forth in it; every moment offers an opportunity to exercise one of these virtues." "At the moment when the State cries out that its very life is at stake, social selfishness must cease and party hatred be hushed. The individual must forget his egoism, and feel that he is a member of the whole body. He should recognize how his own life is nothing worth in comparison with the welfare of the community. War is elevating, because the individual disappears before the great conception of the State. The devotion of the members of a community to each other is nowhere so splendidly conspicuous as in war…. What a perversion of morality to wish to abolish heroism among men!" [H]

[Footnote H: Treitschke, "Politik" i., p. 74.]

Even defeat may bear a rich harvest. It often, indeed, passes an irrevocable sentence on weakness and misery, but often, too, it leads to a healthy revival, and lays the foundation of a new and vigorous constitution. "I recognize in the effect of war upon national character," said Wilhelm von Humboldt, "one of the most salutary elements in the moulding of the human race."

The individual can perform no nobler moral action than to pledge his life on his convictions, and to devote his own existence to the cause which he serves, or even to the conception of the value of ideals to personal morality. Similarly, nations and States can achieve no loftier consummation than to stake their whole power on upholding their independence, their honour, and their reputation.

Such sentiments, however, can only be put into practice in war. The possibility of war is required to give the national character that stimulus from which these sentiments spring, and thus only are nations enabled to do justice to the highest duties of civilization by the fullest development of their moral forces. An intellectual and vigorous nation can experience no worse destiny than to be lulled into a Phaecian existence by the undisputed enjoyment of peace.

From this point of view, efforts to secure peace are extraordinarily detrimental to the national health so soon as they influence politics. The States which from various considerations are always active in this direction are sapping the roots of their own strength. The United States of America, e.g., in June, 1911, championed the ideas of universal peace in order to be able to devote their undisturbed attention to money-making and the enjoyment of wealth, and to save the three hundred million dollars which they spend on their army and navy; they thus incur a great danger, not so much from the possibility of a war with England or Japan, but precisely because they try to exclude all chance of contest with opponents of their own strength, and thus avoid the stress of great political emotions, without which the moral development of the national character is impossible. If they advance farther on this road, they will one day pay dearly for such a policy.

Again, from the Christian standpoint we arrive at the same conclusion. Christian morality is based, indeed, on the law of love. "Love God above all things, and thy neighbour as thyself." This law can claim no significance for the relations of one country to another, since its application to politics would lead to a conflict of duties. The love which a man showed to another country as such would imply a want of love for his own countrymen. Such a system of politics must inevitably lead men astray. Christian morality is personal and social, and in its nature cannot be political. Its object is to promote morality of the individual, in order to strengthen him to work unselfishly in the interests of the community. It tells us to love our individual enemies, but does not remove the conception of enmity. Christ Himself said: "I am not come to send peace on earth, but a sword." His teaching can never be adduced as an argument against the universal law of struggle. There never was a religion which was more combative than Christianity. Combat, moral combat, is its very essence. If we transfer the ideas of Christianity to the sphere of politics, we can claim to raise the power of the State—power in the widest sense, not merely from the material aspect—to the highest degree, with the object of the moral advancement of humanity, and under certain conditions the sacrifice may be made which a war demands. Thus, according to Christianity, we cannot disapprove of war in itself, but must admit that it is justified morally and historically.

Again, we should not be entitled to assume that from the opposite, the purely materialistic, standpoint war is entirely precluded. The individual who holds such views will certainly regard it with disfavour, since it may cost him life and prosperity. The State, however, as such can also come from the materialistic standpoint to a decision to wage war, if it believes that by a certain sacrifice of human lives and happiness the conditions of life of the community may be improved. The loss is restricted to comparatively few, and, since the fundamental notion of all materialistic philosophy inevitably leads to selfishness, the majority of the citizens have no reason for not sacrificing the minority in their own interests. Thus, those who from the materialistic standpoint deny the necessity of war will admit its expediency from motives of self-interest.

Reflection thus shows not only that war is an unqualified necessity, but that it is justifiable from every point of view. The practical methods which the adherents of the peace idea have proposed for the prevention of war are shown to be absolutely ineffective.

It is sometimes assumed that every war represents an infringement of rights, and that not only the highest expression of civilization, but also the true welfare of every nation, is involved in the fullest assertion of these rights, and proposals are made from time to time on this basis to settle the disputes which arise between the various countries by Arbitration Courts, and so to render war impossible. The politician who, without side-interests in these proposals, honestly believes in their practicability must be amazingly short-sighted.

Two questions in this connection are at once suggested: On what right is the finding of this Arbitration Court based? and what sanctions insure that the parties will accept this finding?

To the first question the answer is that such a right does not, and cannot, exist. The conception of right is twofold. It signifies, firstly, the consciousness of right, the living feeling of what is right and good; secondly, the right laid down by society and the State, either written or sanctioned by tradition. In its first meaning it is an indefinite, purely personal conception; in its second meaning it is variable and capable of development. The right determined by law is only an attempt to secure a right in itself. In this sense right is the system of social aims secured by compulsion. It is therefore impossible that a written law should meet all the special points of a particular case. The application of the legal right must always be qualified in order to correspond more or less to the idea of justice. A certain freedom in deciding on the particular case must be conceded to the administration of justice. The established law, within a given and restricted circle of ideas, is only occasionally absolutely just.

The conception of this right is still more obscured by the complex nature of the consciousness of right and wrong. A quite different consciousness of right and wrong develops in individuals, whether persons or peoples, and this consciousness finds its expression in most varied forms, and lives in the heart of the people by the side of, and frequently in opposition to, the established law. In Christian countries murder is a grave crime; amongst a people where blood-vengeance is a sacred duty it can be regarded as a moral act, and its neglect as a crime. It is impossible to reconcile such different conceptions of right.

There is yet another cause of uncertainty. The moral consciousness of the same people alters with the changing ideas of different epochs and schools of philosophy. The established law can seldom keep pace with this inner development, this growth of moral consciousness; it lags behind. A condition of things arises where the living moral consciousness of the people conflicts with the established law, where legal forms are superannuated, but still exist, and Mephistopheles' scoffing words are true:

"Laws are transmitted, as one sees,
Just like inherited disease.
They're handed down from race to race,
And noiseless glide from place to place.
Reason they turn to nonsense; worse,
They make beneficence a curse!
Ah me! That you're a grandson you
As long as you're alive shall rue."
Faust (translation by Sir T. Martin).

Thus, no absolute rights can be laid down even for men who share the same ideas in their private and social intercourse. The conception of the constitutional State in the strictest sense is an impossibility, and would lead to an intolerable state of things. The hard and fast principle must be modified by the progressive development of the fixed law, as well as by the ever-necessary application of mercy and of self-help allowed by the community. If sometimes between individuals the duel alone meets the sense of justice, how much more impossible must a universal international law be in the wide-reaching and complicated relations between nations and States! Each nation evolves its own conception of right, each has its particular ideals and aims, which spring with a certain inevitableness from its character and historical life. These various views bear in themselves their living justification, and may well be diametrically opposed to those of other nations, and none can say that one nation has a better right than the other. There never have been, and never will be, universal rights of men. Here and there particular relations can be brought under definite international laws, but the bulk of national life is absolutely outside codification. Even were some such attempt made, even if a comprehensive international code were drawn up, no self-respecting nation would sacrifice its own conception of right to it. By so doing it would renounce its highest ideals; it would allow its own sense of justice to be violated by an injustice, and thus dishonour itself.

Arbitration treaties must be peculiarly detrimental to an aspiring people, which has not yet reached its political and national zenith, and is bent on expanding its power in order to play its part honourably in the civilized world. Every Arbitration Court must originate in a certain political status; it must regard this as legally constituted, and must treat any alterations, however necessary, to which the whole of the contracting parties do not agree, as an encroachment. In this way every progressive change is arrested, and a legal position created which may easily conflict with the actual turn of affairs, and may check the expansion of the young and vigorous State in favour of one which is sinking in the scale of civilization.

These considerations supply the answer to the second decisive question: How can the judgment of the Arbitration Court be enforced if any State refuses to submit to it? Where does the power reside which insures the execution of this judgment when pronounced?

In America, Elihu Root, formerly Secretary of State, declared in 1908 that the High Court of International Justice established by the second Hague Conference would be able to pronounce definite and binding decisions by virtue of the pressure brought to bear by public opinion. The present leaders of the American peace movement seem to share this idea. With a childlike self-consciousness, they appear to believe that public opinion must represent the view which the American plutocrats think most profitable to themselves. They have no notion that the widening development of mankind has quite other concerns than material prosperity, commerce, and money-making. As a matter of fact, public opinion would be far from unanimous, and real compulsion could only be employed by means of war—the very thing which is to be avoided.

We can imagine a Court of Arbitration intervening in the quarrels of the separate tributary countries when an empire like the Roman Empire existed. Such an empire never can or will arise again. Even if it did, it would assuredly, like a universal peace league, be disastrous to all human progress, which is dependent on the clashing interests and the unchecked rivalry of different groups.

So long as we live under such a State system as at present, the German Imperial Chancellor certainly hit the nail on the head when he declared, in his speech in the Reichstag on March 30, 1911, that treaties for arbitration between nations must be limited to clearly ascertainable legal issues, and that a general arbitration treaty between two countries afforded no guarantee of permanent peace. Such a treaty merely proved that between the two contracting States no serious inducement to break the peace could be imagined. It therefore only confirmed the relations already existing. "If these relations change, if differences develop between the two nations which affect their national existence, which, to use a homely phrase, cut them to the quick, then every arbitration treaty will burn like tinder and end in smoke."

It must be borne in mind that a peaceful decision by an Arbitration Court can never replace in its effects and consequences a warlike decision, even as regards the State in whose favour it is pronounced. If we imagine, for example, that Silesia had fallen to Frederick the Great by the finding of a Court of Arbitration, and not by a war of unparalleled heroism, would the winning of this province have been equally important for Prussia and for Germany? No one will maintain this.

The material increase in power which accrued to Frederick's country by the acquisition of Silesia is not to be underestimated. But far more important was the circumstance that this country could not be conquered by the strongest European coalition, and that it vindicated its position as the home of unfettered intellectual and religious development. It was war which laid the foundations of Prussia's power, which amassed a heritage of glory and honour that can never be again disputed. War forged that Prussia, hard as steel, on which the New Germany could grow up as a mighty European State and a World Power of the future. Here once more war showed its creative power, and if we learn the lessons of history we shall see the same result again and again.

If we sum up our arguments, we shall see that, from the most opposite aspects, the efforts directed towards the abolition of war must not only be termed foolish, but absolutely immoral, and must be stigmatized as unworthy of the human race. To what does the whole question amount? It is proposed to deprive men of the right and the possibility to sacrifice their highest material possessions, their physical life, for ideals, and thus to realize the highest moral unselfishness. It is proposed to obviate the great quarrels between nations and States by Courts of Arbitration—that is, by arrangements. A one-sided, restricted, formal law is to be established in the place of the decisions of history. The weak nation is to have the same right to live as the powerful and vigorous nation. The whole idea represents a presumptuous encroachment on the natural laws of development, which can only lead to the most disastrous consequences for humanity generally.

With the cessation of the unrestricted competition, whose ultimate appeal is to arms, all real progress would soon be checked, and a moral and intellectual stagnation would ensue which must end in degeneration. So, too, when men lose the capacity of gladly sacrificing the highest material blessings—life, health, property, and comfort—for ideals; for the maintenance of national character and political independence; for the expansion of sovereignty and territory in the interests of the national welfare; for a definite influence in the concert of nations according to the scale of their importance in civilization; for intellectual freedom from dogmatic and political compulsion; for the honour of the flag as typical of their own worth—then progressive development is broken off, decadence is inevitable, and ruin at home and abroad is only a question of time. History speaks with no uncertain voice on this subject. It shows that valour is a necessary condition of progress. Where with growing civilization and increasing material prosperity war ceases, military efficiency diminishes, and the resolution to maintain independence under all circumstances fails, there the nations are approaching their downfall, and cannot hold their own politically or racially.

"A people can only hope to take up a firm position in the political world when national character and military tradition act and react upon each." These are the words of Clausewitz, the great philosopher of war, and he is incontestably right.

These efforts for peace would, if they attained their goal, not merely lead to general degeneration, as happens everywhere in Nature where the struggle for existence is eliminated, but they have a direct damaging and unnerving effect. The apostles of peace draw large sections of a nation into the spell of their Utopian efforts, and they thus introduce an element of weakness into the national life; they cripple the justifiable national pride in independence, and support a nerveless opportunist policy by surrounding it with the glamour of a higher humanity, and by offering it specious reasons for disguising its own weakness. They thus play the game of their less scrupulous enemies, just as the Prussian policy, steeped in the ideas of universal peace, did in 1805 and 1806, and brought the State to the brink of destruction.

The functions of true humanity are twofold. On the one hand there is the promotion of the intellectual, moral, and military forces, as well as of political power, as the surest guarantee for the uniform development of character; on the other hand there is the practical realization of ideals, according to the law of love, in the life of the individual and of the community.

It seems to me reasonable to compare the efforts directed towards the suppression of war with those of the Social Democratic Labour party, which goes hand in hand with them. The aims of both parties are Utopian. The organized Labour party strives after an ideal whose realization is only conceivable when the rate of wages and the hours of work are settled internationally for the whole industrial world, and when the cost of living is everywhere uniformly regulated. Until this is the case the prices of the international market determine the standard of wages. The nation which leaves this out of account, and tries to settle independently wages and working hours, runs the risk of losing its position in the international market in competition with nations who work longer hours and at lower rates. Want of employment and extreme misery among the working classes would inevitably be the result. On the other hand, the internationalization of industries would soon, by excluding and preventing any competition, produce a deterioration of products and a profound demoralization of the working population.

The case of the scheme for universal peace is similar. Its execution, as we saw, would be only feasible in a world empire, and this is as impossible as the uniform regulation of the world's industries. A State which disregarded the differently conceived notions of neighbouring countries, and wished to make the idea of universal peace the guiding rule for its policy, would only inflict a fatal injury on itself, and become the prey of more resolute and warlike neighbours. We can, fortunately, assert the impossibility of these efforts after peace ever attaining their ultimate object in a world bristling with arms, where a healthy egotism still directs the policy of most countries. "God will see to it," says Treitschke,[I] "that war always recurs as a drastic medicine for the human race!"

[Footnote I: Treitschke, "Politik," i., p. 76.]

Nevertheless, these tendencies spell for us in Germany no inconsiderable danger. We Germans are inclined to indulge in every sort of unpractical dreams. "The accuracy of the national instinct is no longer a universal attribute with us, as in France." [J] We lack the true feeling for political exigencies. A deep social and religious gulf divides the German people into different political groups, which are bitterly antagonistic to each other. The traditional feuds in the political world still endure. The agitation for peace introduces a new element of weakness, dissension, and indecision, into the divisions of our national and party life.

[Footnote J: Treitschke, "Politik," i., p. 81.]

It is indisputable that many supporters of these ideas sincerely believe in the possibility of their realization, and are convinced that the general good is being advanced by them. Equally true is it, however, that this peace movement is often simply used to mask intensely selfish political projects. Its apparent humanitarian idealism constitutes its danger.

Every means must therefore be employed to oppose these visionary schemes. They must be publicly denounced as what they really are—as an unhealthy and feeble Utopia, or a cloak for political machinations. Our people must learn to see that the maintenance of peace never can or may be the goal of a policy. The policy of a great State has positive aims. It will endeavour to attain this by pacific measures so long as that is possible and profitable. It must not only be conscious that in momentous questions which influence definitely the entire development of a nation, the appeal to arms is a sacred right of the State, but it must keep this conviction fresh in the national consciousness. The inevitableness, the idealism, and the blessing of war, as an indispensable and stimulating law of development, must be repeatedly emphasized. The apostles of the peace idea must be confronted with Goethe's manly words:

"Dreams of a peaceful day?
Let him dream who may!
'War' is our rallying cry,
Onward to victory!"

CHAPTER II.THE DUTY TO MAKE WAR

Prince Bismarck repeatedly declared before the German Reichstag that no one should ever take upon himself the immense responsibility of intentionally bringing about a war. It could not, he said, be foreseen what unexpected events might occur, which altered the whole situation, and made a war, with its attendant dangers and horrors, superfluous. In his "Thoughts and Reminiscences" he expresses himself to this effect: "Even victorious wars can only be justified when they are forced upon a nation, and we cannot see the cards held by Providence so closely as to anticipate the historical development by personal calculation." [A]
[Footnote A: "Gedanken und Erinnerungen," vol. ii., p. 93.]
We need not discuss whether Prince Bismarck wished this dictum to be regarded as a universally applicable principle, or whether he uttered it as a supplementary explanation of the peace policy which he carried out for so long. It is difficult to gauge its true import. The notion of forcing a war upon a nation bears various interpretations. We must not think merely of external foes who compel us to fight. A war may seem to be forced upon a statesman by the state of home affairs, or by the pressure of the whole political situation.
Prince Bismarck did not, however, always act according to the strict letter of that speech; it is his special claim to greatness that at the decisive moment he did not lack the boldness to begin a war on his own initiative. The thought which he expresses in his later utterances cannot, in my opinion, be shown to be a universally applicable principle of political conduct. If we wish to regard it as such, we shall not only run counter to the ideas of our greatest German Prince, but we exclude from politics that independence of action which is the true motive force.
The greatness of true statesmanship consists in a knowledge of the natural trend of affairs, and in a just appreciation of the value of the controlling forces, which it uses and guides in its own interest. It does not shrink from the conflicts, which under the given conditions are unavoidable, but decides them resolutely by war when a favourable position affords prospect of a successful issue. In this way statecraft becomes a tool of Providence, which employs the human will to attain its ends. "Men make history," [B] as Bismarck's actions clearly show.
[Footnote B: Treitschke, "Deutsche Geschichte," i., p. 28.]
No doubt the most strained political situation may unexpectedly admit of a peaceful solution. The death of some one man, the setting of some great ambition, the removal of some master-will, may be enough to change it fundamentally. But the great disputes in the life of a nation cannot be settled so simply. The man who wished to bring the question to a decisive issue may disappear, and the political crisis pass for the moment; the disputed points still exist, and lead once more to quarrels, and finally to war, if they are due to really great and irreconcilable interests. With the death of King Edward VII. of England the policy of isolation, which he introduced with much

adroit statesmanship against Germany, has broken down. The antagonism of Germany and England, based on the conflict of the interests and claims of the two nations, still persists, although the diplomacy which smoothes down, not always profitably, all causes of difference has succeeded in slackening the tension for the moment, not without sacrifices on the side of Germany.

It is clearly an untenable proposition that political action should depend on indefinite possibilities. A completely vague factor would be thus arbitrarily introduced into politics, which have already many unknown quantities to reckon with; they would thus be made more or less dependent on chance.

It may be, then, assumed as obvious that the great practical politician Bismarck did not wish that his words on the political application of war should be interpreted in the sense which has nowadays so frequently been attributed to them, in order to lend the authority of the great man to a weak cause. Only those conditions which can be ascertained and estimated should determine political action.

For the moral justification of the political decision we must not look to its possible consequences, but to its aim and its motives, to the conditions assumed by the agent, and to the trustworthiness, honour, and sincerity of the considerations which led to action. Its practical value is determined by an accurate grasp of the whole situation, by a correct estimate of the resources of the two parties, by a clear anticipation of the probable results—in short, by statesmanlike insight and promptness of decision.

If the statesman acts in this spirit, he will have an acknowledged right, under certain circumstances, to begin a war, regarded as necessary, at the most favourable moment, and to secure for his country the proud privilege of such initiative. If a war, on which a Minister cannot willingly decide, is bound to be fought later under possibly far more unfavourable conditions, a heavy responsibility for the greater sacrifices that must then be made will rest on those whose strength and courage for decisive political action failed at the favourable moment. In the face of such considerations a theory by which a war ought never to be brought about falls to the ground. And yet this theory has in our day found many supporters, especially in Germany.

Even statesmen who consider that the complete abolition of war is impossible, and do not believe that the ultima ratio can be banished from the life of nations, hold the opinion that its advent should be postponed so long as possible.[C]

[Footnote C: Speech of the Imperial Chancellor, v. Bethmann-Hollweg, on
March 30, 1911. In his speech of November 9, 1911, the Imperial
Chancellor referred to the above-quoted words of Prince Bismarck
in order to obtain a peaceful solution of the Morocco question.]

Those who favour this view take up approximately the same attitude as the supporters of the Peace idea, so far as regarding war exclusively as a curse, and ignoring or underestimating its creative and civilizing importance. According to this view, a war recognized as inevitable must be postponed so long as possible, and no statesman is entitled to use exceptionally favourable conditions in order to realize necessary and justifiable aspirations by force of arms.

Such theories only too easily disseminate the false and ruinous notion that the maintenance of peace is the ultimate object, or at least the chief duty, of any policy.

To such views, the offspring of a false humanity, the clear and definite answer must be made that, under certain circumstances, it is not only the right, but the moral and political duty of the statesman to bring about a war.

Wherever we open the pages of history we find proofs of the fact that wars, begun at the right moment with manly resolution, have effected the happiest results, both politically and socially. A feeble policy has always worked harm, since the statesman lacked the requisite firmness to take the risk of a necessary war, since he tried by diplomatic tact to adjust the differences of irreconcilable foes, and deceived himself as to the gravity of the situation and the real importance of the matter. Our own recent history in its vicissitudes supplies us with the most striking examples of this.

The Great Elector laid the foundations of Prussia's power by successful and deliberately incurred wars. Frederick the Great followed in the steps of his glorious ancestor. "He noticed how his state occupied an untenable middle position between the petty states and the great Powers, and showed his determination to give a definite character (décider cet être) to this anomalous existence; it had become essential to enlarge the territory of the State and corriger la figure de la Prusse, if Prussia wished to be independent and to bear with honour the great name of 'Kingdom.'" [D] The King made allowance for this political necessity, and took the bold determination of challenging Austria to fight. None of the wars which he fought had been forced upon him; none of them did he postpone as long as possible. He had always determined to be the aggressor, to anticipate his opponents, and to secure for himself favourable prospects of success. We all know what he achieved. The whole history of the growth of the European nations and of mankind generally would have been changed had the King lacked that heroic power of decision which he showed.

[Footnote D Treitschke, "Deutsche Geschichte," i., p. 51.]

We see a quite different development under the reign of Frederick William III., beginning with the year of weakness 1805, of which our nation cannot be too often reminded.

It was manifest that war with Napoleon could not permanently be avoided. Nevertheless, in spite of the French breach of neutrality, the Prussian Government could not make up its mind to hurry to the help of the allied Russians and Austrians, but tried to maintain peace, though at a great moral cost. According to all human calculation, the participation of Prussia in the war of 1805 would have given the Allies a decisive superiority. The adherence to neutrality led to the crash of 1806, and would have meant the final overthrow of Prussia as a State had not the moral qualities still existed there which Frederick the Great had ingrained on her by his wars. At the darkest moment of defeat they shone most brightly. In spite of the political downfall, the effects of Frederick's victories kept that spirit alive with which he had inspired his State and his people. This is clearly seen in the quite different attitude of the Prussian people and the other Germans under the degrading yoke of the Napoleonic tyranny. The power which had been acquired by the Prussians through long and glorious wars showed itself more valuable than all the material blessings which peace created; it was not to be broken down by the defeat of 1806, and rendered possible the heroic revival of 1813.

The German wars of Unification also belong to the category of wars which, in spite of a thousand sacrifices, bring forth a rich harvest. The instability and political weakness which the Prussian Government showed in 1848, culminating in the disgrace of Olmütz in 1850, had deeply shaken the political and national importance of Prussia. On the other hand, the calm conscious strength with which she faced once more her duties as a nation, when King William I. and Bismarck were at the helm, was soon abundantly manifest. Bismarck, by bringing about our wars of Unification in order to improve radically an untenable position and secure to our people healthy conditions of life, fulfilled the long-felt wish of the German people, and raised Germany to the undisputed rank of a first-class European Power. The military successes and the political position won by the sword laid the foundation for an unparalleled material prosperity. It is difficult to imagine how pitiable the progress of the German people would have been had not these wars been brought about by a deliberate policy.

The most recent history tells the same story. If we judge the Japanese standpoint with an unbiased mind we shall find the resolution to fight Russia was not only heroic, but politically wise and morally justifiable. It was immensely daring to challenge the Russian giant, but the purely military conditions were favourable, and the Japanese nation, which had rapidly risen to a high stage of civilization, needed an extended sphere of influence to complete her development, and to open new channels for her superabundant activities. Japan, from her own point of view, was entitled to claim to be the predominant civilized power in Eastern Asia, and to repudiate the rivalry of Russia. The Japanese statesmen were justified by the result. The victorious campaign created wider conditions of life for the Japanese people and State, and at one blow raised it to be a determining co-factor in international politics, and gave it a political importance which must undeniably lead to great material advancement. If this war had been avoided from weakness or philanthropic illusions, it is reasonable to assume that matters would have taken a very different turn. The growing power of Russia in the Amur district and in Korea would have repelled or at least hindered the Japanese rival from rising to such a height of power as was attained through this war, glorious alike for military prowess and political foresight.

The appropriate and conscious employment of war as a political means has always led to happy results. Even an unsuccessfully waged war may sometimes be more beneficial to a people than the surrender of vital interests without a blow. We find an example of this in the recent heroic struggle of the small Boer States against the British Empire. In this struggle they were inevitably defeated. It was easy to foresee that an armed peasantry could not permanently resist the combined forces of England and her colonies, and that the peasant armies generally could not bear heavy losses. But yet—if all indications are not misleading—the blood shed by the Boer people will yield a free and prosperous future. In spite of much weakness, the resistance was heroic; men like President Stein, Botha, and De Wett, with their gallant followers, performed many great military feats. The whole nation combined and rose unanimously to fight for the freedom of which Byron sings:

"For freedom's battle once begun,
Bequeathed from bleeding sire to son,
Though baffled oft, is ever won."

Inestimable moral gains, which can never be lost in any later developments, have been won by this struggle. The Boers have maintained their place as a nation; in a certain sense they have shown themselves superior to the English. It was only after many glorious victories that they yielded to a crushingly superior force. They accumulated a store of fame and national consciousness which makes them, though conquered, a power to be reckoned with. The result of this development is that the Boers are now the foremost people in South Africa, and that England preferred to grant them self-government than to be faced by their continual hostility. This laid the foundation for the United Free States of South Africa.[E]

[Footnote E: "War and the Arme Blanche," by Erskine Childers: "The truth came like a flash ... that all along we had been conquering the country, not the race; winning positions, not battles" (p. 215).

"To ... aim at so cowing the Boer national spirit, as to gain a permanent political ascendancy for ourselves, was an object beyond our power to achieve. Peaceable political fusion under our own flag was the utmost we could secure. That means a conditional surrender, or a promise of future autonomy" (pp. 227-228). Lord Roberts wrote a very appreciative introduction to this book without any protest against the opinions expressed in it.]

President Kruger, who decided on this most justifiable war, and not Cecil Rhodes, will, in spite of the tragic ending to the war itself, be known in all ages as the great far-sighted statesman of South Africa, who, despite the unfavourable material conditions, knew how to value the inestimable moral qualities according to their real importance.

The lessons of history thus confirm the view that wars which have been deliberately provoked by far-seeing statesmen have had the happiest results. War, nevertheless, must always be a violent form of political agent, which not only contains in itself the danger of defeat, but in every case calls for great sacrifices, and entails incalculable misery. He who determines upon war accepts a great responsibility.

It is therefore obvious that no one can come to such a decision except from the most weighty reasons, more especially under the existing conditions which have created national armies. Absolute clearness of vision is needed to decide how and when such a resolution can be taken, and what political aims justify the use of armed force.

This question therefore needs careful consideration, and a satisfactory answer can only be derived from an examination of the essential duty of the State.

If this duty consists in giving scope to the highest intellectual and moral development of the citizens, and in co-operating in the moral education of the human race, then the State's own acts must necessarily conform to the moral laws. But the acts of the State cannot be judged by the standard of individual morality. If the State wished to conform to this standard it would often find itself at variance with its own particular duties. The morality of the State must be developed out of its own peculiar essence, just as individual morality is rooted in the personality of the man and his duties towards society. The morality of the State must be judged by the nature and raison d'être of the State, and not of the individual citizen. But the end-all and be-all of a State is power, and "he who is not man enough to look this truth in the face should not meddle in politics." [F]

[Footnote F: Treitschke, "Politik," i., p 3, and ii., p 28.]

Machiavelli was the first to declare that the keynote of every policy was the advancement of power. This term, however, has acquired, since the German Reformation, a meaning other than that of the shrewd Florentine. To him power was desirable in itself; for us "the State is not physical power as an end in itself, it is power to protect and promote the higher interests"; "power must justify itself by being applied for the greatest good of mankind." [G]

[Footnote G: Treitschke, "Politik," i., p 3, and ii., p 28.]

The criterion of the personal morality of the individual "rests in the last resort on the question whether he has recognized and developed his own nature to the highest attainable degree of perfection." [H] If the same standard is applied to the State, then "its highest moral duty is to increase its power. The individual must sacrifice himself for the higher community of which he is a member; but the State is itself the highest conception in the wider community of man, and therefore the duty of self-annihilation does not enter into the case. The Christian duty of sacrifice for something higher does not exist for the State, for there is nothing higher than it in the world's history; consequently it cannot sacrifice itself to something higher. When a State sees its downfall staring it in the face, we applaud if it succumbs sword in hand. A sacrifice made to an alien nation not only is immoral, but contradicts the idea of self-preservation, which is the highest ideal of a State." [I]

[Footnote H: Ibid.]

[Footnote I: Ibid., i., p 3.]

I have thought it impossible to explain the foundations of political morality better than in the words of our great national historian. But we can reach the same conclusions by another road. The individual is responsible only for himself. If, either from weakness or from moral reasons, he neglects his own advantage, he only injures himself, the consequences of his actions recoil only on him. The situation is quite different in the case of a State. It represents the ramifying and often conflicting interests of a community. Should it from any reason neglect the interests, it not only to some extent prejudices itself as a legal personality, but it injures also the body of private interests which it represents. This incalculably far-reaching detriment affects not merely one individual responsible merely to himself, but a mass of individuals and the community. Accordingly it is a moral duty of the State to remain loyal to its own peculiar function as guardian and promoter of all higher interests. This duty it cannot fulfil unless it possesses the needful power.

The increase of this power is thus from this standpoint also the first and foremost duty of the State. This aspect of the question supplies a fair standard by which the morality of the actions of the State can be estimated. The crucial question is, How far has the State performed this duty, and thus served the interests of the community? And this not merely in the material sense, but in the higher meaning that material interests are justifiable only so far as they promote the power of the State, and thus indirectly its higher aims.

It is obvious, in view of the complexity of social conditions, that numerous private interests must be sacrificed to the interest of the community, and, from the limitations of human discernment, it is only natural that the view taken of interests of the community may be erroneous. Nevertheless the advancement of the power of the State must be first and foremost the object that guides the statesman's policy. "Among all political sins, the sin of feebleness is the most contemptible; it is the political sin against the Holy Ghost." [J] This argument of political morality is open to the objection that it leads logically to the Jesuitic principle, that the end justifies the means; that, according to it, to increase the power of the State all measures are permissible.

[Footnote J: Treitschke, "Politik," i., p 3.]

A most difficult problem is raised by the question how far, for political objects moral in themselves, means may be employed which must be regarded as reprehensible in the life of the individual. So far as I know, no satisfactory solution has yet been obtained, and I do not feel bound to attempt one at this point. War, with which I am dealing at present, is no reprehensible means in itself, but it may become so if it pursues unmoral or frivolous aims, which bear no comparison with the seriousness of warlike measures. I must deviate here a little from my main theme, and discuss shortly some points which touch the question of political morality.

The gulf between political and individual morality is not so wide as is generally assumed. The power of the State does not rest exclusively on the factors that make up material power— territory, population, wealth, and a large army and navy: it rests to a high degree on moral elements, which are reciprocally related to the material. The energy with which a State promotes its own interests and represents the rights of its citizens in foreign States, the determination which it displays to support them on occasion by force of arms, constitute a real factor of strength, as compared with all such countries as cannot bring themselves to let things come to a crisis in a like case. Similarly a reliable and honourable policy forms an element of strength in dealings with allies as well as with foes. A statesman is thus under no obligation to deceive deliberately. He can from the political standpoint avoid all negotiations which compromise his personal integrity, and he will thereby serve the reputation and power of his State no less than when he holds aloof from political menaces, to which no acts correspond, and renounces all political formulas and phrases.

In antiquity the murder of a tyrant was thought a moral action, and the Jesuits have tried to justify regicide.[K] At the present day political murder is universally condemned from the standpoint of political morality. The same holds good of preconcerted political deception. A State which employed deceitful methods would soon sink into disrepute. The man who pursues moral ends with unmoral means is involved in a contradiction of motives, and nullifies the object at which he aims, since he denies it by his actions. It is not, of course, necessary that a man communicate all his intentions and ultimate objects to an opponent; the latter can be left to form his own opinion on this point. But it is not necessary to lie deliberately or to practise crafty deceptions. A fine frankness has everywhere been the characteristic of great statesmen. Subterfuges and duplicity mark the petty spirit of diplomacy.

[Footnote K: Mariana, "De rege et regis institutione." Toledo, 1598.]

Finally, the relations between two States must often be termed a latent war, which is provisionally being waged in peaceful rivalry. Such a position justifies the employment of hostile methods, cunning, and deception, just as war itself does, since in such a case both parties are determined to employ them. I believe after all that a conflict between personal and political morality may be avoided by wise and prudent diplomacy, if there is no concealment of the desired end, and it is recognized that the means employed must correspond to the ultimately moral nature of that end.

Recognized rights are, of course, often violated by political action. But these, as we have already shown, are never absolute rights; they are of human origin, and therefore imperfect and variable. There are conditions under which they do not correspond to the actual truth of things; in this case the summum jus summa injuria holds good, and the infringement of the right appears morally justified. York's decision to conclude the convention of Tauroggen was indisputably a violation of right, but it was a moral act, for the Franco-Prussian alliance was made under compulsion, and was antagonistic to all the vital interests of the Prussian State; it was essentially untrue and immoral. Now it is always justifiable to terminate an immoral situation.

As regards the employment of war as a political means, our argument shows that it becomes the duty of a State to make use of the ultima ratio not only when it is attacked, but when by the policy of other States the power of the particular State is threatened, and peaceful methods are insufficient to secure its integrity. This power, as we saw, rests on a material basis, but finds expression in ethical values. War therefore seems imperative when, although the material basis of power is not threatened, the moral influence of the State (and this is the ultimate point at issue) seems to be prejudiced. Thus apparently trifling causes may under certain circumstances constitute a fully justifiable casus belli if the honour of the State, and consequently its moral prestige, are endangered. This prestige is an essential part of its power. An antagonist must never be allowed to believe that there is any lack of determination to assert this prestige, even if the sword must be drawn to do so.

In deciding for war or peace, the next important consideration is whether the question under discussion is sufficiently vital for the power of the State to justify the determination to fight; whether the inevitable dangers and miseries of a war do not threaten to inflict greater injury on the interests of the State than the disadvantages which, according to human calculation, must result if war is not declared. A further point to be considered is whether the general position of affairs affords some reasonable prospect of military success. With these considerations of expediency certain other weighty aspects of the question must also be faced.

It must always be kept in mind that a State is not justified in looking only to the present, and merely consulting the immediate advantage of the existing generation. Such policy would be opposed to all that constitutes the essential nature of the State. Its conduct must be guided by the moral duties incumbent on it, which, as one step is gained, point to the next higher, and prepare the present for the future. "The true greatness of the State is that it links the past with the present and the future; consequently the individual has no right to regard the State as a means for attaining his own ambitions in life." [L]

[Footnote L: Treitschke, "Politik," i., p 3.]

The law of development thus becomes a leading factor in politics, and in the decision for war this consideration must weigh more heavily than the sacrifices necessarily to be borne in the present. "I cannot conceive," Zelter once wrote to Goethe, "how any right deed can be performed without sacrifice; all worthless actions must lead to the very opposite of what is desirable."

A second point of view which must not be neglected is precisely that which Zelter rightly emphasizes. A great end cannot be attained except by staking large intellectual and material resources, and no certainty of success can ever be anticipated. Every undertaking implies a greater or less venture. The daily intercourse of civic life teaches us this lesson; and it cannot be otherwise in politics where account must be taken of most powerful antagonists whose strength can only be vaguely estimated. In questions of comparatively trifling importance much may be done by agreements and compromises, and mutual concessions may produce a satisfactory status. The solution of such problems is the sphere of diplomatic activity. The state of things is quite different when vital questions are at issue, or when the opponent demands concession, but will guarantee none, and is clearly bent on humiliating the other party. Then is the time for diplomatists to be silent and for great statesmen to act. Men must be resolved to stake everything, and cannot shun the solemn decision of war. In such questions any reluctance to face the opponent, every abandonment of important interests, and every attempt at a temporizing settlement, means not only a momentary loss of political prestige, and frequently of real power, which may possibly be made good in another place, but a permanent injury to the interests of the State, the full gravity of which is only felt by future generations.

Not that a rupture of pacific relations must always result in such a case. The mere threat of war and the clearly proclaimed intention to wage it, if necessary, will often cause the opponent to give way. This intention must, however, be made perfectly plain, for "negotiations without arms are like music-books without instruments," as Frederick the Great said. It is ultimately the actual strength of a nation to which the opponent's purpose yields. When, therefore, the threat of war is insufficient to call attention to its own claims the concert must begin; the obligation is unconditional, and the right to fight becomes the duty to make war, incumbent on the nation and statesman alike.

Finally, there is a third point to be considered. Cases may occur where war must be made simply as a point of honour, although there is no prospect of success. The responsibility of this has also to be borne. So at least Frederick the Great thought. His brother Henry, after the battle of Kolin, had advised him to throw himself at the feet of the Marquise de Pompadour in order to purchase a peace with France. Again, after the battle of Kunersdorf his position seemed quite hopeless, but the King absolutely refused to abandon the struggle. He knew better what suited the honour and the moral value of his country, and preferred to die sword in hand than to conclude a degrading peace. President Roosevelt, in his message to the Congress of the United States of America on December 4, 1906, gave expression to a similar thought. "It must ever be kept in mind," so the manly and inspiriting words ran, "that war is not merely justifiable, but imperative, upon honourable men and upon an honourable nation when peace is only to be obtained by the sacrifice of conscientious conviction or of national welfare. A just war is in the long-run far better for a nation's soul than the most prosperous peace obtained by an acquiescence in wrong or injustice…. It must be remembered that even to be defeated in war may be better than not to have fought at all."

To sum up these various views, we may say that expediency in the higher sense must be conclusive in deciding whether to undertake a war in itself morally justifiable. Such decision is rendered more easy by the consideration that the prospects of success are always the greatest when the moment for declaring war can be settled to suit the political and military situation. It must further be remembered that every success in foreign policy, especially if obtained by a demonstration of military strength, not only heightens the power of the State in foreign affairs, but adds to the reputation of the Government at home, and thus enables it better to fulfil its moral aims and civilizing duties.

No one will thus dispute the assumption that, under certain circumstances, it is the moral and political duty of the State to employ war as a political means. So long as all human progress and all natural development are based on the law of conflict, it is necessary to engage in such conflict under the most favourable conditions possible.

When a State is confronted by the material impossibility of supporting any longer the warlike preparations which the power of its enemies has forced upon it, when it is clear that the rival States must gradually acquire from natural reasons a lead that cannot be won back, when there are indications of an offensive alliance of stronger enemies who only await the favourable moment to strike—the moral duty of the State towards its citizens is to begin the struggle while the prospects of success and the political circumstances are still tolerably favourable. When, on the other hand, the hostile States are weakened or hampered by affairs at home and abroad, but its own warlike strength shows elements of superiority, it is imperative to use the favourable circumstances to promote its own political aims. The danger of a war may be faced the more readily if there is good prospect that great results may be obtained with comparatively small sacrifices.

These obligations can only be met by a vigorous, resolute, active policy, which follows definite ideas, and understands how to arouse and concentrate all the living forces of the State, conscious of the truth of Schiller's lines:

"The chance that once thou hast refused
Will never through the centuries recur."

The verdict of history will condemn the statesman who was unable to take the responsibility of a bold decision, and sacrificed the hopes of the future to the present need of peace.

It is obvious that under these circumstances it is extremely difficult to answer the question whether in any special case conditions exist which justify the determination to make war. The difficulty is all the greater because the historical significance of the act must be considered, and the immediate result is not the final criterion of its justification.

War is not always the final judgment of Heaven. There are successes which are transitory while the national life is reckoned by centuries. The ultimate verdict can only be obtained by the survey of long epochs.[M]

[Footnote M: Treitschke, "Politik," i., p 2.] 54 The man whose high and responsible lot is to steer the fortunes of a great State must be able to disregard the verdict of his contemporaries; but he must be all the clearer as to the motives of his own policy, and keep before his eyes, with the full weight of the categorical imperative, the teaching of Kant: "Act so that the maxim of thy will can at the same time hold good as a principle of universal legislation." [N]

[Footnote N: Kant, "Kritik der praktischen Vernuft," p. 30.]

He must have a clear conception of the nature and purpose of the State, and grasp this from the highest moral standpoint. He can in no other way settle the rules of his policy and recognize clearly the laws of political morality.

He must also form a clear conception of the special duties to be fulfilled by the nation, the guidance of whose fortunes rests in his hands. He must clearly and definitely formulate these duties as the fixed goal of statesmanship. When he is absolutely clear upon this point he can judge in each particular case what corresponds to the true interests of the State; then only can he act systematically in the definite prospect of smoothing the paths of politics, and securing favourable conditions for the inevitable conflicts; then only, when the hour for combat strikes and the decision to fight faces him, can he rise with a free spirit and a calm breast to that standpoint which Luther once described in blunt, bold language: "It is very true that men write and say often what a curse war is. But they ought to consider how much greater is that curse which is averted by war. Briefly, in the business of war men must not regard the massacres, the burnings, the battles, and the marches, etc.—that is what the petty and simple do who only look with the eyes of children at the surgeon, how he cuts off the hand or saws off the leg, but do not see or notice that he does it in order to save the whole body. Thus we must look at the business of war or the sword with the eyes of men, asking, Why these murders and horrors? It will be shown that it is a business, divine in itself, and as needful and necessary to the world as eating or drinking, or any other work."[O]

[Footnote O: Luther, "Whether soldiers can be in a state of salvation."]

Thus in order to decide what paths German policy must take in order to further the interests of the German people, and what possibilities of war are involved, we must first try to estimate the problems of State and of civilization which are to be solved, and discover what political purposes correspond to these problems.

CHAPTER III.A BRIEF SURVEY OF GERMANY'S HISTORICAL DEVELOPMENT

The life of the individual citizen is valuable only when it is consciously and actively employed for the attainment of great ends. The same holds good of nations and States. They are, as it were, personalities in the framework of collective humanity, infinitely various in their endowments and their characteristic qualities, capable of the most different achievements, and serving the most multifarious purposes in the great evolution of human existence.

Such a theory will not be accepted from the standpoint of the materialistic philosophy which prevails among wide circles of our nation to-day.

According to it, all that happens in the world is a necessary consequence of given conditions; free will is only necessity become conscious. It denies the difference between the empiric and the intelligible Ego, which is the basis of the notion of moral freedom.

This philosophy cannot stand before scientific criticism. It seems everywhere arbitrarily restricted by the narrow limits of the insufficient human intelligence. The existence of the universe is opposed to the law of a sufficient cause; infinity and eternity are incomprehensible to our conceptions, which are confined to space and time.

The essential nature of force and volition remains inexplicable. We recognize only a subjectively qualified phenomenon in the world; the impelling forces and the real nature of things are withdrawn from our understanding. A systematic explanation of the universe is quite impossible from the human standpoint. So much seems clear—although no demonstrable certainty attaches to this theory—that spiritual laws beyond the comprehension of us men govern the world according to a conscious plan of development in the revolving cycles of a perpetual change. Even the gradual evolution of mankind seems ruled by a hidden moral law. At any rate we recognize in the growing spread of civilization and common moral ideas a gradual progress towards purer and higher forms of life.

It is indeed impossible for us to prove design and purpose in every individual case, because our attitude to the universal whole is too limited and anomalous. But within the limitations of our knowledge of things and of the inner necessity of events we can at least try to understand in broad outlines the ways of Providence, which we may also term the principles of development. We shall thus obtain useful guidance for our further investigation and procedure.

The agency and will of Providence are most clearly seen in the history of the growth of species and races, of peoples and States. "What is true," Goethe once said in a letter to Zelter, "can but be raised and supported by its history; what is false only lowered and dissipated by its history." The formation of peoples and races, the rise and fall of States, the laws which govern the common life, teach us to recognize which forces have a creative, sustaining, and beneficent influence, and which work towards disintegration, and thus produce inevitable downfall. We are here following the working of universal laws, but we must not forget that States are personalities endowed with very different human attributes, with a peculiar and often very marked character, and that these subjective qualities are distinct factors in the development of States as a whole. Impulses and influences exercise a very different effect on the separate national individualities. We must endeavour to grasp history in the spirit of the psychologist rather than of the naturalist. Each nation must be judged from its own standpoint if we wish to learn the general trend of its development. We must study the history of the German people in its connection with that of the other European States, and ask first what paths its development has hitherto followed, and what guidance the past gives for Our future policy. From the time of their first appearance in history the Germans showed themselves a first-class civilized people.

When the Roman Empire broke up before the onslaught of the barbarians there were two main elements which shaped the future of the West, Christianity and the Germans. The Christian teaching preached equal rights for all men and community of goods in an empire of masters and slaves, but formulated the highest moral code, and directed the attention of a race, which only aimed at luxury, to the world beyond the grave as the true goal of existence. It made the value of man as man, and the moral development of personality according to the laws of the individual conscience, the starting-point of all development. It thus gradually transformed the philosophy of the ancient world, whose morality rested solely on the relations with the state. Simultaneously with this, hordes of Germans from the thickly-populated North poured victoriously in broad streams over the Roman Empire and the decaying nations of the Ancient World. These masses could not keep their nationality pure and maintain their position as political powers. The States which they founded were short-lived. Even then men recognized how difficult it is for a lower civilization to hold its own against a higher. The Germans were gradually merged in the subject nations. The German element, however, instilled new life into these nations, and offered new opportunities for growth. The stronger the admixture of German blood, the more vigorous and the more capable of civilization did the growing nations appear.

In the meantime powerful opponents sprung up in this newly-formed world. The Latin race grew up by degrees out of the admixture of the Germans with the Roman world and the nations subdued by them, and separated itself from the Germans, who kept themselves pure on the north of the Alps and in the districts of Scandinavia. At the same time the idea of the Universal Empire, which the Ancient World had embraced, continued to flourish.

In the East the Byzantine Empire lasted until A.D. 1453. In the West, however, the last Roman Emperor had been deposed by Odoacer in 476. Italy had fallen into the hands of the East Goths and Lombards successively. The Visigoths had established their dominion in Spain, and the Franks and Burgundians in Gaul.

A new empire rose from the latter quarter. Charles the Great, with his powerful hand, extended the Frankish Empire far beyond the boundaries of Gaul. By the subjugation of the Saxons he became lord of the country between the Rhine and the Elbe; he obtained the sovereignty in Italy by the conquest of the Lombards, and finally sought to restore the Western Roman Empire. He was crowned Emperor in Rome in the year 800. His successors clung to this claim; but the Frankish Empire soon fell to pieces. In its partition the western half formed what afterwards became France, and the East Frankish part of the Empire became the later Germany. While the Germans in the West Frankish Empire, in Italy and Spain, had abandoned their speech and customs, and had gradually amalgamated with the Romans, the inhabitants of the East Frankish Empire, especially the Saxons and their neighbouring tribes, maintained their Germanic characteristics, language, and customs. A powerful German [A] kingdom arose which renewed the claims of Charles the Great to the Western Roman Empire. Otto the Great was the first German King who took this momentous step. It involved him and his successors in a quarrel with the Bishops of Rome, who wished to be not only Heads of the Church, but lords of Italy, and did not hesitate to falsify archives in order to prove their pretended title to that country.

[Footnote A: German (Deutsch=diutisk) signifies originally "popular," opposed to "foreign"— e.g., the Latin Church dialect. It was first used as the name of a people, in the tenth century A.D.]

The Popes made good this right, but they did not stop there. Living in Rome, the sacred seat of the world-empire, and standing at the head of a Church which claimed universality, they, too, laid hold in their own way of the idea of universal imperium. The notion was one of the boldest creations of the human intellect—to found and maintain a world-sovereignty almost wholly by the employment of spiritual powers.

Naturally these Papal pretensions led to feuds with the Empire. The freedom of secular aspirations clashed with the claims of spiritual dominion. In the portentous struggle of the two Powers for the supremacy, a struggle which inflicted heavy losses on the German Empire, the Imperial cause was worsted. It was unable to mould the widely different and too independent subdivisions of the empire into a homogeneous whole, and to crush the selfish particularism of the estates. The last Staufer died on the scaffold at Naples under the axe of Charles of Anjou, who was a vassal of the Church.

The great days of the German-Roman Empire were over. The German power lay on the ground in fragments. A period of almost complete anarchy followed. Dogmatism and lack of patriotic sentiment, those bad characteristics of the German people, contributed to extend this destruction to the economic sphere. The intellectual life of the German people deteriorated equally. At the time when the Imperial power was budding and under the rule of the highly-gifted Staufers, German poetry was passing through a first classical period. Every German country was ringing with song; the depth of German sentiment found universal expression in ballads and poems, grave or gay, and German idealism inspired the minnesingers. But with the disappearance of the Empire every string was silent, and even the plastic arts could not rise above the coarseness and confusion of the political conditions. The material prosperity of the people indeed improved, as affairs at home were better regulated, and developed to an amazing extent; the Hanseatic League bore its flag far and wide over the northern seas, and the great trade-routes, which linked the West and Orient, led from Venice and Genoa through Germany. But the earlier political power was never again attained.

Nevertheless dislike of spiritual despotism still smouldered in the breasts of that German people, which had submitted to the Papacy, and was destined, once more to blaze up into bright flames, and this time in the spiritual domain. As she grew more and more worldly, the Church had lost much of her influence on men's minds. On the other hand, a refining movement had grown up in humanism, which, supported by the spirit of antiquity, could not fail from its very nature to become antagonistic to the Church. It found enthusiastic response in Germany, and was joined by everyone whose thoughts and hopes were centred in freedom. Ulrich von Hutten's battle-cry, "I have dared the deed," rang loud through the districts of Germany.

Humanism was thus in a sense the precursor of the Reformation, which conceived in the innermost heart of the German people, shook Europe to her foundations. Once more it was the German people which, as formerly in the struggle between the Arian Goths and the Orthodox Church, shed it's heart's blood in a religious war for spiritual liberty, and now for national independence also. No struggle more pregnant with consequences for the development of humanity had been fought out since the Persian wars. In this cause the German people nearly disappeared, and lost all political importance. Large sections of the Empire were abandoned to foreign States. Germany became a desert. But this time the Church did not remain victorious as she did against the Arian Goths and the Staufers. It is true she was not laid prostrate; she still remained a mighty force, and drew new strength from the struggle itself. Politically the Catholic States, under Spanish leadership, won an undisputed supremacy. But, on the other hand, the right to spiritual freedom was established. This most important element of civilization was retained for humanity in the reformed Churches, and has become ever since the palladium of all progress, though even after the Peace of Westphalia protracted struggles were required to assert religious freedom.

The States of the Latin race on their side now put forward strong claims to the universal imperium in order to suppress the German ideas of freedom. Spain first, then France: the two soon quarrelled among themselves about the predominance. At the same time, in Germanized England a firs-class Protestant power was being developed, and the age of discoveries, which coincided roughly with the end of the Reformation and the Thirty Years' War, opened new and unsuspected paths to human intellect and human energy. Political life also acquired a fresh stimulus. Gradually a broad stream of immigrants poured into the newly-discovered districts of America, the northern part of which fell to the lot of the Germanic and the southern part to that of the Latin race. Thus was laid the foundation of the great colonial empires, and consequently, of world politics. Germany remained excluded from this great movement, since she wasted her forces in ecclesiastical disputes and religious wars. On the other hand, in combination with England, the Low Countries and Austria, which latter had at the same time to repel the inroad of Turks from the East, she successfully curbed the French ambition for sovereignty in a long succession of wars. England by these wars grew to be the first colonial and maritime power in the world. Germany forfeited large tracts of territory, and lost still more in political power. She broke up into numerous feeble separate States, which were entirely void of any common sympathy with the German cause. But this very disintegration lent her fresh strength. A centre of Protestant power was established in the North—i.e., Prussia.

After centuries of struggle the Germans had succeeded in driving back the Slavs, who poured in from the East, in wrestling large tracts from them, and in completely Germanizing them. This struggle, like that with the niggard soil, produced a sturdy race, conscious of its strength, which extended its power to the coasts of the Baltic, and successfully planted Germanic culture in the far North. The German nation was finally victorious also against Swedes, who disputed the command of the Baltic. In that war the Great Elector had laid the foundations of a strong political power, which, under his successors, gradually grew into an influential force in Germany. The headship of Protestant Germany devolved more and more on this state, and a counterpoise to Catholic Austria grew up. This latter State had developed out of Germany into an independent great Power, resting its supremacy not only on a German population, but also on Hungarians and Slavs. In the Seven Years' War Prussia broke away from Catholic Austria and the Empire, and confronted France and Russia as an independent Protestant State.

But yet another dark hour was in store for Germany, as she once more slowly struggled upwards. In France the Monarchy has exhausted the resources of the nation for its own selfish ends. The motto of the monarchy, L'état c'est moi, carried to an extreme, provoked a tremendous revulsion of ideas, which culminated in the stupendous revolution of 1789, and everywhere in Europe, and more specially in Germany, shattered and swept away the obsolete remnants of medievalism. The German Empire as such disappeared; only fragmentary States survived, among which Prussia alone showed any real power. France once again under Napoleon was fired with the conception of the universal imperium, and bore her victorious eagles to Italy, Egypt, Syria, Germany, and Spain, and even to the inhospitable plains of Russia, which by a gradual political absorption of the Slavonic East, and a slow expansion of power in wars with Poland, Sweden, Turkey, and Prussia, had risen to an important place among the European nations. Austria, which had become more and more a congeries of different nationalities, fell before the mighty Corsican. Prussia, which seemed to have lost all vigour in her dream of peace, collapsed before his onslaught.

But the German spirit emerged with fresh strength from the deepest humiliation. The purest and mightiest storm of fury against the yoke of the oppressor that ever honoured an enslaved nation burst out in the Protestant North. The wars of liberation, with their glowing enthusiasm, won back the possibilities of political existence for Prussia and for Germany, and paved the way for further world-wide historical developments.

While the French people in savage revolt against spiritual and secular despotism had broken their chains and proclaimed their rights, another quite different revolution was working in Prussia— the revolution of duty. The assertion of the rights of the individual leads ultimately to individual irresponsibility and to a repudiation of the State. Immanuel Kant, the founder of critical philosophy, taught, in opposition to this view, the gospel of moral duty, and Scharnhorst grasped the idea of universal military service. By calling upon each individual to sacrifice property and life for the good of the community, he gave the clearest expression to the idea of the State, and created a sound basis on which the claim to individual rights might rest at the same time Stein laid the foundations of self-employed-government in Prussia.

While measures of the most far-reaching historical importance were thus being adopted in the State on which the future fate of Germany was to depend, and while revolution was being superseded by healthy progress, a German Empire of the first rank, the Empire of intellect, grew up in the domain of art and science, where German character and endeavour found the deepest and fullest expression. A great change had been effected in this land of political narrowness and social sterility since the year 1750. A literature and a science, born in the hearts of the nation, and deeply rooted in the moral teaching of Protestantism, had raised their minds far beyond the boundaries of practical life into the sunlit heights of intellectual liberty, and manifested the power and superiority of the German spirit. "Thus the new poetry and science became for many decades the most effectual bond of union for this dismembered people, and decided the victory of Protestantism in German life." [B]

[Footnote B: Treitschke, "Deutsche Geschichte", i., p. 88.]

Germany was raised to be once more "the home of heresy, since she developed the root-idea of the Reformation into the right of unrestricted and unprejudiced inquiry". [C] Moral obligations, such as no nation had ever yet made the standard of conduct, were laid down in the philosophy of Kant and Fichte, and a lofty idealism inspired the songs of her poets. The intense effect of these spiritual agencies was realized in the outburst of heroic fury in 1813. "Thus our classical literature, starting from a different point, reached the same goal as the political work of the Prussian monarchy", [D] and of those men of action who pushed this work forward in the hour of direst ruin.

[Footnote C: Ibid., i., p. 90.]
[Footnote D: Ibid.]

The meeting of Napoleon and Goethe, two mighty conquerors, was an event in the world's history. On one side the scourge of God, the great annihilator of all survivals from the past, the gloomy despot, the last abortion of the revolution—a

"Part of the power that still
Produces Good, while still devising Ill";

on the other, the serenely grave Olympian who uttered the words, "Let man be noble, resourceful, and good"; who gave a new content to the religious sentiment, since he conceived all existence as a perpetual change to higher conditions, and pointed out new paths in science; who gave the clearest expression to all aspirations of the human intellect, and all movements of the German mind, and thus roused his people to consciousness; who finally by his writings on every subject showed that the whole realm of human knowledge was concentrated in the German brain; a prophet of truth, an architect of imperishable monuments which testify to the divinity in man. The great conqueror of the century was met by the hero of intellect, to whom was to fall the victory of the future. The mightiest potentate of the Latin race faced the great Germanic who stood in the forefront of humanity.

Truly a nation which in the hour of its deepest political degradation could give birth to men like Fichte, Scharnhorst, Stein, Schiller, and Goethe, to say nothing about the great soldier-figures of the wars of Liberation, must be called to a mighty destiny.

We must admit that in the period immediately succeeding the great struggle of those glorious days, the short-sightedness, selfishness, and weakness of its Sovereigns, and the jealousy of its neighbours, robbed the German people of the full fruits of its heroism, devotion, and pure enthusiasm. The deep disappointment of that generation found expression in the revolutionary movement of 1848, and in the emigration of thousands to the free country of North America, where the Germans took a prominent part in the formation of a new nationality, but were lost to their mother-country. The Prussian monarchy grovelled before Austria and Russia, and seemed to have forgotten its national duties.

Nevertheless in the centre of the Prussian State there was springing up from the blood of the champions of freedom a new generation that no longer wished to be the anvil, but to wield the hammer. Two men came to the front, King William I. and the hero of the Saxon forest. Resolutely they united the forces of the nation, which at first opposed them from ignorance, and broke down the selfishness and dogmatic positivism of the popular representatives. A victorious campaign settled matters with Austria, who did not willingly cede the supremacy in Germany, and left the German Imperial confederation without forfeiting her place as a Great Power. France was brought to the ground with a mighty blow; the vast majority of the German peoples united under the Imperial crown which the King of Prussia wore; the old idea of the German Empire was revived in a federal shape by the Triple Alliance of Germany, Austria, and Italy. The German idea, as Bismarck fancied it, ruled from the North Sea to the Adriatic and the Mediterranean. Like a phoenix from the ashes, the German giant rose from the sluggard-bed of the old German Confederation, and stretched his mighty limbs.

It was an obvious and inevitable result that this awakening of Germany vitally affected the other nations which had hitherto divided the economic and political power. Hostile combinations threatened us on all sides in order to check the further expansion of our power. Hemmed in between France and Russia, who allied themselves against us, we failed to gather the full fruits of our victories. The short-sightedness and party feuds of the newly-formed Reichstag—the old hereditary failings of our nation—prevented any colonial policy on broad lines. The intense love of peace, which the nation and Government felt, made us fall behind in the race with other countries.

In the most recent partition of the earth, that of Africa, victorious Germany came off badly. France, her defeated opponent, was able to found the second largest colonial Empire in the world; England appropriated the most important portions; even small and neutral Belgium claimed a comparatively large and valuable share; Germany was forced to be content with some modest strips of territory. In addition to, and in connection with, the political changes, new views and new forces have come forward.

Under the influence of the constitutional ideas of Frederick the Great, and the crop of new ideas borne by the French Revolution, the conception of the State has completely changed since the turn of the century. The patrimonial state of the Middle Ages was the hereditary possession of the Sovereign. Hence sprung the modern State, which represents the reverse of this relation, in which the Sovereign is the first servant of the State, and the interest of the State, and not of the ruler, is the key to the policy of the Government. With this altered conception of the State the principle of nationality has gradually developed, of which the tendency is as follows: Historical boundaries are to be disregarded, and the nations combined into a political whole; the State will thus acquire a uniform national character and common national interests.

This new order of things entirely altered the basis of international relations, and set new and unknown duties before the statesman. Commerce and trade also developed on wholly new lines. After 1815 the barriers to every activity—guilds and trade restrictions—were gradually removed. Landed property ceased to be a monopoly. Commerce and industries flourished conspicuously. "England introduced the universal employment of coal and iron and of machinery into industries, thus founding immense industrial establishments; by steamers and railways she brought machinery into commerce, at the same time effecting an industrial revolution by physical science and chemistry, and won the control of the markets of the world by cotton. There came, besides, the enormous extension of the command of credit in the widest sense, the exploitation of India, the extension of colonization over Polynesia, etc." England at the same time girdled the earth with her cables and fleets. She thus attained to a sort of world-sovereignty. She has tried to found a new universal Empire; not, indeed, by spiritual or secular weapons, like Pope and Emperor in bygone days, but by the power of money, by making all material interests dependent on herself. Facing her, between the Atlantic and Pacific Oceans, linking the West and the East, the United States of North America have risen to be an industrial and commercial power of the first rank. Supported by exceptionally abundant natural resources, and the unscrupulously pushing character of her inhabitants, this mighty Empire aims at a suitable recognition of her power in the council of the nations, and is on the point of securing this by the building of a powerful navy. Russia has not only strengthened her position in Europe, but has extended her power over the entire North of Asia, and is pressing farther into the centre of that continent. She has already crossed swords with the States of the Mongolian race. This vast population, which fills the east of the Asiatic continent, has, after thousands of years of dormant civilization, at last awakened to political life, and categorically claims its share in international life. The entrance of Japan into the circle of the great World Powers means a call to arms. "Asia for the Asiatics," is the phrase which she whispers beneath her breath, trusting in the strength of her demand. The new Great Power has emerged victoriously from its first encounter with a European foe. China, too, is preparing to expand her forces outwardly. A mighty movement is thrilling Asia—the awakening of a new epoch.

Dangers, then, which have already assumed a profound importance for the civilized countries of Europe, are threatening from Asia, the old cradle of the nations. But even in the heart of the European nations, forces which have slumbered hitherto are now awake. The persisting ideas of the French Revolution and the great industrial progress which characterized the last century, have roused the working classes of every country to a consciousness of their importance and their social power. The workers, originally concerned only in the amelioration of their material position, have, in theory, abandoned the basis of the modern State, and seek their salvation in the revolution which they preach. They do not wish to obtain what they can within the limitations of the historically recognized State, but they wish to substitute for it a new State, in which they themselves are the rulers. By this aspiration they not only perpetually menace State and society, but endanger in the separate countries the industries from which they live, since they threaten to destroy the possibility of competing in the international markets by continuous increase of wages and decrease of work. Even in Germany this movement has affected large sections of the population.

Until approximately the middle of the last century, agriculture and cattle-breeding formed the chief and most important part of German industries. Since then, under the protection of wise tariffs, and in connection with the rapid growth of the German merchant navy, trade has marvellously increased. Germany has become an industrial and trading nation; almost the whole of the growing increase of the population finds work and employment in this sphere. Agriculture has more and more lost its leading position in the economic life of the people. The artisan class has thus become a power in our State. It is organized in trade unions, and has politically fallen under the influence of the international social democracy. It is hostile to the national class distinctions, and strains every nerve to undermine the existing power of the State.

It is evident that the State cannot tolerate quietly this dangerous agitation, and that it must hinder, by every means, the efforts of the anti-constitutionalist party to effect their purpose. The law of self-preservation demands this; but it is clear that, to a certain point, the pretensions of the working classes are justified. The citizen may fairly claim to protect himself from poverty by work, and to have an opportunity of raising himself in the social scale, if he willingly devotes his powers. He is entitled to demand that the State should grant this claim, and should be bound to protect him against the tyranny of capital.

Two means of attaining such an object are open to the State: first, it may create opportunities of work, which secure remunerative employment to all willing hands; secondly, it may insure the workman by legislation against every diminution in his capacity to work owing to sickness, age, or accident; may give him material assistance when temporarily out of work, and protect him against compulsion which may hinder him from working.

The economical prosperity of Germany as the visible result of three victorious campaigns created a labour market sufficiently large for present purposes, although without the conscious intention of the State. German labour, under the protection of the political power, gained a market for itself. On the other hand, the German State has intervened with legislation, with full consciousness of the end and the means. As Scharnhorst once contrasted the duty of the citizen with the rights of man, so the Emperor William I. recognized the duty of the State towards those who were badly equipped with the necessaries of life. The position of the worker was assured, so far as circumstances allowed, by social legislation. No excuse, therefore, for revolutionary agitation now existed.

A vigorous opposition to all the encroachments of the social democrats indicated the only right way in which the justifiable efforts of the working class could be reconciled with the continuance of the existing State and of existing society, the two pillars of all civilization and progress. This task is by no means completed. The question still is, How to win back the working class to the ideals of State and country? Willing workers must be still further protected against social democratic tyranny.

Germany, nevertheless, is in social-political respects at the head of all progress in culture. German science has held its place in the world. Germany certainly took the lead in political sciences during the last century, and in all other domains of intellectual inquiry has won a prominent position through the universality of her philosophy and her thorough and unprejudiced research into the nature of things.

The achievements of Germany in the sphere of science and literature are attested by the fact that the annual export of German books to foreign countries is, according to trustworthy estimates, twice as large as that of France, England, and America combined. It is only in the domain of the exact sciences that Germany has often been compelled to give precedence to foreign countries. German art also has failed to win a leading position. It shows, indeed, sound promise in many directions, and has produced much that is really great; but the chaos of our political conditions is, unfortunately, reflected in it. The German Empire has politically been split up into numerous parties. Not only are the social democrats and the middle class opposed, but they, again, are divided among themselves; not only are industries and agriculture bitter enemies, but the national sentiment has not yet been able to vanquish denominational antagonisms, and the historical hostility between North and South has prevented the population from growing into a completely united body.

So stands Germany to-day, torn by internal dissensions, yet full of sustained strength; threatened on all sides by dangers, compressed into narrow, unnatural limits, she still is filled with high aspirations, in her nationality, her intellectual development, in her science, industries, and trade. And now, what paths does this history indicate to us for the future?

What duties are enforced on us by the past?

It is a question of far-reaching importance; for on the way in which the German State answers this question, depend not only our own further development, but to some extent the subsequent shaping of the history of the world.

CHAPTER IV.GERMANY'S HISTORICAL MISSION

Let us pass before our mind's eye the whole course of our historical development, and let us picture to ourselves the life-giving streams of human beings, that in every age have poured forth from the Empire of Central Europe to all parts of the globe; let us reflect what rich seeds of intellectual and moral development were sown by the German intellectual life: the proud conviction forces itself upon us with irresistible power that a high, if not the highest, importance for the entire development of the human race is ascribable to this German people.

This conviction is based on the intellectual merits of our nation, on the freedom and the universality of the German spirit, which have ever and again been shown in the course of its history. There is no nation whose thinking is at once so free from prejudice and so historical as the German, which knows how to unite so harmoniously the freedom of the intellectual and the restraint of the practical life on the path of free and natural development. The Germans have thus always been the standard-bearers of free thought, but at the same time a strong bulwark against revolutionary anarchical outbreaks. They have often been worsted in the struggle for intellectual freedom, and poured out their best heart's blood in the cause. Intellectual compulsion has sometimes ruled the Germans; revolutionary tremors have shaken the life of this people—the great peasant war in the sixteenth century, and the political attempts at revolution in the middle of the nineteenth century. But the revolutionary movement has been checked and directed into the paths of a healthy natural advancement. The inevitable need of a free intellectual self-determination has again and again disengaged itself from the inner life of the soul of the people, and broadened into world-historical importance.

Thus two great movements were born from the German intellectual life, on which, henceforth, all the intellectual and moral progress of man must rest: the Reformation and the critical philosophy. The Reformation, which broke the intellectual yoke, imposed by the Church, which checked all free progress; and the Critique of Pure Reason, which put a stop to the caprice of philosophic speculation by defining for the human mind the limitations of its capacity for knowledge, and at the same time pointed out in what way knowledge is really possible. On this substructure was developed the intellectual life of our time, whose deepest significance consists in the attempt to reconcile the result of free inquiry with the religious needs of the heart, and to lay a foundation for the harmonious organization of mankind. Torn this way and that, between hostile forces, in a continuous feud between faith and knowledge, mankind seems to have lost the straight road of progress. Reconciliation only appears possible when the thought of religious reformation leads to a permanent explanation of the idea of religion, and science remains conscious of the limits of its power, and does not attempt to explain the domain of the supersensual world from the results of natural philosophy.

The German nation not only laid the foundations of this great struggle for an harmonious development of humanity, but took the lead in it. We are thus incurring an obligation for the future, from which we cannot shrink. We must be prepared to be the leaders in this campaign, which is being fought for the highest stake that has been offered to human efforts. Our nation is not only bound by its past history to take part in this struggle, but is peculiarly adapted to do so by its special qualities.

No nation on the face of the globe is so able to grasp and appropriate all the elements of culture, to add to them from the stores of its own spiritual endowment, and to give back to mankind richer gifts than it received. It has "enriched the store of traditional European culture with new and independent ideas and ideals, and won a position in the great community of civilized nations which none else could fill." "Depth of conviction, idealism, universality, the power to look beyond all the limits of a finite existence, to sympathize with all that is human, to traverse the realm of ideas in companionship with the noblest of all nations and ages—this has at all times been the German characteristic; this has been extolled as the prerogative of German culture." [A] To no nation, except the German, has it been given to enjoy in its inner self "that which is given to mankind as a whole." We often see in other nations a greater intensity of specialized ability, but never the same capacity for generalization and absorption. It is this quality which specially fits us for the leadership in the intellectual world, and imposes on us the obligation to maintain that position.

[Footnote A: Treitschke, "Deutsche Geschichte," i., p. 95.]

There are numerous other tasks to be fulfilled if we are to discharge our highest duty. They form the necessary platform from which we can mount to the highest goal. These duties lie in the domains of science and politics, and also in that borderland where science and politics touch, and where the latter is often directly conditioned by the results of scientific inquiry.

First and foremost it is German science which must regain its superiority in unwearying and brilliant research in order to vindicate our birthright. On the one hand, we must extend the theory of the perceptive faculty; on the other, we must increase man's dominion over Nature by exploring her hidden secrets, and thus make human work more useful and remunerative. We must endeavour to find scientific solutions of the great problems which deeply concern mankind. We need not restrict ourselves to the sphere of pure theory, but must try to benefit civilization by the practical results of research, and thus create conditions of life in which a purer conception of the ideal life can find its expression.

It is, broadly speaking, religious and social controversies which exercise the most permanent influence on human existence, and condition not only our future development, but the higher life generally. These problems have occupied the minds of no people more deeply and permanently than our own. Yet the revolutionary spirit, in spite of the empty ravings of social democratic agitators, finds no place in Germany. The German nature tends towards a systematic healthy development, which works slowly in opposition to the different movements. The Germans thus seem thoroughly qualified to settle in their own country the great controversies which are rending other nations, and to direct them into the paths of a natural progress in conformity with the laws of evolution.

We have already started on the task in the social sphere, and shall no doubt continue it, so far as it is compatible with the advantages of the community and the working class itself. We must not spare any efforts to find other means than those already adopted to inspire the working class with healthy and patriotic ambitions.

It is to be hoped, in any case, that if ever a great and common duty, requiring the concentration of the whole national strength, is imposed upon us, that the labour classes will not withhold their co-operation, and that, in face of a common danger, our nation will recover that unity which is lamentably deficient to-day.

No attempt at settlement has been made in the religious domain. The old antagonists are still bitterly hostile to each other, especially in Germany. It will be the duty of the future to mitigate the religious and political antagonism of the denominations, under guarantees of absolute liberty of thought and all personal convictions, and to combine the conflicting views into a harmonious and higher system. At present there appears small probability of attaining this end. The dogmatism of Protestant orthodoxy and the Jesuitic tendencies and ultramontanism of the Catholics, must be surmounted, before any common religious movement can be contemplated. But no German statesman can disregard this aspect of affairs, nor must he ever forget that the greatness of our nation is rooted exclusively on Protestantism. Legally and socially all denominations enjoy equal rights, but the German State must never renounce the leadership in the domain of free spiritual development. To do so would mean loss of prestige.

Duties of the greatest importance for the whole advance of human civilization have thus been transmitted to the German nation, as heir of a great and glorious past. It is faced with problems of no less significance in the sphere of its international relations. These problems are of special importance, since they affect most deeply the intellectual development, and on their solution depends the position of Germany in the world.

The German Empire has suffered great losses of territory in the storms and struggles of the past. The Germany of to-day, considered geographically, is a mutilated torso of the old dominions of the Emperors; it comprises only a fraction of the German peoples. A large number of German fellow-countrymen have been incorporated into other States, or live in political independence, like the Dutch, who have developed into a separate nationality, but in language and national customs cannot deny their German ancestry. Germany has been robbed of her natural boundaries; even the source and mouth of the most characteristically German stream, the much lauded German Rhine, lie outside the German territory. On the eastern frontier, too, where the strength of the modern German Empire grew up in centuries of war against the Slavs, the possessions of Germany are menaced. The Slavonic waves are ever dashing more furiously against the coast of that Germanism, which seems to have lost its old victorious strength.

Signs of political weakness are visible here, while for centuries the overflow of the strength of the German nation has poured into foreign countries, and been lost to our fatherland and to our nationality; it is absorbed by foreign nations and steeped with foreign sentiments. Even to-day the German Empire possesses no colonial territories where its increasing population may find remunerative work and a German way of living.

This is obviously not a condition which can satisfy a powerful nation, or corresponds to the greatness of the German nation and its intellectual importance.

At an earlier epoch, to be sure, when Germans had in the course of centuries grown accustomed to the degradation of being robbed of all political significance, a large section of our people did not feel this insufficiency. Even during the age of our classical literature the patriotic pride of that idealistic generation "was contented with the thought that no other people could follow the bold flights of German genius or soar aloft to the freedom of our world citizenship." [B]

[Footnote B: Treitschke, "Deutsche Geschichte," i., p. 195.]

Schiller, in 1797, could write the lines:

"German majesty and honour
Fall not with the princes' crown;
When amid the flames of war
German Empire crashes down,
German greatness stands unscathed." [C]

[Footnote C: Fragment of a poem on "German Greatness," published in 1905 by Bernhard Suphan.]

The nobler and better section of our nation, at any rate, holds different sentiments to-day. We attach a higher value to the influence of the German spirit on universal culture than was then possible, since we must now take into consideration the immense development of Germany in the nineteenth century, and can thus better estimate the old importance of our classical literature. Again, we have learnt from the vicissitudes of our historical growth to recognize that the full and due measure of intellectual development can only be achieved by the political federation of our nation. The dominion of German thought can only be extended under the aegis of political power, and unless we act in conformity to this idea, we shall be untrue to our great duties towards the human race.

Our first and positive duty consists, therefore, in zealously guarding the territories of Germany, as they now are, and in not surrendering a foot's breadth of German soil to foreign nationalities. On the west the ambitious schemes of the Latin race have been checked, and it is hard to imagine that we shall ever allow this prize of victory to be snatched again from our hands. On the southeast the Turks, who formerly threatened the civilized countries of Europe, have been completely repulsed. They now take a very different position in European politics from that which they filled at the time of their victorious advance westwards. Their power on the Mediterranean is entirely destroyed. On the other hand, the Slavs have become a formidable power. Vast regions which were once under German influence are now once more subject to Slavonic rule, and seem permanently lost to us. The present Russian Baltic provinces were formerly flourishing seats of German culture. The German element in Austria, our ally, is gravely menaced by the Slavs; Germany herself is exposed to a perpetual peaceful invasion of Slavonic workmen. Many Poles are firmly established in the heart of Westphalia. Only faint-hearted measures are taken to-day to stem this Slavonic flood. And yet to check this onrush of Slavism is not merely an obligation inherited from our fathers, but a duty in the interests of self-preservation and European civilization. It cannot yet be determined whether we can keep off this vast flood by pacific precautions. It is not improbable that the question of Germanic or Slavonic supremacy will be once more decided by the sword. The probability of such a conflict grows stronger as we become more lax in pacific measures of defence, and show less determination to protect the German soil at all costs.

The further duty of supporting the Germans in foreign countries in their struggle for existence and of thus keeping them loyal to their nationality, is one from which, in our direct interests, we cannot withdraw. The isolated groups of Germans abroad greatly benefit our trade, since by preference they obtain their goods from Germany; but they may also be useful to us politically, as we discover in America. The American-Germans have formed a political alliance with the Irish, and thus united, constitute a power in the State, with which the Government must reckon. Finally, from the point of view of civilization, it is imperative to preserve the German spirit, and by so doing to establish foci of universal culture.

Even if we succeed in guarding our possessions in the East and West, and in preserving the German nationality in its present form throughout the world, we shall not be able to maintain our present position, powerful as it is, in the great competition with the other Powers, if we are contented to restrict ourselves to our present sphere of power, while the surrounding countries are busily extending their dominions. If we wish to compete further with them, a policy which our population and our civilization both entitle and compel us to adopt, we must not hold back in the hard struggle for the sovereignty of the world.

Lord Rosebery, speaking at the Royal Colonial Institute on March 1, 1893, expressed himself as follows: "It is said that our Empire is already large enough and does not need expansion.... We shall have to consider not what we want now, but what we want in the future.... We have to remember that it is part of our responsibility and heritage to take care that the world, so far as it can be moulded by us, should receive the Anglo-Saxon and not another character." [D]

[Footnote D: This passage is quoted in the book of the French ex-Minister Hanotaux, "Fashoda et le partage de l'Afrique."]

That is a great and proud thought which the Englishman then expressed.

If we count the nations who speak English at the present day, and if we survey the countries which acknowledge the rule of England, we must admit that he is justified from the English point of view. He does not here contemplate an actual world-sovereignty, but the predominance of the English spirit is proclaimed in plain language.

England has certainly done a great work of civilization, especially from the material aspect; but her work is one-sided. All the colonies which are directly subject to English rule are primarily exploited in the interest of English industries and English capital. The work of civilization, which England undeniably has carried out among them, has always been subordinated to this idea; she has never justified her sovereignty by training up a free and independent population, and by transmitting to the subject peoples the blessings of an independent culture of their own. With regard to those colonies which enjoy self-government, and are therefore more or less free republics, as Canada, Australia, South Africa, it is very questionable whether they will permanently retain any trace of the English spirit. They are not only growing States, but growing nations, and it seems uncertain at the present time whether England will be able to include them permanently in the Empire, to make them serviceable to English industries, or even to secure that the national character is English. Nevertheless, it is a great and proud ambition that is expressed in Lord Rosebery's words, and it testifies to a supreme national self-confidence.

The French regard with no less justifiable satisfaction the work done by them in the last forty years. In 1909 the former French Minister, Hanotaux, gave expression to this pride in the following words: "Ten years ago the work of founding our colonial Empire was finished. France has claimed her rank among the four great Powers. She is at home in every quarter of the globe. French is spoken, and will continue to be spoken, in Africa, Asia, America, Oceania. Seeds of sovereignty are sown in all parts of the world. They will prosper under the protection of Heaven." [E]

[Footnote E: Hanotaux, "Fashoda et le partage de l'Afrique."]

The same statesman criticized, with ill-concealed hatred, the German policy: "It will be for history to decide what has been the leading thought of Germany and her Government during the complicated disputes under which the partition of Africa and the last phase of French colonial policy were ended. We may assume that at first the adherents to Bismarck's policy saw with satisfaction how France embarked on distant and difficult undertakings, which would fully occupy the attention of the country and its Government for long years to come. Nevertheless, it is not certain that this calculation has proved right in the long-run, since Germany ultimately trod the same road, and, somewhat late, indeed, tried to make up for lost time. If that country deliberately abandoned colonial enterprise to others, it cannot be surprised if these have obtained the best shares."

This French criticism is not altogether unfair. It must be admitted with mortification and envy that the nation vanquished in 1870, whose vital powers seemed exhausted, which possessed no qualification for colonization from want of men to colonize, as is best seen in Algeria, has yet created the second largest colonial Empire in the world, and prides herself on being a World Power, while the conqueror of Gravelotte and Sedan in this respect lags far behind her, and only recently, in the Morocco controversy, yielded to the unjustifiable pretensions of France in a way which, according to universal popular sentiment, was unworthy alike of the dignity and the interests of Germany.

The openly declared claims of England and France are the more worthy of attention since an entente prevails between the two countries. In the face of these claims the German nation, from the standpoint of its importance to civilization, is fully entitled not only to demand a place in the sun, as Prince Bülow used modestly to express it, but to aspire to an adequate share in the sovereignty of the world far beyond the limits of its present sphere of influence. But we can only reach this goal, by so amply securing our position in Europe, that it can never again be questioned. Then only we need no longer fear that we shall be opposed by stronger opponents whenever we take part in international politics. We shall then be able to exercise our forces freely in fair rivalry with the other World Powers, and secure to German nationality and German spirit throughout the globe that high esteem which is due to them.

Such an expansion of power, befitting our importance, is not merely a fanciful scheme—it will soon appear as a political necessity.

The fact has already been mentioned that, owing to political union and improved economic conditions during the last forty years, an era of great prosperity has set in, and that German industries have been widely extended and German trade has kept pace with them. The extraordinary capacity of the German nation for trade and navigation has once more brilliantly asserted itself. The days of the Hanseatic League have returned. The labour resources of our nation increase continuously. The increase of the population in the German Empire alone amounts yearly to a million souls, and these have, to a large extent, found remunerative industrial occupation.

There is, however, a reverse side to this picture of splendid development. We are absolutely dependent on foreign countries for the import of raw materials, and to a considerable extent also for the sale of our own manufactures. We even obtain a part of our necessaries of life from abroad. Then, again, we have not the assured markets which England possesses in her colonies. Our own colonies are unable to take much of our products, and the great foreign economic spheres try to close their doors to outsiders, especially Germans, in order to encourage their own industries, and to make themselves independent of other countries. The livelihood of our working classes directly depends on the maintenance and expansion of our export trade. It is a question of life and death for us to keep open our oversea commerce. We shall very soon see ourselves compelled to find for our growing population means of life other than industrial employment. It is out of the question that this latter can keep pace permanently with the increase of population. Agriculture will employ a small part of this increase, and home settlements may afford some relief. But no remunerative occupation will ever be found within the borders of the existing German Empire for the whole population, however favourable our international relations. We shall soon, therefore, be faced by the question, whether we wish to surrender the coming generations to foreign countries, as formerly in the hour of our decline, or whether we wish to take steps to find them a home in our own German colonies, and so retain them for the fatherland. There is no possible doubt how this question must be answered. If the unfortunate course of our history has hitherto prevented us from building a colonial Empire, it is our duty to make up for lost time, and at once to construct a fleet which, in defiance of all hostile Powers, may keep our sea communications open.

We have long underestimated the importance of colonies. Colonial possessions which merely serve the purpose of acquiring wealth, and are only used for economic ends, while the owner-State does not think of colonizing in any form or raising the position of the aboriginal population in the economic or social scale, are unjustifiable and immoral, and can never be held permanently. "But that colonization which retains a uniform nationality has become a factor of immense importance for the future of the world. It will determine the degree in which each nation shares in the government of the world by the white race. It is quite imaginable that a count owns no colonies will no longer count among the European Great Powers, however powerful it may otherwise be." [F]

[Footnote F: Treitschke, "Politik," i., Section 8.]

We are already suffering severely from the want of colonies to meet our requirements. They would not merely guarantee a livelihood to our growing working population, but would supply raw materials and foodstuffs, would buy goods, and open a field of activity to that immense capital of intellectual labour forces which is to-day lying unproductive in Germany, or is in the service of foreign interests. We find throughout the countries of the world German merchants, engineers, and men of every profession, employed actively in the service of foreign masters, because German colonies, when they might be profitably engaged, do not exist. In the future, however, the importance of Germany will depend on two points: firstly, how many millions of men in the world speak German? secondly, how many of them are politically members of the German Empire?

These are heavy and complicated duties, which have devolved on us from the entire past development of our nation, and are determined by its present condition as regards the future. We must be quite clear on this point, that no nation has had to reckon with the same difficulties and hostility as ours. This is due to the many restrictions of our political relations, to our unfavourable geographical position, and to the course of our history. It was chiefly our own fault that we were condemned to political paralysis at the time when the great European States built themselves up, and sometimes expanded into World Powers. We did not enter the circle of the Powers, whose decision carried weight in politics, until late, when the partition of the globe was long concluded. All which other nations attained in centuries of natural development—political union, colonial possessions, naval power, international trade—was denied to our nation until quite recently. What we now wish to attain must be fought for, and won, against a superior force of hostile interests and Powers.

It is all the more emphatically our duty plainly to perceive what paths we wish to take, and what our goals are, so as not to split up our forces in false directions, and involuntarily to diverge from the straight road of our intended development.

The difficulty of our political position is in a certain sense an advantage. By keeping us in a continually increasing state of tension, it has at least protected us so far from the lethargy which so often follows a long period of peace and growing wealth. It has forced us to stake all our spiritual and material forces in order to rise to every occasion, and has thus discovered and strengthened resources which will be of great value whenever we shall be called upon to draw the sword.

CHAPTER V. WORLD POWER OR DOWNFALL

In discussing the duties which fall to the German nation from its history and its general as well as particular endowments, we attempted to prove that a consolidation and expansion of our position among the Great Powers of Europe, and an extension of our colonial possessions, must be the basis of our future development.

The political questions thus raised intimately concern all international relations, and should be thoroughly weighed. We must not aim at the impossible. A reckless policy would be foreign to our national character and our high aims and duties. But we must aspire to the possible, even at the risk of war. This policy we have seen to be both our right and our duty. The longer we look at things with folded hands, the harder it will be to make up the start which the other Powers have gained on us.

"The man of sense will by the forelock clutch
Whatever lies within his power,
Stick fast to it, and neither shirk,
Nor from his enterprise be thrust,

But, having once begun to work,
Go working on because he must."
                    Faust
            (translated by Sir Theodore Martin).

The sphere in which we can realize our ambition is circumscribed by the hostile intentions of the other World Powers, by the existing territorial conditions, and by the armed force which is at the back of both. Our policy must necessarily be determined by the consideration of these conditions. We must accurately, and without bias or timidity, examine the circumstances which turn the scale when the forces which concern us are weighed one against the other.

These considerations fall partly within the military, but belong mainly to the political sphere, in so far as the political grouping of the States allows a survey of the military resources of the parties. We must try to realize this grouping. The shifting aims of the politics of the day need not be our standard; they are often coloured by considerations of present expediency, and offer no firm basis for forming an opinion. We must rather endeavour to recognize the political views and intentions of the individual States, which are based on the nature of things, and therefore will continually make their importance felt. The broad lines of policy are ultimately laid down by the permanent interests of a country, although they may often be mistaken from short-sightedness or timidity, and although policy sometimes takes a course which does not seem warranted from the standpoint of lasting national benefits. Policy is not an exact science, following necessary laws, but is made by men who impress on it the stamp of their strength or their weakness, and often divert it from the path of true national interests. Such digressions must not be ignored. The statesman who seizes his opportunity will often profit by these political fluctuations. But the student who considers matters from the standpoint of history must keep his eyes mainly fixed on those interests which seem permanent. We must therefore try to make the international situation in this latter sense clear, so far as it concerns Germany's power and ambitions.

We see the European Great Powers divided into two great camps.

On the one side Germany, Austria, and Italy have concluded a defensive alliance, whose sole object is to guard against hostile aggression. In this alliance the two first-named States form the solid, probably unbreakable, core, since by the nature of things they are intimately connected. The geographical conditions force this result. The two States combined form a compact series of territories from the Adriatic to the North Sea and the Baltic. Their close union is due also to historical national and political conditions. Austrians have fought shoulder to shoulder with Prussians and Germans of the Empire on a hundred battlefields; Germans are the backbone of the Austrian dominions, the bond of union that holds together the different nationalities of the Empire. Austria, more than Germany, must guard against the inroads of Slavism, since numerous Slavonic races are comprised in her territories. There has been no conflict of interests between the two States since the struggle for the supremacy in Germany was decided. The maritime and commercial interests of the one point to the south and south-east, those of the other to the north. Any feebleness in the one must react detrimentally on the political relations of the other. A quarrel between Germany and Austria would leave both States at the mercy of overwhelmingly powerful enemies. The possibility of each maintaining its political position depends on their standing by each other. It may be assumed that the relations uniting the two States will be permanent so long as Germans and Magyars are the leading nationalities in the Danubian monarchy. It was one of the master-strokes of Bismarck's policy to have recognized the community of Austro-German interests even during the war of 1866, and boldly to have concluded a peace which rendered such an alliance possible.

xliii

The weakness of the Austrian Empire lies in the strong admixture of Slavonic elements, which are hostile to the German population, and show many signs of Pan-Slavism. It is not at present, however, strong enough to influence the political position of the Empire.

Italy, also, is bound to the Triple Alliance by her true interests. The antagonism to Austria, which has run through Italian history, will diminish when the needs of expansion in other spheres, and of creating a natural channel for the increasing population, are fully recognized by Italy. Neither condition is impossible. Irredentism will then lose its political significance, for the position, which belongs to Italy from her geographical situation and her past history, and will promote her true interests if attained, cannot be won in a war with Austria. It is the position of a leading political and commercial Mediterranean Power. That is the natural heritage which she can claim. Neither Germany nor Austria is a rival in this claim, but France, since she has taken up a permanent position on the coast of North Africa, and especially in Tunis, has appropriated a country which would have been the most natural colony for Italy, and has, in point of fact, been largely colonized by Italians. It would, in my opinion, have been politically right for us, even at the risk of a war with France, to protest against this annexation, and to preserve the territory of Carthage for Italy. We should have considerably strengthened Italy's position on the Mediterranean, and created a cause of contention between Italy and France that would have added to the security of the Triple Alliance.

The weakness of this alliance consists in its purely defensive character. It offers a certain security against hostile aggression, but does not consider the necessary development of events, and does not guarantee to any of its members help in the prosecution of its essential interests. It is based on a status quo, which was fully justified in its day, but has been left far behind by the march of political events. Prince Bismarck, in his "Thoughts and Reminiscences," pointed out that this alliance would not always correspond to the requirements of the future. Since Italy found the Triple Alliance did not aid her Mediterranean policy, she tried to effect a pacific agreement with England and France, and accordingly retired from the Triple Alliance. The results of this policy are manifest to-day. Italy, under an undisguised arrangement with England and France, but in direct opposition to the interests of the Triple Alliance, attacked Turkey, in order to conquer, in Tripoli, the required colonial territory. This undertaking brought her to the brink of a war with Austria, which, as the supreme Power in the Balkan Peninsula, can never tolerate the encroachment of Italy into those regions.

The Triple Alliance, which in itself represents a natural league, has suffered a rude shock. The ultimate reason for this result is found in the fact that the parties concerned with a narrow, short-sighted policy look only to their immediate private interests, and pay no regard to the vital needs of the members of the league. The alliance will not regain its original strength until, under the protection of the allied armies, each of the three States can satisfy its political needs. We must therefore be solicitous to promote Austria's position in the Balkans, and Italy's interests on the Mediterranean. Only then can we calculate on finding in our allies assistance towards realizing our own political endeavours. Since, however, it is against all our interests to strengthen Italy at the cost of Turkey, which is, as we shall see, an essential member of the Triple Alliance, we must repair the errors of the past, and in the next great war win back Tunis for Italy. Only then will Bismarck's great conception of the Triple Alliance reveal its real meaning. But the Triple Alliance, so long as it only aims at negative results, and leaves it to the individual allies to pursue their vital interests exclusively by their own resources, will be smitten with sterility. On the surface, Italy's Mediterranean interests do not concern us closely. But their real importance for us is shown by the consideration that the withdrawal of Italy from the Triple Alliance, or, indeed, its secession to an Anglo-Franco-Russian entente, would probably be the signal for a great European war against us and Austria. Such a development would gravely prejudice the lasting interests of Italy, for she would forfeit her political independence by so doing, and incur the risk of sinking to a sort of vassal state of France. Such a contingency is not unthinkable, for, in judging the policy of Italy, we must not disregard her relations with England as well as with France.

England is clearly a hindrance in the way of Italy's justifiable efforts to win a prominent position in the Mediterranean. She possesses in Gibraltar, Malta, Cyprus, Egypt, and Aden a chain of strong bases, which secure the sea-route to India, and she has an unqualified interest in commanding this great road through the Mediterranean. England's Mediterranean fleet is correspondingly strong and would—especially in combination with the French Mediterranean squadron—seriously menace the coasts of Italy, should that country be entangled in a war against England and France. Italy is therefore obviously concerned in avoiding such a war, as long as the balance of maritime power is unchanged. She is thus in an extremely difficult double position; herself a member of the Triple Alliance, she is in a situation which compels her to make overtures to the opponents of that alliance, so long as her own allies can afford no trustworthy assistance to her policy of development. It is our interest to reconcile Italy and Turkey so far as we can.

France and Russia have united in opposition to the Central European Triple Alliance. France's European policy is overshadowed by the idea of revanche. For that she makes the most painful sacrifices; for that she has forgotten the hundred years' enmity against England and the humiliation of Fashoda. She wishes first to take vengeance for the defeats of 1870-71, which wounded her national pride to the quick; she wishes to raise her political prestige by a victory over Germany, and, if possible, to regain that former supremacy on the continent of Europe which she so long and brilliantly maintained; she wishes, if fortune smiles on her arms, to reconquer Alsace and Lorraine. But she feels too weak for an attack on Germany. Her whole foreign policy, in spite of all protestations of peace, follows the single aim of gaining allies for this attack. Her alliance with Russia, her entente with England, are inspired with this spirit; her present intimate relations with this latter nation are traceable to the fact that the French policy hoped, and with good reason, for more active help from England's hostility to Germany than from Russia.

The colonial policy of France pursues primarily the object of acquiring a material, and, if possible, military superiority over Germany. The establishment of a native African army, the contemplated introduction of a modified system of conscription in Algeria, and the political annexation of Morocco, which offers excellent raw material for soldiers, so clearly exhibit this intention, that there can be no possible illusion as to its extent and meaning.

Since France has succeeded in bringing her military strength to approximately the same level as Germany, since she has acquired in her North African Empire the possibility of considerably increasing that strength, since she has completely outstripped Germany in the sphere of colonial policy, and has not only kept up, but also revived, the French sympathies of Alsace and Lorraine, the conclusion is obvious: France will not abandon the paths of an anti-German policy, but will do her best to excite hostility against us, and to thwart German interests in every quarter of the globe. When she came to an understanding with the Italians, that she should be given a free hand in Morocco if she allowed them to occupy Tripoli, a wedge was driven into the Triple Alliance which threatens to split it. It may be regarded as highly improbable that she will maintain honourably and with no arrière-pensée the obligations undertaken in the interests of German commerce in Morocco. The suppression of these interests was, in fact, a marked feature of the French Morocco policy, which was conspicuously anti-German. The French policy was so successful that we shall have to reckon more than ever on the hostility of France in the future. It must be regarded as a quite unthinkable proposition that an agreement between France and Germany can be negotiated before the question between them has been once more decided by arms. Such an agreement is the less likely now that France sides with England, to whose interest it is to repress Germany but strengthen France. Another picture meets our eyes if we turn to the East, where the giant Russian Empire towers above all others.

The Empire of the Czar, in consequence of its defeat in Manchuria, and of the revolution which was precipitated by the disastrous war, is following apparently a policy of recuperation. It has tried to come to an understanding with Japan in the Far East, and with England in Central Asia; in the Balkans its policy aims at the maintenance of the status quo. So far it does not seem to have entertained any idea of war with Germany. The Potsdam agreement, whose importance cannot be overestimated, shows that we need not anticipate at present any aggressive policy on Russia's part. The ministry of Kokowzew seems likely to wish to continue this policy of recuperation, and has the more reason for doing so, as the murder of Stolypin with its accompanying events showed, as it were by a flash of lightning, a dreadful picture of internal disorder and revolutionary intrigue. It is improbable, therefore, that Russia would now be inclined to make armed intervention in favour of France. The Russo-French alliance is not, indeed, swept away, and there is no doubt that Russia would, if the necessity arose, meet her obligations; but the tension has been temporarily relaxed, and an improvement in the Russo-German relations has been effected, although this state of things was sufficiently well paid for by the concessions of Germany in North Persia.

It is quite obvious that this policy of marking time, which Russia is adopting for the moment, can only be transitory. The requirements of the mighty Empire irresistibly compel an expansion towards the sea, whether in the Far East, where it hopes to gain ice-free harbours, or in the direction of the Mediterranean, where the Crescent still glitters on the dome of St. Sophia. After a successful war, Russia would hardly hesitate to seize the mouth of the Vistula, at the possession of which she has long aimed, and thus to strengthen appreciably her position in the Baltic.

Supremacy in the Balkan Peninsula, free entrance into the Mediterranean, and a strong position on the Baltic, are the goals to which the European policy of Russia has naturally long been directed. She feels herself, also, the leading power of the Slavonic races, and has for many years been busy in encouraging and extending the spread of this element into Central Europe. Pan-Slavism is still hard at work.

It is hard to foresee how soon Russia will come out from her retirement and again tread the natural paths of her international policy. Her present political attitude depends considerably on the person of the present Emperor, who believes in the need of leaning upon a strong monarchical State, such as Germany is, and also on the character of the internal development of the mighty Empire. The whole body of the nation is so tainted with revolutionary and moral infection, and the peasantry is plunged in such economic disorder, that it is difficult to see from what elements a vivifying force may spring up capable of restoring a healthy condition. Even the agrarian policy of the present Government has not produced any favourable results, and has so far disappointed expectations. The possibility thus has always existed that, under the stress of internal affairs, the foreign policy may be reversed and an attempt made to surmount the difficulties at home by successes abroad. Time and events will decide whether these successes will be sought in the Far East or in the West. On the one side Japan, and possibly China, must be encountered; on the other, Germany, Austria, and, possibly, Turkey.

Doubtless these conditions must exercise a decisive influence on the Franco-Russian Alliance. The interests of the two allies are not identical. While France aims solely at crushing Germany by an aggressive war, Russia from the first has more defensive schemes in view. She wished to secure herself against any interference by the Powers of Central Europe in the execution of her political plans in the South and East, and at the same time, at the price of an alliance, to raise, on advantageous terms in France, the loans which were so much needed. Russia at present has no inducement to seek an aggressive war with Germany or to take part in one. Of course, every further increase of the German power militates against the Russian interests. We shall therefore always find her on the side of those who try to cross our political paths.

England has recently associated herself with the Franco-Russian Alliance. She has made an arrangement in Asia with Russia by which the spheres of influence of the two parties are delimited, while with France she has come to terms in the clear intention of suppressing Germany under all circumstances, if necessary by force of arms.

The actually existing conflict of Russian and English interests in the heart of Asia can obviously not be terminated by such agreements. So, also, no natural community of interests exists between England and France. A strong French fleet may be as great a menace to England as to any other Power. For the present, however, we may reckon on an Anglo—French entente. This union is cemented by the common hostility to Germany. No other reason for the political combination of the two States is forthcoming. There is not even a credible pretext, which might mask the real objects.

This policy of England is, on superficial examination, not very comprehensible. Of course, German industries and trade have lately made astounding progress, and the German navy is growing to a strength which commands respect. We are certainly a hindrance to the plans which England is prosecuting in Asiatic Turkey and Central Africa. This may well be distasteful to the English from economic as well as political and military aspects. But, on the other hand, the American competition in the domain of commercial politics is far keener than the German. The American navy is at the present moment stronger than the German, and will henceforth maintain this precedence. Even the French are on the point of building a formidable fleet, and their colonial Empire, so far as territory is concerned, is immensely superior to ours. Yet, in spite of all these considerations, the hostility of the English is primarily directed against us. It is necessary to adopt the English standpoint in order to understand the line of thought which guides the English politicians. I believe that the solution of the problem is to be found in the wide ramifications of English interests in every part of the world.

Since England committed the unpardonable blunder, from her point of view, of not supporting the Southern States in the American War of Secession, a rival to England's world-wide Empire has appeared on the other side of the Atlantic in the form of the United States of North America, which are a grave menace to England's fortunes. The keenest competition conceivable now exists between the two countries. The annexation of the Philippines by America, and England's treaty with Japan, have accentuated the conflict of interests between the two nations. The trade and industries of America can no longer be checked, and the absolutely inexhaustible and ever-growing resources of the Union are so prodigious that a naval war with America, in view of the vast distances and wide extent of the enemies' coasts, would prove a very bold, and certainly very difficult, undertaking. England accordingly has always diplomatically conceded the claims of America, as quite recently in the negotiations about fortifying the Panama Canal; the object clearly is to avoid any collision with the United States, from fearing the consequences of such collision. The American competition in trade and industries, and the growth of the American navy, are tolerated as inevitable, and the community of race is borne in mind. In this sense, according to the English point of view, must be understood the treaty by which a Court of Arbitration between the two countries was established.

England wishes, in any case, to avert the danger of a war with America. The natural opposition of the two rival States may, however, in the further development of things, be so accentuated that England will be forced to assert her position by arms, or at least to maintain an undisputed naval supremacy, in order to emphasize her diplomatic action. The relations of the two countries to Canada may easily become strained to a dangerous point, and the temporary failure of the Arbitration Treaty casts a strong light on the fact that the American people does not consider that the present political relations of the two nations are permanent.

There is another danger which concerns England more closely and directly threatens her vitality. This is due to the nationalist movement in India and Egypt, to the growing power of Islam, to the agitation for independence in the great colonies, as well as to the supremacy of the Low-German element in South Africa.

Turkey is the only State which might seriously threaten the English position in Egypt by land. This contingency gives to the national movement in Egypt an importance which it would not otherwise possess; it clearly shows that England intensely fears every Pan-Islamitic movement. She is trying with all the resources of political intrigue to undermine the growing power of Turkey, which she officially pretends to support, and is endeavouring to create in Arabia a new religious centre in opposition to the Caliphate.

The same views are partially responsible for the policy in India, where some seventy millions of Moslems live under the English rule. England, so far, in accordance with the principle of divide et impera, has attempted to play off the Mohammedan against the Hindu population. But now that a pronounced revolutionary and nationalist tendency shows itself among these latter, the danger is imminent that Pan-Islamism, thoroughly roused, should unite with the revolutionary elements of Bengal. The co-operation of these elements might create a very grave danger, capable of shaking the foundations of England's high position in the world.

While so many dangers, in the future at least, threaten both at home and abroad, English imperialism has failed to link the vast Empire together, either for purposes of commerce or defence, more closely than hitherto. Mr. Chamberlain's dream of the British Imperial Customs Union has definitely been abandoned. No attempt was made at the Imperial Conference in 1911 to go back to it. "A centrifugal policy predominated. .... When the question of imperial defence came up, the policy was rejected which wished to assure to Great Britain the help of the oversea dominions in every imaginable eventuality." The great self-ruled colonies represent allies, who will stand by England in the hour of need, but "allies with the reservation that they are not to be employed wrongfully for objects which they cannot ascertain or do not approve." [A] There are clear indications that the policy of the dominions, though not yet planning a separation from England, is contemplating the future prospect of doing so. Canada, South Africa, and Australia are developing, as mentioned in Chapter IV., into independent nations and States, and will, when their time comes, claim formal independence.

[Footnote A: Th. Schiemann in the Kreuzzeitung of July 5, 1911.]

All these circumstances constitute a grave menace to the stability of England's Empire, and these dangers largely influence England's attitude towards Germany.

England may have to tolerate the rivalry of North America in her imperial and commercial ambitions, but the competition of Germany must be stopped. If England is forced to fight America, the German fleet must not be in a position to help the Americans. Therefore it must be destroyed.

A similar line of thought is suggested by the eventuality of a great English colonial war, which would engage England's fleets in far distant parts of the world. England knows the German needs and capabilities of expansion, and may well fear that a German Empire with a strong fleet might use such an opportunity for obtaining that increase of territory which England grudges. We may thus explain the apparent indifference of England to the French schemes of aggrandizement. France's capability of expansion is exhausted from insufficient increase of population. She can no longer be dangerous to England as a nation, and would soon fall victim to English lust of Empire, if only Germany were conquered.

The wish to get rid of the dangers presumably threatening from the German quarter is all the more real since geographical conditions offer a prospect of crippling the German overseas commerce without any excessive efforts. The comparative weakness of the German fleet, contrasted with the vast superiority of the English navy, allows a correspondingly easy victory to be anticipated, especially if the French fleet co-operates. The possibility, therefore, of quickly and completely getting rid of one rival, in order to have a free hand for all other contingencies, looms very near and undoubtedly presents a practicable means of placing the naval power of England on a firm footing for years to come, of annihilating German commerce and of checking the importance of German interests in Africa and Northern Asia.

The hostility to Germany is also sufficiently evident in other matters. It has always been England's object to maintain a certain balance of power between the continental nations of Europe, and to prevent any one of them attaining a pronounced supremacy. While these States crippled and hindered each other from playing any active part on the world's stage, England acquired an opportunity of following out her own purposes undisturbed, and of founding that world Empire which she now holds. This policy she still continues, for so long as the Powers of Europe tie each other's hands, her own supremacy is uncontested. It follows directly from this that England's aim must be to repress Germany, but strengthen France; for Germany at the present moment is the only European State which threatens to win a commanding position; but France is her born rival, and cannot keep on level terms with her stronger neighbour on the East, unless she adds to her forces and is helped by her allies. Thus the hostility to Germany, from this aspect also, is based on England's most important interests, and we must treat it as axiomatic and self-evident.

The argument is often adduced that England by a war with Germany would chiefly injure herself, since she would lose the German market, which is the best purchaser of her industrial products, and would be deprived of the very considerable German import trade. I fear that from the English point of view these conditions would be an additional incentive to war. England would hope to acquire, in place of the lost German market, a large part of those markets which had been supplied by Germany before the war, and the want of German imports would be a great stimulus, and to some extent a great benefit, to English industries.

After all, it is from the English aspect of the question quite comprehensible that the English Government strains every nerve to check the growing power of Germany, and that a passionate desire prevails in large circles of the English nation to destroy the German fleet which is building, and attack the objectionable neighbour.

English policy might, however, strike out a different line, and attempt to come to terms with Germany instead of fighting. This would be the most desirable course for us. A Triple

Alliance—Germany, England, and America—has been suggested.[B] But for such a union with Germany to be possible, England must have resolved to give a free course to German development side by side with her own, to allow the enlargement of our colonial power, and to offer no political hindrances to our commercial and industrial competition. She must, therefore, have renounced her traditional policy, and contemplate an entirely new grouping of the Great Powers in the world.

[Footnote B: "The United States and the War Cloud in Europe," by Th. Schiemann, McClure's Magazine, June, 1910.]

It cannot be assumed that English pride and self-interest will consent to that. The continuous agitation against Germany, under the tacit approval of the Government, which is kept up not only by the majority of the Press, but by a strong party in the country, the latest statements of English politicians, the military preparations in the North Sea, and the feverish acceleration of naval construction, are unmistakable indications that England intends to persist in her anti-German policy. The uncompromising hostility of England and her efforts to hinder every expansion of Germany's power were openly shown in the very recent Morocco question. Those who think themselves capable of impressing on the world the stamp of their spirit, do not resign the headship without a struggle, when they think victory is in their grasp.

A pacific agreement with England is, after all, a will-o'-the-wisp which no serious German statesman would trouble to follow. We must always keep the possibility of war with England before our eyes, and arrange our political and military plans accordingly. We need not concern ourselves with any pacific protestations of English politicians, publicists, and Utopians, which, prompted by the exigencies of the moment, cannot alter the real basis of affairs. When the Unionists, with their greater fixity of purpose, replace the Liberals at the helm, we must be prepared for a vigorous assertion of power by the island Empire.

On the other hand, America, which indisputably plays a decisive part in English policy, is a land of limitless possibilities. While, on the one side, she insists on the Monroe doctrine, on the other she stretches out her own arms towards Asia and Africa, in order to find bases for her fleets. The United States aim at the economic and, where possible, the political command of the American continent, and at the naval supremacy in the Pacific. Their interests, both economic and political, notwithstanding all commercial and other treaties, clash emphatically with those of Japan and England. No arbitration treaties could alter this.

No similar opposition to Germany, based on the nature of things, has at present arisen from the ambitions of the two nations; certainly not in the sphere of politics. So far as can be seen, an understanding with Germany ought to further the interests of America. It is unlikely that the Americans would welcome any considerable addition to the power of England. But such would be the case if Great Britain succeeded in inflicting a political and military defeat on Germany. For a time it seemed as if the Anglo-American negotiations about Arbitration Courts would definitely end in an alliance against Germany. There has, at any rate, been a great and widespread agitation against us in the United States. The Americans of German and Irish stock resolutely opposed it, and it is reasonable to assume that the anti-German movement in the United States was a passing phase, with no real foundation in the nature of things. In the field of commerce there is, no doubt, keen competition between the two countries, especially in South America; there is, however, no reason to assume that this will lead to political complications. Japan has, for the time being, a direct political interest for us only in her influence on the affairs of Russia, America, England, and China. In the Far East, since Japan has formed an alliance with England, and seems recently to have effected an arrangement with Russia, we have to count more on Japanese hostility than Japanese friendship. Her attitude to China may prove exceptionally important to our colonial possessions in East Asia. If the two nations joined hands—a hardly probable eventuality at present—it would become difficult for us to maintain an independent position between them. The political rivalry between the two nations of yellow race must therefore be kept alive. If they are antagonistic, they will both probably look for help against each other in their relations with Europe, and thus enable the European Powers to retain their possessions in Asia.

While the aspiring Great Powers of the Far East cannot at present directly influence our policy, Turkey—the predominant Power of the Near East—is of paramount importance to us. She is our natural ally; it is emphatically our interest to keep in close touch with her. The wisest course would have been to have made her earlier a member of the Triple Alliance, and so to have prevented the Turco-Italian War, which threatens to change the whole political situation, to our disadvantage. Turkey would gain in two ways: she assures her position both against Russia and against England—the two States, that is, with whose hostility we have to reckon. Turkey, also, is the only Power which can threaten England's position in Egypt, and thus menace the short sea-route and the land communications to India. We ought to spare no sacrifices to secure this country as an ally for the eventuality of a war with England or Russia. Turkey's interests are ours. It is also to the obvious advantage of Italy that Turkey maintain her commanding position on the Bosphorus and at the Dardanelles, that this important key should not be transferred to the keeping of foreigners, and belong to Russia or England.

If Russia gained the access to the Mediterranean, to which she has so long aspired, she would soon become a prominent Power in its eastern basin, and thus greatly damage the Italian projects in those waters. Since the English interests, also, would be prejudiced by such a development, the English fleet in the Mediterranean would certainly be strengthened. Between England, France, and Russia it would be quite impossible for Italy to attain an independent or commanding position, while the opposition of Russia and Turkey leaves the field open to her. From this view of the question, therefore, it is advisable to end the Turco-Italian conflict, and to try and satisfy the justifiable wishes of Italy at the cost of France, after the next war, it may be.

Spain alone of the remaining European Powers has any independent importance. She has developed a certain antagonism to France by her Morocco policy, and may, therefore, become eventually a factor in German policy. The petty States, on the contrary, form no independent centres of gravity, but may, in event of war, prove to possess a by no means negligible importance: the small Balkan States for Austria and Turkey; Denmark, Holland, Belgium, and Switzerland, and eventually Sweden, for Germany.

Switzerland and Belgium count as neutral. The former was declared neutral at the Congress of Vienna on November 20, 1815, under the collective guarantee [C] of the signatory Powers; Belgium, in the Treaties of London of November 15,1831, and of April 19,1839, on the part of the five Great Powers, the Netherlands, and Belgium itself.

[Footnote C: By a collective guarantee is understood the duty of the contracting Powers to take steps to protect this neutrality when all agree that it is menaced. Each individual Power has the right to interfere if it considers the neutrality menaced.]

If we look at these conditions as a whole, it appears that on the continent of Europe the power of the Central European Triple Alliance and that of the States united against it by alliance and agreement balance each other, provided that Italy belongs to the league. If we take into calculation the imponderabilia, whose weight can only be guessed at, the scale is inclined slightly in favour of the Triple Alliance. On the other hand, England indisputably rules the sea.

In consequence of her crushing naval superiority when allied with France, and of the geographical conditions, she may cause the greatest damage to Germany by cutting off her maritime trade. There is also a not inconsiderable army available for a continental war. When all considerations are taken into account, our opponents have a political superiority not to be underestimated. If France succeeds in strengthening her army by large colonial levies and a strong English landing-force, this superiority would be asserted on land also. If Italy really withdraws from the Triple Alliance, very distinctly superior forces will be united against Germany and Austria.

Under these conditions the position of Germany is extraordinarily difficult. We not only require for the full material development of our nation, on a scale corresponding to its intellectual importance, an extended political basis, but, as explained in the previous chapter, we are compelled to obtain space for our increasing population and markets for our growing industries. But at every step which we take in this direction England will resolutely oppose us. English policy may not yet have made the definite decision to attack us; but it doubtless wishes, by all and every means, even the most extreme, to hinder every further expansion of German international influence and of German maritime power. The recognized political aims of England and the attitude of the English Government leave no doubt on this point. But if we were involved in a struggle with England, we can be quite sure that France would not neglect the opportunity of attacking our flank. Italy, with her extensive coast-line, even if still a member of the Triple Alliance, will have to devote large forces to the defence of the coast to keep off the attacks of the Anglo-French Mediterranean Fleet, and would thus be only able to employ weaker forces against France. Austria would be paralyzed by Russia; against the latter we should have to leave forces in the East. We should thus have to fight out the struggle against France and England practically alone with a part of our army, perhaps with some support from Italy. It is in this double menace by sea and on the mainland of Europe that the grave danger to our political position lies, since all freedom of action is taken from us and all expansion barred.

Since the struggle is, as appears on a thorough investigation of the international question, necessary and inevitable, we must fight it out, cost what it may. Indeed, we are carrying it on at the present moment, though not with drawn swords, and only by peaceful means so far. On the one hand it is being waged by the competition in trade, industries and warlike preparations; on the other hand, by diplomatic methods with which the rival States are fighting each other in every region where their interests clash.

With these methods it has been possible to maintain peace hitherto, but not without considerable loss of power and prestige. This apparently peaceful state of things must not deceive us; we are facing a hidden, but none the less formidable, crisis—perhaps the most momentous crisis in the history of the German nation.

We have fought in the last great wars for our national union and our position among the Powers of Europe; we now must decide whether we wish to develop into and maintain a World Empire, and procure for German spirit and German ideas that fit recognition which has been hitherto withheld from them.

Have we the energy to aspire to that great goal? Are we prepared to make the sacrifices which such an effort will doubtless cost us? or are we willing to recoil before the hostile forces, and sink step by step lower in our economic, political, and national importance? That is what is involved in our decision.

"To be, or not to be," is the question which is put to us to-day, disguised, indeed, by the apparent equilibrium of the opposing interests and forces, by the deceitful shifts of diplomacy, and the official peace-aspirations of all the States; but by the logic of history inexorably demanding an answer, if we look with clear gaze beyond the narrow horizon of the day and the mere surface of things into the region of realities.

There is no standing still in the world's history. All is growth and development. It is obviously impossible to keep things in the status quo, as diplomacy has so often attempted. No true statesman will ever seriously count on such a possibility; he will only make the outward and temporary maintenance of existing conditions a duty when he wishes to gain time and deceive an opponent, or when he cannot see what is the trend of events. He will use such diplomatic means only as inferior tools; in reality he will only reckon with actual forces and with the powers of a continuous development.

We must make it quite clear to ourselves that there can be no standing still, no being satisfied for us, but only progress or retrogression, and that it is tantamount to retrogression when we are contented with our present place among the nations of Europe, while all our rivals are straining with desperate energy, even at the cost of our rights, to extend their power. The process of our decay would set in gradually and advance slowly so long as the struggle against us was waged with peaceful weapons; the living generation would, perhaps, be able to continue to exist in peace and comfort. But should a war be forced upon us by stronger enemies under conditions unfavourable to us, then, if our arms met with disaster, our political downfall would not be delayed, and we should rapidly sink down. The future of German nationality would be sacrificed, an independent German civilization would not long exist, and the blessings for which German blood has flowed in streams—spiritual and moral liberty, and the profound and lofty aspirations of German thought—would for long ages be lost to mankind.

If, as is right, we do not wish to assume the responsibility for such a catastrophe, we must have the courage to strive with every means to attain that increase of power which we are entitled to claim, even at the risk of a war with numerically superior foes.

Under present conditions it is out of the question to attempt this by acquiring territory in Europe. The region in the East, where German colonists once settled, is lost to us, and could only be recovered from Russia by a long and victorious war, and would then be a perpetual incitement to renewed wars. So, again, the reannexation of the former South Prussia, which was united to Prussia on the second partition of Poland, would be a serious undertaking, on account of the Polish population.

Under these circumstances we must clearly try to strengthen our political power in other ways. In the first place, our political position would be considerably consolidated if we could finally get rid of the standing danger that France will attack us on a favourable occasion, so soon as we find ourselves involved in complications elsewhere. In one way or another we must square our account with France if we wish for a free hand in our international policy. This is the first and foremost condition of a sound German policy, and since the hostility of France once for all cannot be removed by peaceful overtures, the matter must be settled by force of arms. France must be so completely crushed that she can never again come across our path.

Further, we must contrive every means of strengthening the political power of our allies. We have already followed such a policy in the case of Austria when we declared our readiness to protect, if necessary with armed intervention, the final annexation of Bosnia and Herzegovina by our ally on the Danube. Our policy towards Italy must follow the same lines, especially if in any Franco-German war an opportunity should be presented of doing her a really valuable service. It is equally good policy in every way to support Turkey, whose importance for Germany and the Triple Alliance has already been discussed.

Our political duties, therefore, are complicated, and during the Turco-Italian War all that we can do at first is to use our influence as mediators, and to prevent a transference of hostilities to the Balkan Peninsula. It cannot be decided at this moment whether further intervention will be necessary. Finally, as regards our own position in Europe, we can only effect an extension of our own political influence, in my opinion, by awakening in our weaker neighbours, through the integrity and firmness of our policy, the conviction that their independence and their interests are bound up with Germany, and are best secured under the protection of the German arms. This conviction might eventually lead to an enlargement of the Triple Alliance into a Central European Federation. Our military strength in Central Europe would by this means be considerably increased, and the extraordinarily unfavourable geographical configuration of our dominions would be essentially improved in case of war. Such a federation would be the expression of a natural community of interests, which is founded on the geographical and natural conditions, and would insure the durability of the political community based on it.

We must employ other means also for the widening of our colonial territory, so that it may be able to receive the overflow of our population. Very recent events have shown that, under certain circumstances, it is possible to obtain districts in Equatorial Africa by pacific negotiations. A financial or political crash in Portugal might give us the opportunity to take possession of a portion of the Portuguese colonies. We may assume that some understanding exists between England and Germany which contemplates a division of the Portuguese colonial possessions, but has never become publici juris. It cannot, indeed, be certain that England, if the contingency arrives, would be prepared honestly to carry out such a treaty, if it actually exists. She might find ways and means to invalidate it. It has even been often said, although disputed in other quarters, that Great Britain, after coming to an agreement with Germany about the partition of the Portuguese colonies, had, by a special convention, guaranteed Portugal the possession of all her colonies.

Other possible schemes may be imagined, by which some extension of our African territory would be possible. These need not be discussed here more particularly. If necessary, they must be obtained as the result of a successful European war. In all these possible acquisitions of territory the point must be strictly borne in mind that we require countries which are climatically suited to German settlers. Now, there are even in Central Africa large regions which are adapted to the settlement of German farmers and stock-breeders, and part of our overflow population might be diverted to those parts. But, generally speaking, we can only obtain in tropical colonies markets for our industrial products and wide stretches of cultivated ground for the growth of the raw materials which our industries require. This represents in itself a considerable advantage, but does not release us from the obligation to acquire land for actual colonization.

A part of our surplus population, indeed—so far as present conditions point—will always be driven to seek a livelihood outside the borders of the German Empire. Measures must be taken to the extent at least of providing that the German element is not split up in the world, but remains united in compact blocks, and thus forms, even in foreign countries, political centres of gravity in our favour, markets for our exports, and centres for the diffusion of German culture.

An intensive colonial policy is for us especially an absolute necessity. It has often been asserted that a "policy of the open door" can replace the want of colonies of our own, and must constitute our programme for the future, just because we do not possess sufficient colonies. This notion is only justified in a certain sense. In the first place, such a policy does not offer the possibility of finding homes for the overflow population in a territory of our own; next, it does not guarantee the certainty of an open and unrestricted trade competition. It secures to all trading nations equal tariffs, but this does not imply by any means competition under equal conditions. On the contrary, the political power which is exercised in such a country is the determining factor in the economic relations. The principle of the open door prevails everywhere—in Egypt, Manchuria, in the Congo State, in Morocco—and everywhere the politically dominant Power controls the commerce: in Manchuria Japan, in Egypt England, in the Congo State Belgium, and in Morocco France. The reason is plain. All State concessions fall naturally to that State which is practically dominant; its products are bought by all the consumers who are any way dependent on the power of the State, quite apart from the fact that by reduced tariffs and similar advantages for the favoured wares the concession of the open door can be evaded in various ways. A "policy of the open door" must at best be regarded as a makeshift, and as a complement of a vigorous colonial policy. The essential point is for a country to have colonies or its own and a predominant political influence in the spheres where its markets lie. Our German world policy must be guided by these considerations.

The execution of such political schemes would certainly clash with many old-fashioned notions and vested rights of the traditional European policy. In the first place, the principle of the balance of power in Europe, which has, since the Congress of Vienna, led an almost sacrosanct but entirely unjustifiable existence, must be entirely disregarded.

The idea of a balance of power was gradually developed from the feeling that States do not exist to thwart each other, but to work together for the advancement of culture. Christianity, which leads man beyond the limits of the State to a world citizenship of the noblest kind, and lays the foundation of all international law, has exercised a wide influence in this respect. Practical interests, too, have strengthened the theory of balance of power. When it was understood that the State was a power, and that, by its nature, it must strive to extend that power, a certain guarantee of peace was supposed to exist in the balance of forces. The conviction was thus gradually established that every State had a close community of interests with the other States, with which it entered into political and economic relations, and was bound to establish some sort of understanding with them. Thus the idea grew up in Europe of a State-system, which was formed after the fall of Napoleon by the five Great Powers—England, France, Russia, Austria, and Prussia, which latter had gained a place in the first rank by force of arms; in 1866 Italy joined it as the sixth Great Power.

"Such a system cannot be supported with an approximate equilibrium among the nations." "All theory must rest on the basis of practice, and a real equilibrium—an actual equality of power—is postulated,"[D] This condition does not exist between the European nations. England by herself rules the sea, and the 65,000,000 of Germans cannot allow themselves to sink to the same level of power as the 40,000,000 of French. An attempt has been made to produce a real equilibrium by special alliances. One result only has been obtained—the hindrance of the free development of the nations in general, and of Germany in particular. This is an unsound condition. A European balance of power can no longer be termed a condition which corresponds to the existing state of things; it can only have the disastrous consequences of rendering the forces of the continental European States mutually ineffective, and of thus favouring the plans of the political powers which stand outside that charmed circle. It has always been England's policy to stir up enmity between the respective continental States, and to keep them at approximately the same standard of power, in order herself undisturbed to conquer at once the sovereignty of the seas and the sovereignty of the world.

[Footnote D: Treitschke.]

We must put aside all such notions of equilibrium. In its present distorted form it is opposed to our weightiest interests. The idea of a State system which has common interests in civilization must not, of course, be abandoned; but it must be expanded on a new and more just basis. It is now not a question of a European State system, but of one embracing all the States in the world, in which the equilibrium is established on real factors of power. We must endeavour to obtain in this system our merited position at the head of a federation of Central European States, and thus reduce the imaginary European equilibrium, in one way or the other, to its true value, and correspondingly to increase our own power.

A further question, suggested by the present political position, is whether all the political treaties which were concluded at the beginning of the last century under quite other conditions—in fact, under a different conception of what constitutes a State—can, or ought to be, permanently observed. When Belgium was proclaimed neutral, no one contemplated that she would lay claim to a large and valuable region of Africa. It may well be asked whether the acquisition of such territory is not ipso facto a breach of neutrality, for a State from which—theoretically at least—all danger of war has been removed, has no right to enter into political competition with the other States. This argument is the more justifiable because it may safely be assumed that, in event of a war of Germany against France and England, the two last mentioned States would try to unite their forces in Belgium. Lastly, the neutrality of the Congo State [E] must be termed more than problematic, since Belgium claims the right to cede or sell it to a non-neutral country. The conception of permanent neutrality is entirely contrary to the essential nature of the State, which can only attain its highest moral aims in competition with other States. Its complete development presupposes such competition.

[Footnote E: The Congo State was proclaimed neutral, but without guarantees, by Acts of February 26, 1885.]

Again, the principle that no State can ever interfere in the internal affairs of another State is repugnant to the highest rights of the State. This principle is, of course, very variously interpreted, and powerful States have never refrained from a higher-handed interference in the internal affairs of smaller ones. We daily witness instances of such conduct. Indeed, England quite lately attempted to interfere in the private affairs of Germany, not formally or by diplomatic methods, but none the less in point of fact, on the subject of our naval preparations. It is, however, accepted as a principle of international intercourse that between the States of one and the same political system a strict non-interference in home affairs should be observed. The unqualified recognition of this principle and its application to political intercourse under all conditions involves serious difficulties. It is the doctrine of the Liberals, which was first preached in France in 1830, and of which the English Ministry of Lord Palmerston availed themselves for their own purpose. Equally false is the doctrine of unrestricted intervention, as promulgated by the States of the Holy Alliance at Troppau in 1820. No fixed principles for international politics can be laid down.

After all, the relation of States to each other is that of individuals; and as the individual can decline the interference of others in his affairs, so naturally, the same right belongs to the State. Above the individual, however, stands the authority of the State, which regulates the relations of the citizens to each other. But no one stands above the State, which regulates the relations of the citizens to each other. But no one stands above the State; it is sovereign and must itself decide whether the internal conditions or measures of another state menace its own existence or interests. In no case, therefore, may a sovereign State renounce the right of interfering in the affairs of other States, should circumstances demand. Cases may occur at any time, when the party disputes or the preparations of the neighboring country becomes a threat to the existence of a State. "It can only be asserted that every State acts at its own risk when it interferes in the internal affairs of another State, and that experience shows how very dangerous such an interference may become." On the other hand, it must be remembered that the dangers which may arise from non-intervention are occasionally still graver, and that the whole discussion turns, not on an international right, but simply and solely on power and expediency.

I have gone closely into these questions of international policy because, under conditions which are not remote, they may greatly influence the realization of our necessary political aspirations, and may give rise to hostile complications. Then it becomes essential that we do not allow ourselves to be cramped in our freedom of action by considerations, devoid of any inherent political necessity, which only depend on political expediency, and are not binding on us. We must remain conscious in all such eventualities that we cannot, under any circumstances, avoid fighting for our position in the world, and that the all-important point is, not to postpone that war as long as possible, but to bring it on under the most favourable conditions possible. "No man," so wrote Frederick the Great to Pitt on July 3, 1761, "if he has a grain of sense, will leave his enemies leisure to make all preparations in order to destroy him; he will rather take advantage of his start to put himself in a favourable position."

If we wish to act in this spirit of prompt and effective policy which guided the great heroes of our past, we must learn to concentrate our forces, and not to dissipate them in centrifugal efforts. The political and national development of the German people has always, so far back as German history extends, been hampered and hindered by the hereditary defects of its character—that is, by the particularism of the individual races and States, the theoretic dogmatism of the parties, the incapacity to sacrifice personal interests for great national objects from want of patriotism and of political common sense, often, also, by the pettiness of the prevailing ideas. Even to-day it is painful to see how the forces of the German nation, which are so restricted and confined in their activities abroad, are wasted in fruitless quarrels among themselves.

Our primary and most obvious moral and political duty is to overcome these hereditary failings, and to lay a secure foundation for a healthy, consistent development of our power.

It must not be denied that the variety of forms of intellectual and social life arising from the like variety of the German nationality and political system offers valuable advantages. It presents countless centres for the advancement of science, art, technical skill, and a high spiritual and material way of life in a steadily increasing development. But we must resist the converse of these conditions, the transference of this richness in variety and contrasts into the domain of politics.

Above all must we endeavour to confirm and consolidate the institutions which are calculated to counteract and concentrate the centrifugal forces of the German nature—the common system of defence of our country by land and sea, in which all party feeling is merged, and a strong national empire.

No people is so little qualified as the German to direct its own destinies, whether in a parliamentarian or republican constitution; to no people is the customary liberal pattern so inappropriate as to us. A glance at the Reichstag will show how completely this conviction, which is forced on us by a study of German history, holds good to-day.

The German people has always been incapable of great acts for the common interest except under the irresistible pressure of external conditions, as in the rising of 1813, or under the leadership of powerful personalities, who knew how to arouse the enthusiasm of the masses, to stir the German spirit to its depths, to vivify the idea of nationality, and force conflicting aspirations into concentration and union.

We must therefore take care that such men are assured the possibility of acting with a confident and free hand in order to accomplish great ends through and for our people.

Within these limits, it is in harmony with the national German character to allow personality to have a free course for the fullest development of all individual forces and capacities, of all spiritual, scientific, and artistic aims. "Every extension of the activities of the State is beneficial and wise, if it arouses, promotes, and purifies the independence of free and reasoning men; it is evil when it kills and stunts the independence of free men." [F] This independence of the individual, within the limits marked out by the interests of the State, forms the necessary complement of the wide expansion of the central power, and assures an ample scope to a liberal development of all our social conditions.

[Footnote F: Treitschke, "Politik," i., Section 2.]

We must rouse in our people the unanimous wish for power in this sense, together with the determination to sacrifice on the altar of patriotism, not only life and property, but also private views and preferences in the interests of the common welfare. Then alone shall we discharge our great duties of the future, grow into a World Power, and stamp a great part of humanity with the impress of the German spirit. If, on the contrary, we persist in that dissipation of energy which now marks our political life, there is imminent fear that in the great contest of the nations, which we must inevitably face, we shall be dishonourably beaten; that days of disaster await us in the future, and that once again, as in the days of our former degradation, the poet's lament will be heard:

"O Germany, thy oaks still stand,
But thou art fallen, glorious land!"
                    KÖRNER.

CHAPTER VI. THE SOCIAL AND POLITICAL SIGNIFICANCE OF ARMING FOR WAR

Germany has great national and historical duties of policy and culture to fulfil, and her path towards further progress is threatened by formidable enmities. If we realize this, we shall see that it will be impossible to maintain our present position and secure our future without an appeal to arms.

Knowing this, as every man must who impartially considers the political situation, we are called upon to prepare ourselves as well as possible for this war. The times are passed when a stamp of the foot raised an army, or when it was sufficient to levy the masses and lead them to battle. The armaments of the present day must be prepared in peace-time down to the smallest detail, if they are to be effective in time of need.

Although this fact is known, the sacrifices which are required for warlike preparations are no longer so willingly made as the gravity of the situation demands. Every military proposal is bitterly contested in the Reichstag, frequently in a very petty spirit, and no one seems to understand that an unsuccessful war would involve our nation in economic misery, with which the most burdensome charges for the army (and these for the most part come back again into the coffers of the country) cannot for an instant be compared. A victorious war, on the other hand, brings countless advantages to the conqueror, and, as our last great wars showed, forms a new departure in economic progress. The fact is often forgotten that military service and the observance of the national duty of bearing arms are in themselves a high moral gain for our people, and improve the strength and capacity for work. Nor can it be ignored that a nation has other than merely economic duties to discharge. I propose to discuss the question, what kind and degree of preparation for war the great historical crisis through which we are passing demands from us. First, however, it will be profitable to consider the importance of preparations for war generally, and not so much from the purely military as from the social and political aspect; we shall thus strengthen the conviction that we cannot serve the true interests of the country better than by improving its military capabilities.

Preparation for war has a double task to discharge. Firstly, it must maintain and raise the military capabilities of the nation as a national asset; and, secondly, it must make arrangements for the conduct of the war and supply the requisite means.

This capability of national defence has a pronounced educative value in national development. As in the social competition the persons able to protect themselves hold the field—the persons, that is, who, well equipped intellectually, do not shirk the contest, but fight it out with confidence and certainty of victory—so in the rivalry of nations and States victory rests with the people able to defend itself, which boldly enters the lists, and is capable of wielding the sword with success. Military service not only educates nations in warlike capacity, but it develops the intellectual and moral qualities generally for the occupations of peace. It educates a man to the full mastery of his body, to the exercise and improvement of his muscles; it develops his mental powers, his self-reliance and readiness of decision; it accustoms him to order and subordination for a common end; it elevates his self-respect and courage, and thus his capacity for every kind of work.

It is a quite perverted view that the time devoted to military service deprives economic life of forces which could have been more appropriately and more profitably employed elsewhere. These forces are not withdrawn from economic life, but are trained for economic life. Military training produces intellectual and moral forces which richly repay the time spent, and have their real value in subsequent life. It is therefore the moral duty of the State to train as many of its countrymen as possible in the use of arms, not only with the prospect of war, but that they may share in the benefits of military service and improve their physical and moral capacities of defence. The sums which the State applies to the military training of the nation are distinctly an outlay for social purposes; the money so spent serves social and educative ends, and raises the nation spiritually and morally; it thus promotes the highest aims of civilization more directly than achievements of mechanics, industries, trades, and commerce, which certainly discharge the material duties of culture by improving the national livelihood and increasing national wealth, but bring with them a number of dangers, such as craving for pleasure and tendency to luxury, thus slackening the moral and productive fibres of the nations. Military service as an educational instrument stands on the same level as the school, and, as will be shown in a later section, each must complete and assist the other. But a people which does not willingly bear the duties and sacrifices entailed by school and military service renounces its will to live, and sacrifices objects which are noble and assure the future for the sake of material advantages which are one-sided and evanescent.

It is the duty, therefore, of every State, conscious of its obligations towards civilization and society, remorselessly to put an end to all tendencies inimical to the full development of the power of defence. The method by which the maintenance and promotion of this defensive power can be practically carried out admits of great variety. It depends largely on the conditions of national life, on the geographical and political circumstances, as well as on past history, and consequently ranges between very wide extremes.

In the Boer States, as among most uncivilized peoples, the military training was almost exclusively left to the individual. That was sufficient to a certain point, since their method of life in itself made them familiar with carrying arms and with riding, and inured them to hard bodily exertions. The higher requirements of combination, subordination, and campaigning, could not be met by such a military system, and the consequences of this were felt disastrously in the conduct of the war. In Switzerland and other States an attempt is made to secure national defence by a system of militia, and to take account of political possibilities. The great European States maintain standing armies in which all able-bodied citizens have to pass a longer or shorter period of military training. England alone keeps up a mercenary army, and by the side of it a territorial army, whose ranks are filled by volunteers.

In these various ways different degrees of military efficiency are obtained, but, generally, experience shows that the more thorough and intelligent this training in arms, the greater the development of the requisite military qualities in the units; and the more these qualities become a second nature, the more complete will be their warlike efficiency.

When criticizing the different military systems, we must remember that with growing civilization the requisite military capacities are always changing. The duties expected from the Roman legionary or the soldiers who fought in line under Frederick the Great were quite different from those of the rifleman and cavalryman of to-day. Not merely have the physical functions of military service altered, but the moral qualities expected from the fighting man are altered. This applies to the individual soldier as much as to the whole army. The character of warfare has continually been changing. To fight in the Middle Ages or in the eighteenth century with comparatively small forces was one thing; it is quite another to handle the colossal armies of to-day. The preparations for war, therefore, in the social as well as military sense, must be quite different in a highly developed modern civilized State from those in countries, standing on a lower level of civilization, where ordinary life is full of military elements, and war is fought under relatively simple conditions.

The crushing superiority of civilized States over people with a less developed civilization and military system is due to this altered form of military efficiency. It was thus that Japan succeeded in raising herself in a brief space to the supremacy in Eastern Asia. She now reaps in the advancement of her culture what she sowed on the battlefield, and proves once again the immeasurable importance, in its social and educational aspects, of military efficiency. Our own country, by employing its military powers, has attained a degree of culture which it never could have reached by the methods of peaceful development.

When we regard the change in the nature of military efficiency, we find ourselves on ground where the social duty of maintaining the physical and moral power of the nation to defend itself comes into direct contact with the political duty of preparing for warfare itself.

A great variety of procedure is possible, and actually exists, in regard to the immediate preparations for war. This is primarily expressed in the choice of the military system, but it is manifested in various other ways. We see the individual States—according to their geographical position, their relations to other States and the military strength of their neighbours, according to their historic claims and their greater or less importance in the political system of the world—making their military preparations with more or less energy, earnestness, and expenditure. When we consider the complex movements of the life of civilized nations, the variety of its aims and the multiplicity of its emotions, we must agree that the growth or decrease of armaments is everywhere affected by these considerations. War is only a means of attaining political ends and of supporting moral strength.

Thus, if England attaches most weight to her navy, her insular position and the wide oversea interests which she must protect thoroughly justify her policy. If, on the other hand, England develops her land forces only with the objects of safeguarding the command of her colonies, repelling a very improbable hostile invasion, and helping an allied Power in a continental war, the general political situation explains the reason. As a matter of fact, England can never be involved in a great continental European war against her will.

So Switzerland, which has been declared neutral by political treaties, and can therefore only take the field if she is attacked, rightly lays most stress on the social importance of military service, and tries to develop a scheme of defence which consists mainly in increasing the security afforded by her own mountains. The United States of America, again, are justified in keeping their land forces within very modest limits, while devoting their energies to the increase of their naval power. No enemy equal to them in strength can ever spring up on the continent of America; they need not fear the invasion of any considerable forces. On the other hand, they are threatened by oversea conflicts, of epoch-making importance, with the yellow race, which has acquired formidable strength opposite their western coast, and possibly with their great trade rival England, which has, indeed, often made concessions, but may eventually see herself compelled to fight for her position in the world.

While in some States a restriction of armaments is natural and justifiable, it is easily understood that France must strain every nerve to secure her full recognition among the great military nations of Europe. Her glorious past history has fostered in her great political pretensions which she will not abandon without a struggle, although they are no longer justified by the size of her population and her international importance. France affords a conspicuous example of self-devotion to ideals and of a noble conception of political and moral duties.

In the other European States, as in France, external political conditions and claims, in combination with internal politics, regulate the method and extent of warlike preparations, and their attitude, which necessity forces upon them, must be admitted to carry its own justification. A State may represent a compact unity, from the point of view of nationality and civilization; it may have great duties to discharge in the development of human culture, and may possess the national strength to safeguard its independence, to protect its own interests, and, under certain circumstances, to persist in its civilizing mission and political schemes in defiance of other nations. Another State may be deficient in the conditions of individual national life and in elements of culture; it may lack the resources necessary for the defence and maintenance of its political existence single-handed in the teeth of all opposition. There is a vast difference between these two cases.

A State like the latter is always more or less dependent on the friendliness of stronger neighbours, whether it ranks in public law as fully independent or has been proclaimed neutral by international conventions. If it is attacked on one side, it must count on support from the other. Whether it shall continue to exist as a State and under what conditions must depend on the result of the ensuing war and the consequent political position—factors that lie wholly outside its own sphere of power.

This being the case, the question may well be put whether such a State is politically justified in requiring from its citizens in time of peace the greatest military efforts and correspondingly large pecuniary expenditure. It will certainly have to share the contest in which it is itself, perhaps, the prize, and theoretically will do best to have the largest possible military force at its disposal. But there is another aspect of the question which is at least arguable. The fighting power of such a State may be so small that it counts for nothing in comparison with the millions of a modern army. On the other hand, where appreciable military strength exists, it may be best not to organize the army with a view to decisive campaigning, but to put the social objects of military preparation into the foreground, and to adopt in actual warfare a defensive policy calculated to

lxi

gain time, with a view to the subsequent interference of the prospective allies with whom the ultimate decision will rest. Such an army must, if it is to attain its object, represent a real factor of strength. It must give the probable allies that effective addition of strength which may insure a superiority over the antagonist. The ally must then be forced to consider the interests of such secondary State. The forces of the possible allies will thus exercise a certain influence on the armament of the State, in combination with the local conditions, the geographical position, and the natural configuration of the country.

It is only to be expected that, since such various conditions exist, the utmost variety should also prevail among the military systems; and such is, in fact, the case.

In the mountain stronghold of Switzerland, which has to reckon with the political and military circumstances of Germany, France, and Italy, preparations for war take a different shape from those of Holland, situated on the coast and secured by numerous waterways, whose political independence is chiefly affected by the land forces of Germany and the navy of England.

The conditions are quite otherwise for a country which relies wholly on its own power.

The power of the probable antagonists and of the presumable allies will have a certain importance for it, and its Government will in its plans and military preparations pay attention to their grouping and attitudes; but these preparations must never be motived by such considerations alone. The necessity for a strong military force is permanent and unqualified; the political permutations and combinations are endless, and the assistance of possible allies is always an uncertain and shifting factor, on which no reliance can be reposed.

The military power of an independent State in the true sense must guarantee the maintenance of a force sufficient to protect the interests of a great civilized nation and to secure to it the necessary freedom of development. If from the social standpoint no sacrifice can be considered too great which promotes the maintenance of national military efficiency, the increase in these sacrifices due to political conditions must be willingly and cheerfully borne, in consideration of the object thereby to be gained. This object—of which each individual must be conscious—if conceived in the true spirit of statesmanship, comprises the conditions which are decisive for the political and moral future of the State as well as for the livelihood of each individual citizen.

A civilization which has a value of its own, and thus forms a vital factor in the development of mankind, can only flourish where all the healthy and stimulating capacities of a nation find ample scope in international competition. This is also an essential condition for the unhindered and vigorous exercise of individual activities. Where the natural capacity for growth is permanently checked by external circumstances, nation and State are stunted and individual growth is set back.

Increasing political power and the consequent multiplication of possibilities of action constitute the only healthy soil for the intellectual and moral strength of a vigorous nation, as is shown by every phase of history.

The wish for culture must therefore in a healthy nation express itself first in terms of the wish for political power, and the foremost duty of statesmanship is to attain, safeguard, and promote this power, by force of arms in the last resort. Thus the first and most essential duty of every great civilized people is to prepare for war on a scale commensurate with its political needs. Even the superiority of the enemy cannot absolve from the performance of this requirement. On the contrary, it must stimulate to the utmost military efforts and the most strenuous political action in order to secure favourable conditions for the eventuality of a decisive campaign. Mere numbers count for less than ever in modern fighting, although they always constitute a very important factor of the total strength. But, within certain limits, which are laid down by the law of numbers, the true elements of superiority under the present system of gigantic armies are seen to be spiritual and moral strength, and larger masses will be beaten by a small, well-led and self-devoting army. The Russo-Japanese War has proved this once more.

Granted that the development of military strength is the first duty of every State, since all else depends upon the possibility to assert power, it does not follow that the State must spend the total of its personal and financial resources solely on military strength in the narrower sense of army and navy. That is neither feasible nor profitable. The military power of a people is not exclusively determined by these external resources; it consists, rather, in a harmonious development of physical, spiritual, moral, financial, and military elements of strength. The highest and most effective military system cannot be developed except by the co-operation of all these factors. It needs a broad and well-constructed basis in order to be effective. In the Manchurian War at the critical moment, when the Japanese attacking strength seemed spent, the Russian military system broke down, because its foundation was unstable; the State had fallen into political and moral ruin, and the very army was tainted with revolutionary ideas.

The social requirement of maintaining military efficiency, and the political necessity for so doing, determine the nature and degree of warlike preparations; but it must be remembered that this standard may be very variously estimated, according to the notion of what the State's duties are. Thus, in Germany the most violent disputes burst out whenever the question of the organization of the military forces is brought up, since widely different opinions prevail about the duties of the State and of the army.

It is, indeed, impossible so to formulate and fix the political duties of the State that they cannot be looked at from another standpoint. The social democrat, to whom agitation is an end in itself, will see the duty of the State in a quite different light from the political dilettante, who lives from hand to mouth, without making the bearing of things clear to himself, or from the sober Statesman who looks to the welfare of the community and keeps his eyes fixed on the distant beacons on the horizon of the future.

Certain points of view, however, may be laid down, which, based on the nature of things, check to some degree any arbitrary decision on these momentous questions, and are well adapted to persuade calm and experienced thinkers.

First, it must be observed that military power cannot be improvised in the present political world, even though all the elements for it are present.

Although the German Empire contains 65,000,000 inhabitants, compared to 40,000,000 of French, this excess in population represents merely so much dead capital, unless a corresponding majority of recruits are annually enlisted, and unless in peace-time the necessary machinery is set up for their organization. The assumption that these masses would be available for the army in the moment of need is a delusion. It would not mean a strengthening, but a distinct weakening, of the army, not to say a danger, if these untrained masses were at a crisis suddenly sent on active service. Bourbaki's campaign shows what is to be expected from such measures. Owing to the complexity of all modern affairs, the continuous advance in technical skill and in the character of warlike weapons, as also in the increased requirements expected from the individual, long and minute preparations are necessary to procure the highest military values. Allusion has already been made to this at the beginning of this chapter. It takes a year to complete a 30-centimetre cannon. If it is to be ready for use at a given time, it must have been ordered long beforehand. Years will pass before the full effect of the strengthening of the army, which is now being decided on, appears in the rolls of the Reserve and the Landwehr. The recruit who begins his service to-day requires a year's training to become a useful soldier. With the hasty training of substitute reservists and such expedients, we merely deceive ourselves as to the necessity of serious preparations. We must not regard the present only, but provide for the future.

The same argument applies to the political conditions. The man who makes the bulk of the preparations for war dependent on the shifting changes of the politics of the day, who wishes to slacken off in the work of arming because no clouds in the political horizon suggest the necessity of greater efforts, acts contrary to all real statesmanship, and is sinning against his country. The moment does not decide; the great political aspirations, oppositions, and tensions, which are based on the nature of things—these turn the scale.

When King William at the beginning of the sixties of the last century undertook the reorganization of the Prussian army, no political tension existed. The crisis of 1859 had just subsided. But the King had perceived that the Prussian armament was insufficient to meet the requirements of the future. After a bitter struggle he extorted from his people a reorganization of the army, and this laid the foundations without which the glorious progress of our State would never have begun. In the same true spirit of statesmanship the Emperor William II. has powerfully aided and extended the evolution of our fleet, without being under the stress of any political necessity; he has enjoyed the cheerful co-operation of his people, since the reform at which he aimed was universally recognized as an indisputable need of the future, and accorded with traditional German sentiment.

While the preparation for war must be completed irrespectively of the political influences of the day, the military power of the probable opponents marks a limit below which the State cannot sink without jeopardizing the national safety.

Further, the State is bound to enlist in its service all the discoveries of modern science, so far as they can be applied to warfare, since all these methods and engines of war, should they be exclusively in the hands of the enemy, would secure him a distinct superiority. It is an obvious necessity to keep the forces which can be put into the field as up-to-date as possible, and to facilitate their military operations by every means which science and mechanical skill supply. Further, the army must be large enough to constitute a school for the whole nation, in which a thoroughgoing and no mere superficial military efficiency may be attained.

Finally, the nature of the preparation for war is to some degree regulated by the political position of the State. If the State has satisfied its political ambitions and is chiefly concerned with keeping its place, the military policy will assume a more or less defensive character. States, on the other hand, which are still desirous of expansion, or such as are exposed to attacks on different sides, must adopt a predominantly offensive military system.

Preparations for war in this way follow definite lines, which are dictated by necessity and circumstances; but it is evident that a wide scope is still left for varieties of personal opinion, especially where the discussion includes the positive duties of the State, which may lead to an energetic foreign policy, and thus possibly to an offensive war, and where very divergent views exist as to the preparation for war. In this case the statesman's only resource is to use persuasion, and to so clearly expound and support his conceptions of the necessary policy that the majority of the nation accept his view. There are always and everywhere conditions which have a persuasive character of their own, and appeal to the intellects and the feelings of the masses. Every Englishman is convinced of the necessity to maintain the command of the sea, since he realizes that not only the present powerful position of the country, but also the possibility of feeding the population in case of war, depend on it. No sacrifice for the fleet is too great, and every increase of foreign navies instantly disquiets public opinion. The whole of France, except a few anti-military circles, feels the necessity of strengthening the position of the State, which was shaken by the defeats of 1870-71, through redoubled exertions in the military sphere, and this object is being pursued with exemplary unanimity.

Even in neutral Switzerland the feeling that political independence rests less on international treaties than on the possibility of self-defence is so strong and widespread that the nation willingly supports heavy taxation for its military equipment. In Germany, also, it should be possible to arouse a universal appreciation of the great duties of the State, if only our politicians, without any diplomatic evasion, which deceives no one abroad and is harmful to the people at home, disclosed the true political situation and the necessary objects of our policy.

To be sure, they must be ready to face a struggle with public opinion, as King William I. did: for when public opinion does not stand under the control of a master will or a compelling necessity, it can be led astray too easily by the most varied influences. This danger is particularly great in a country so torn asunder internally and externally as Germany. He who in such a case listens to public opinion runs a danger of inflicting immense harm on the interests of State and people.

One of the fundamental principles of true statesmanship is that permanent interests should never be abandoned or prejudiced for the sake of momentary advantages, such as the lightening of the burdens of the taxpayer, the temporary maintenance of peace, or suchlike specious benefits, which, in the course of events, often prove distinct disadvantages.

The statesman, therefore, led astray neither by popular opinion nor by the material difficulties which have to be surmounted, nor by the sacrifices required of his countrymen, must keep these objects carefully in view. So long as it seems practicable he will try to reconcile the conflicting interests and bring them into harmony with his own. But where great fundamental questions await decision, such as the actual enforcement of universal service or of the requirements on which readiness for war depends, he must not shrink from strong measures in order to create the forces which the State needs, or will need, in order to maintain its vitality.

One of the most essential political duties is to initiate and sanction preparations for war on a scale commensurate with the existing conditions; to organize them efficiently is the duty of the military authorities—a duty which belongs in a sense to the sphere of strategy, since it supplies the machinery with which commanders have to reckon. Policy and strategy touch in this sphere. Policy has a strategic duty to perform, since it sanctions preparations for war and defines their limit.

It would, therefore, be a fatal and foolish act of political weakness to disregard the military and strategic standpoint, and to make the bulk of the preparations for war dependent on the financial moans momentarily available. "No expenditure without security," runs the formula in which this policy clothes itself. It is justified only when the security is fixed by the expenditure. In a great civilized State it is the duties which must be fulfilled—as Treitschke, our great historian and national politician, tells us—that determine the expenditure, and the great Finance Minister is not the man who balances the national accounts by sparing the national forces, while renouncing the politically indispensable outlay, but he who stimulates all the live forces of the nation to cheerful activity, and so employs them for national ends that the State revenue suffices to meet the admitted political demands. He can only attain this purpose if he works in harmony with the Ministers for Commerce, Agriculture, Industries, and Colonies, in order to break down the restrictions which cramp the enterprise and energy of the individual, to make all dead values remunerative, and to create favourable conditions for profitable business. A great impulse must thrill the whole productive and financial circles of the State, if the duties of the present and the future are to be fulfilled.

Thus the preparation for war, which, under modern conditions, calls for very considerable expenditure, exercises a marked influence on the entire social and political life of the people and on the financial policy of the State.

CHAPTER VII.THE CHARACTER OF OUR NEXT WAR

The social necessity of maintaining the power of the nation to defend itself, the political claims which the State puts forward, the strength of the probable hostile combinations, are the chief factors which determine the conditions of preparation for war.

I have already tried to explain and formulate the duties in the spheres of policy and progress which our history and our national character impose on us. My next task is to observe the possible military combinations which we must be prepared to face.

In this way only can we estimate the dangers which threaten us, and can judge whether, and to what degree, we can carry out our political intentions. A thorough understanding of these hostile counter-movements will give us a clear insight into the character of the next war; and this war will decide our future.

It is not sufficient to know the military fighting forces of our probable antagonists, although this knowledge constitutes the necessary basis for further inquiry; but we must picture to ourselves the intensity of the hostility with which we have to reckon and the probable efficiency of oar enemies. The hostility which we must anticipate is determined by the extent to which mutual political schemes and ambitions clash, and by the opposition in national character. Our opinion as to the military efficiency of our rivals must be based on the latest data available.

If we begin by looking at the forces of the individual States and groups of States which may be hostile to us, we have the following results: According to the recent communications of the French Finance Minister Klotz (in a speech made at the unveiling of a war memorial in Issoudan), the strength of the French army on a peace footing in the year 1910 amounted in round figures to 580,000 men. This included the "Colonial Corps," stationed in France itself, which, in case of war, belongs to the field army in the European theatre of war, and the "Service auxiliaire "—that is, some 30,000 non-efficients, who are drafted in for service without arms. The entire war establishment, according to the information of the same Minister, including field army and reserves, consists of 2,800,000 men available on mobilization. A reduction from this number must be made in event of mobilization, which French sources put down at 20 per cent. The whole strength of the French field army and reserves may therefore be reckoned at some 2,300,000.

To this must be added, as I rather from the same source, 1,700,000 Territorials, with their "reserve," from which a reduction of 25 per cent., or roughly 450,000 men, must be made.

If it is assumed that, in case of war, the distribution of the arms will correspond to that in peace, the result is, on the basis of the strength of separate arms, which the Budget of 1911 anticipates, that out of the 2,300,000 field and reserve troops there must be assigned—to the infantry, about 1,530.000; to the cavalry, about 230,000 (since a considerable part of the reservists of these arms are employed in the transport service); to the artillery, about 380,000; to the pioneers, 70,000: to train and administration services (trains, columns, medical service, etc.), 90,000.

No further increase in these figures is possible, since in France 90 per cent, of all those liable to serve have been called up, and the birth-rate is steadily sinking. While in 1870 it reached 940,000 yearly, it has sunk in 1908 to 790.000. Recourse already has been had to the expedient of requiring smaller qualifications than before, and of filling the numerous subsidiary posts (clerks, waiters, etc.) with less efficient men, in order to relieve the troops themselves.

Under these conditions, it was necessary to tap new sources, and the plan has been formed of increasing the troops with native-born Algerians and Tunisians, in order to be able to strengthen the European army with them in event of war. At the same time negroes, who are excellent and trustworthy material, are to be enrolled in West Africa. A limited conscription, such as exists in Tunis, is to be introduced into Algeria. The black army is at first to be completed by volunteers, and conscription will only be enforced at a crisis. These black troops are in the first place to garrison Algeria and Tunis, to release the troops stationed there for service in Europe, and to protect the white settlers against the natives. Since the negroes raised for military service are heathen, it is thought that they will be a counterpoise to the Mohammedan natives. It has been proved that negro troops stand the climate of North Africa excellently, and form very serviceable troops. The two black battalions stationed in the Schauja, who took part in the march to Fez, bore the climate well, and thoroughly proved their value. There can be no doubt that this plan will be vigorously prosecuted, with every prospect of success. It is so far in an early stage. Legislative proposals on the use of the military resources offered by the native Algerians and the West African negroes have not yet been laid before Parliament by the Government. It cannot yet be seen to what extent the native and black troops will be increased. The former Minister of War, Messimy, had advocated a partial conscription of the native Algerians. An annual muster is made of the Algerian males of eighteen years of age available for military service. The Commission appointed for the purpose reported in 1911 that, after the introduction of the limited service in the army and the reserve, there would be in Algeria and Tunisia combined some 100,000 to 120,000 native soldiers available in war-time. They could also be employed in Europe, and are thus intended to strengthen the Rhine army by three strong army corps of first-class troops, who, in the course of years, may probably be considerably increased by the formation of reserves. As regards the black troops, the matter is different. France, in her West African possessions combined, has some 16,000 negro troops available. As the black population numbers 10,000,000 to 12,000,000, these figures may be considerably raised.

Since May, 1910, there has been an experimental battalion of Senegalese sharp-shooters in Southern Algeria, and in the draft War Budget for 1912 a proposal was made to transfer a second battalion of Senegalese to Algeria. The conclusion is forced upon us that the plan of sending black troops in larger numbers to Algeria will be vigorously prosecuted. There is, however, no early probability of masses of black troops being transported to North Africa, since there are not at present a sufficient number of trained men available. The Senegalese Regiments 1, 2 and 3, stationed in Senegambia, are hardly enough to replace and complete the Senegalese troops quartered in the other African colonies of France. Although there is no doubt that France is in a position to raise a strong black army, the probability that black divisions will be available for a European war is still remote. But it cannot be questioned that they will be so some day.

Still less is any immediate employment of native Moroccan troops in Europe contemplated. Morocco possesses very good native warriors, but the Sultan exerts effective sovereignty only over a part of the territory termed "Morocco." There cannot be, therefore, for years to come any question of employing this fighting material on a large scale. The French and Moroccan Governments are for the moment occupied in organizing a serviceable Sultan's army of 20,000 men to secure the command of the country and to release the French troops in Morocco.

The annexation of Morocco may for the time being mean no great addition to military strength; but, as order is gradually established, the country will prove to be an excellent recruiting depot, and France will certainly use this source of power with all her accustomed energy in military matters.

For the immediate future we have, therefore, only to reckon with the reinforcements of the French European army which can be obtained from Algeria and Tunisia, so soon as the limited system of conscription is universally adopted there. This will supply a minimum of 120,000 men, and the tactical value of these troops is known to any who have witnessed their exploits on the battlefields of Weissenburg and Wörth. At least one strong division of Turcos is already available.

Next to the French army, we are chiefly concerned with the military power of Russia. Since the peace and war establishments are not published, it is hard to obtain accurate statistics; no information is forthcoming as to the strength of the various branches of the service, but the totals of the army may be calculated approximately. According to the recruiting records of the last three years, the strength of the Russian army on a peace footing amounts to 1,346,000 men, inclusive of Cossacks and Frontier Guards. Infantry and sharp-shooters are formed into 37 army corps (1 Guards, 1 Grenadiers, and 25 army corps in Europe; 3 Caucasian, 2 Turkistanian, and 5 Siberian corps). The cavalry is divided into divisions, independent brigades, and separate independent regiments.

In war, each army corps consists of 2 divisions, and is in round figures 42,000 strong; each infantry division contains 2 brigades, at a strength of 20,000. Each sharp-shooter brigade is about 9,000 strong, the cavalry divisions about 4,500 strong. On the basis of these numbers, we arrive at a grand total of 1,800,000 for all the army corps, divisions, sharp-shooter brigades, and cavalry divisions. To this must be added unattached troops and troops on frontier or garrison duty, so that the war strength of the standing army can be reckoned at some 2,000,000.

This grand total is not all available in a European theatre of war. The Siberian and Turkistanian army corps must be deducted, as they would certainly be left in the interior and on the eastern frontier. For the maintenance of order in the interior, it would probably be necessary to leave the troops in Finland, the Guards at St. Petersburg, at least one division at Moscow, and the Caucasian army corps in the Caucasus. This would mean a deduction of thirteen army corps, or 546,000 men; so that we have to reckon with a field army, made up of the standing army, 1,454,000 men strong. To this must be added about 100 regiments of Cossacks of the Second and Third Ban, which may be placed at 50,000 men, and the reserve and Empire-defence formations to be set on foot in case of war. For the formation of reserves, there are sufficient trained men available to constitute a reserve division of the first and second rank for each corps respectively. These troops, if each division is assumed to contain 20,000 men, would be 1,480,000 men strong. Of course, a certain reduction must be made in these figures. Also it is not known which of these formations would be really raised in event of mobilization. In any case, there will be an enormous army ready to be put into movement for a great war. After deducting all the forces which must be left behind in the interior, a field army of 2,000,000 men could easily be organized in Europe. It cannot be stated for certain whether arms, equipment, and ammunition for such a host can be supplied in sufficient quantity. But it will be best not to undervalue an Empire like Russia in this respect.

Quite another picture is presented to us when we turn our attention to England, the third member of the Triple Entente.

The British Empire is divided from the military point of view into two divisions: into the United Kingdom itself with the Colonies governed by the English Cabinet, and the self-governing Colonies. These latter have at their disposal a militia, which is sometimes only in process of formation. They can be completely ignored so far as concerns any European theatre of war. The army of the parts of the Empire administered by the English Cabinet divides into the regular army, which is filled up by enlistment, the native troops, commanded by English officers, and the Territorial army, a militia made up of volunteers which has not reached the intended total of 300,000. It is now 270,000 strong, and is destined exclusively for home defence. Its military value cannot at present be ranked very highly. For a Continental European war it may be left out of account. We have in that case only to deal with a part of the regular English army. This is some 250,000 strong. The men serve twelve years, of which seven are with the colours and five in the reserve. The annual supply of recruits is 35,000. The regular reserve is now 136,000 strong. There is also a special reserve, with a militia-like training, which is enlisted for special purposes, so that the grand total of the reserve reaches the figure of 200,000.

Of the regular English army, 134,000 men are stationed in England, 74,500 in India (where, in combination with 159,000 native troops, they form the Anglo-Indian army), and about 39,000 in different stations—Gibraltar, Malta, Egypt, Aden, South Africa, and the other Colonies and Protectorates. In this connection the conditions in Egypt are the most interesting: 6,000 English are stationed there, while in the native Egyptian army (17,000 strong; in war-time, 29,000 strong) one-fifth of the officers are Englishmen. It may be supposed that, in view of the great excitement in the Moslem world, the position of the English is precarious. The 11,000 troops now stationed in South Africa are to be transferred as soon as possible to Mediterranean garrisons. In event of war, a special division will, on emergency, be organized there.

For a war in Continental Europe, we have only to take into account the regular army stationed in England. When mobilized, it forms the "regular field army" of 6 infantry divisions, 1 cavalry division, 2 mounted brigades and army troops, and numbers 130,000 men, without columns and trains. The regular troops in the United Kingdom which do not form part of the regular field army are some 100,000 strong. They consist of a very small number of mobile units, foot artillery, and engineers for coast defence, as well as the reserve formations. These troops, with some 13,000 militia artillery and militia engineers, constitute the Home Army, under whose protection the Territorial field army is completing its organization. Months must certainly elapse before portions of this army can strengthen the regular field army. At the most 150,000 men may be reckoned upon for an English expeditionary force. These troops compose at the same time the reserve of the troops stationed in the Colonies, which require reinforcements at grave crises. This constitutes the weak point in the British armament. England can employ her regular army in a Continental war so long only as all is quiet in the Colonies. This fact brings into prominence how important it will be, should war break out, to threaten England in her colonial possessions, and especially in Egypt.

Against the powerful hosts which the Powers of the Triple Entente can put into the field, Germany can command an active army of 589,705 men (on peace establishment, including non-commissioned officers) and about 25,500 officers; while Austria has an army which on a peace footing is 361,553 men and about 20,000 officers strong. The combined war strength of the two States may be estimated as follows:

In Germany there were drafted into the army, including volunteers and non-combatants, in 1892, 194,664 men; in 1909, 267,283 men; or on an average for seventeen years, 230,975 men annually. This gives a total of 3,926,575 men. If we estimate the natural decrease at 25 per cent., we have 2,944,931 trained men left. By adding the peace establishment to it, we arrive at an estimated strength of 3,534,636, which the French can match with about the same figures.

The annual enlistment in Austria amounts to some 135,000. Liability to serve lasts twelve years, leaving out of account service in the Landsturm. Deducting the three years of active service, this gives a total of 1,215,000, or, after the natural decrease by 25 per cent., 911,250 men. To this must be added the nine yearly batches of trained Landsturm, which, after the same deductions, will come likewise to 911,250. The addition of the peace strength of the army will produce a grand total of 2,184,053 men on a war footing; approximately as many as Russia, after all deductions, can bring into the field in Europe.

In what numbers the existing soldiers would in case of war be available for field formations in Germany and Austria is not known, and it would be undesirable to state. It depends partly on the forces available, partly on other circumstances winch are not open to public discussion. However high our estimate of the new formations may be, we shall never reach the figures which the combined forces of France and Russia present. We must rather try to nullify the numerical superiority of the enemy by the increased tactical value of the troops, by intelligent generalship, and a prompt use of opportunity and locality. Even the addition of the Italian army to the forces of Germany and Austria would not, so far as I know, restore numerical equality in the field.

In France it has been thought hitherto that two or three army corps must be left on the Italian frontier. Modern French writers [A] are already reckoning so confidently on the withdrawal of Italy from the Triple Alliance that they no longer think it necessary to put an army in the field against Italy, but consider that the entire forces of France are available against Germany.

[Footnote A: Colonel Boucher, "L'offensive contre l'Allemagne."]

The peace establishment of the Italian army amounts, in fact, to 250,000 men, and is divided into 12 army corps and 25 divisions. The infantry, in 96 regiments, numbers 140,000; there are besides 12 regiments of Bersaglieri, with which are 12 cyclist battalions and 8 Alpine regiments in 78 companies. The cavalry consists of 29 regiments, 12 of which are united in 3 cavalry divisions. The artillery has a strength of 24 field artillery regiments and 1 mounted regiment of artillery, and numbers 193 field and 8 mounted batteries. Besides this there are 27 mountain batteries and 10 regiments of garrison artillery in 98 companies. Lastly, there are 6 engineer regiments, including a telegraph regiment and an airship battalion. The Gendarmerie contains 28,000 men.

On a war footing the strength of the field army is 775,000. Some 70,000 men are enrolled in other formations of the first and second line. The militia is some 390,000 strong. The strength of the reserves who might be mobilized is not known. The field army is divided into 3 armies of 9 army corps in all, to which are added 8 to 12 divisions of the Territorial army and 4 cavalry divisions.

As to colonial troops, Italy can command in Benadir the services of 48 officers and 16 non-commissioned officers of Italian birth, and 3,500 native soldiers; in Eritrea there are 131 officers, 644 non-commissioned officers and privates of Italian birth, and 3,800 natives.

Italy thus can put a considerable army into the field; but it is questionable whether the South Italian troops have much tactical value. It is possible that large forces would be required for coast-defence, while the protection of Tripoli, by no means an easy task, would claim a powerful army if it is to be held against France.

The Turkish military forces would be of great importance if they joined the coalition of Central European Powers or its opponents.

The regular peace establishment of the Turkish army amounts to 275,000 men. In the year 1910 there were three divisions of it:

I. The Active Army (Nizam):

  Infantry 133,000
  Cavalry 26,000
  Artillery 43,000

Pioneers 4,500
Special troops 7,500
Train formations 3,000
Mechanics 3,000
A total, that is, of 220,000 men.
2. The Redif (militia) cadres, composed of infantry, 25,000 men. Within this limit, according to the Redif law, men are enlisted in turns for short trainings.
3. Officers in the Nizam and Redif troops, military employés, officials, and others, more than 30,000.
The entire war strength of the Turkish army amounts to 700,000 men. We need only to take into consideration the troops from Europe, Anatolia, Armenia, and Syria. All these troops even are not available in a European theatre of war. On the other hand, the "Mustafiz" may be regarded as an "extraordinary reinforcement"; this is usually raised for local protection or the maintenance of quiet and order in the interior. To raise 30,000 or 40,000 men of this militia in Europe is the simplest process. From the high military qualities of the Turkish soldiers, the Turkish army must be regarded as a very important actor. Turkey thus is a very valuable ally to whichever party she joins.
The smaller Balkan States are also able to put considerable armies into the field.
Montenegro can put 40,000 to 45,000 men into the field, with 104 cannons and 44 machine guns, besides 11 weak reserve battalions for frontier and home duties.
Servia is supposed to have an army 28,000 strong on a peace footing; this figure is seldom reached, and sinks in winter to 10,000 men. The war establishment consists of 250,000 men, comprising about 165,000 rifles, 5,500 sabres, 432 field and mountain guns (108 batteries of 4 guns); besides this there are 6 heavy batteries of 4 to 6 cannons and 228 machine guns available. Lastly come the reserve formations (third line), so that in all some 305,000 men can be raised, exclusive of the militia, an uncertain quantity.
The Bulgarian army has a peace establishment of 59,820 men. It is not known how they are distributed among the various branches of the service. On a war footing an army of 330,000 is raised, including infantry at a strength of 230,000 rifles, with 884 cannons, 232 machine guns, and 6,500 sabres. The entire army, inclusive of the reserves and national militia, which latter is only available for home service and comprises men from forty-one to forty-six years of age, is said to be 400,000 strong.
Rumania, which occupies a peculiar position politically, forms a power in herself. There is in Rumania, besides the troops who according to their time of service are permanently with the colours, a militia cavalry called "Calarashi" (intelligent young yeomen on good horses of their own), whose units serve intermittently for short periods.
In peace the army is composed of 5,000 officers and 90,000 men of the permanent establishment, and some 12,000 serving intermittently. The infantry numbers some 2,500 officers and 57,000 men, the permanent cavalry (Rosiori) some 8,000 men with 600 officers, and the artillery 14,000 men with 700 officers.
For war a field army can be raised of some 6,000 officers and 274,000 men, with 550 cannons. Of these 215,000 men belong to the infantry, 7,000 to the cavalry, and 20,000 to the artillery. The cavalry is therefore weaker than on the peace footing, since, as it seems, a part of the Calarashi is not to be employed as cavalry. Inclusive of reserves and militia, the whole army will be 430,000 strong. There are 650,000 trained men available for service.
Although the Balkan States, from a military point of view, chiefly concern Austria, Turkey, and

Russia, and only indirectly come into relations with Germany, yet the armies of the smaller Central European States may under some circumstances be of direct importance to us, if they are forced or induced to take part with us or against us in a European war.

Of our western neighbours, Switzerland and Holland come first under consideration, and then Belgium.

Switzerland can command, in case of war, a combined army of 263,000 men. The expeditionary force, which is of first importance for an offensive war, consists of 96,000 infantry and 5,500 cavalry, with 288 field guns and 48 field howitzers (the howitzer batteries are in formation), a total of 141,000 men.

The Landwehr consists of 50.000 infantry and 4,000 cavalry, with 36 12-centimetre cannons belonging to foot artillery. It has a total strength of 69,000 men. The Landsturm finally has a strength of 53,000 men.

The Dutch army has a peace establishment averaging 30,000 men, which varies much owing to the short period of service. There are generally available 13,000 infantry, 3,000 cavalry, 5,000 field artillery, 3,400 garrison artillery, and 1,400 engineers, pontonniers, and transport troops. The field army in war is 80,000 strong, and is made up of 64,000 infantry, cyclist, and machine-gun sections, 2,600 cavalry, 4,400 artillery, and goo engineers. It is formed into 4 army divisions each of 15 battalions, 4 squadrons, 6 batteries, and 1 section engineers. There is, further, a garrison army of 80,000 men, which consists of 12 active and 48 Landwehr infantry battalions, 44 active and 44 Landwehr foot artillery companies, and 10 companies engineers and pontonniers, including Landwehr. The Dutch coast also is fortified. At Holder, Ymuiden, Hook of Holland, at Völkerack and Haringvliet there are various outworks, while the fortifications at Flushing are at present unimportant. Amsterdam is also a fortress with outlying fortifications in the new Dutch water-line (Fort Holland).

Holland is thus well adapted to cause serious difficulties to an English landing, if her coast batteries are armed with effective cannons. It would easily yield to a German invasion, if it sided against us.

Belgium in peace has 42,800 troops available, distributed as follows: 26,000 infantry, 5,400 cavalry, 4,650 field artillery, 3,400 garrison artillery, 1,550 engineers and transport service. On a war footing the field army will be 100,000 strong, comprising 74,000 infantry, 7,250 cavalry, 10,000 field artillery, 1,900 engineers and transport service, and is formed into 4 army divisions and 2 cavalry divisions. The latter are each 20 squadrons and 2 batteries strong; each of the army divisions consists nominally of 17 battalions infantry, 1 squadron, 12 batteries, and 1 section engineers. In addition there is a garrison army of 80,000, which can be strengthened by the garde civique, Antwerp forms the chief military base, and may be regarded as a very strong fortress. Besides this, on the line of the Maas, there are the fortified towns of Liege, Huy, and Namur. There are no coast fortifications.

Denmark, as commanding the approaches to the Baltic, is of great military importance to us. Copenhagen, the capital, is a strong fortress. The Army, on the other hand, is not an important factor of strength, as the training of the units is limited to a few months. This State maintains on a peace footing some 10,000 infantry, 800 cavalry, 2,300 artillery, and 1,100 special arms, a total of 14,200 men; but the strength varies between 7,500 and 26.000. In war-time an army of 62,000 men and 10,000 reserves can be put into the field, composed numerically of 58,000 infantry, 3,000 cavalry, 9,000 artillery, and 2,000 special arms.

Sweden can command eight classes of the First Ban, which comprises units from twenty-one to twenty-eight years of age, and is 200,000 strong, as well as four classes of the Second Ban, with a strength of 90,000, which is made up of units from twenty-eight to thirty-two years of age. There are also available 30,000 trained volunteers, students and ex-students from twenty-one to thirty-two years of age.

The eight classes of the Landsturm are 165,000 men strong. It can, accordingly, be roughly calculated what field army can be raised in case of war. The entire First Ban certainly comes under this head.

In Greece, which does not signify much for a European war, but might in combination with the small Balkan States prove very troublesome to Turkey, and is therefore important for us, an active army of 146,000 men can be put into the field; there are besides this 83,000 men in the Landwehr and 63,000 men in the Landsturm.

Spain has a peace army of 116,232 men, of whom 34,000 are permanently stationed in Africa. In war she can raise 327,000 men (140,000 active army, 154,000 garrison troops, 33,000 gendarmerie). The mobilization is so badly organized that at the end of a month 70,000 to 80,000 men could at most be put into the field.

As regards the naval forces of the States which concern us to-day, the accompanying table, which is taken from the Nauticus of 1911, affords a comparative epitome, which applies to May, 1911. It shows that, numerically, the English fleet is more than double as strong as ours. This superiority is increased if the displacements and the number of really modern ships are compared. In May we possessed only four battleships and one armed cruiser of the latest type; the English have ten ships-of-the-line and four armed cruisers which could be reckoned battleships. The new ships do not materially alter this proportion. The comparative number of the ships-of-the-line is becoming more favourable, that of the armoured cruisers will be less so than it now is. It may be noticed that among our cruisers are a number of vessels which really have no fighting value, and that the coast-defence ironclads cannot be counted as battleships. France, too, was a little ahead of us in the number of battleships in May, 1911, but, from all that is hitherto known about the French fleet, it cannot be compared with the German in respect of good material and trained crews. It would, however, be an important factor if allied with the English.

```
        |Battle- |Armoured |Armoured| Armoured |Protected |Number |N S
Nation. |ships   |Coast    |Gunboats| Cruisers |Cruisers  |of |u u
        |above   |Defence  |and     | |        |Torpedo   |m b
        |5,000   |Vessels  |Armoured| | |      |Vessels   |b m
        |Tons.   |from     |Ships   | | | |e a
        |        |3000 Tons|under   | | | |r r
        |        |to 5,000 |3,000   | | | | |i
        |        |Tons     |Tons    | | | | |i
        +—+————-+—+——————+—+—+———+—+———-+—+——-+—+———+—+———+—+———+o n
        |No|Displ. |No|Displ.|No|Displ|No|Displ. |No|Displ. | |From|f e
        | | | | | | | | | | | |200+|80- | s
        | | | | | | | | | | | |Tons| 200|
        | | | | | | | | | | | |Tons|
————————————-+—+————————-+—+—+———————+—+———+—+———+—+———+—+———+—+———-+—+———+—+———
GERMANY:| | | | | | | | | | | |
Ready |25|332,410| 5|20,600| -| —- |10|114,590|33|122,130| 117| 70| 12
Voted or | | | | | | | | | | | | |
building|12| —- | -| —- | -| —- | 4| —- | 7| —- | 14| —| —
        | | | | | | | | | | | |
```

ENGLAND: |||||||||||||
Ready |50|793,260| -| —- | -| —- |38|484,970|66|333,540| 223| 36| 53
Voted or |||||||||||||
 building|12|286,640| -| —- | -| —- | 6|145,320|20|101,320| 51| —- | 19
 |||||||||||||
FRANCE: |||||||||||||
Ready |22|314,930| -| —- | -| —- |22|214,670|10| 50,780| 71| 191| 52
Voted or |||||||||||||
 building| 4| 93,880| -| —- | -|—- | -|—- | -| —- | 13| —- | 19
 |||||||||||||
ITALY: |||||||||||||
Ready | 8| 96,980| -| —- | -| —- |10| 79,530| 4| 10,040| 53| 39| 7
Voted or |||||||||||||
 building| 4| 84,000| -| —- | -|—- | -|—- | 3| 10,200| 14| 28| 13
 |||||||||||||
AUSTRIA- ||||||||||||||
 HUNGARY ||||||||||||||
Ready |11|102,620| -| —- | -|—- | 3| 18,870| 4| 10,590| 18| 66| 7
Voted or |||||||||||||
 building| 5| 94,500| -| —- | -|—- | -|—- | 3| —- | 6| — | —
 |||||||||||||
RUSSIA: |||||||||||||
Baltic |||||||||||||
Fleet |||||||||||||
 Ready | 4| 62,300| -| —- | 1|1,760| 6| 64,950| 4| 27,270| 60| 19| 13
Voted or |||||||||||||
 building| 8| —- | -|—- | -|—- | -|—- | -| —- | 1| — | 1
Black Sea| |||||||||||||
 Fleet |||||||||||||
 Ready | 6| 72,640| -| —- | -|—- | -|—- | 3| 13,620| 17| 10| 4
Voted or |||||||||||||
 building| 4| —- | -|—- | -|—- | -|—- | -| —- | 14| — | 7
Siberian |||||||||||||
 Fleet |—| —- | -| -|—- | -|—- | -|—- | 2| 9,180| 20| 7| 13
 |||||||||||||
UNITED |||||||||||||
 STATES: |||||||||||||
Ready |30|434,890| 4|13,120| -| —- |14|181,260|16| 65,270| 40| 28| 19
Voted or |||||||||||||
 building| 7|190,000| -| —- | -| —- | -|—- | -|—- | 14| — | 20
 |||||||||||||
JAPAN: |||||||||||||
Ready |13|194,690| 2| 8,540| -| —- |13|139,830|12| 49,170| 59| 49| 12
Voted or |||||||||||||
 building| 3| —- | -|—- | -|—- | 4|107,120| 3| 15,000| 2| — | 1
————————-+—-+————-+—-+————-+—-+—————+—-+————————-+—-+———-+—-+——

Let us assume that in event of war England as well as France must leave a certain naval force in the Mediterranean, which need not be stronger than the combined Italian and Austrian fleets, but might be smaller, in event of a change in the grouping of the States; let us further assume that numerous cruisers will be detained at the extra-European stations—the fact, however, remains that England and France together can collect against Germany in the North Sea a fleet of battleships alone three times as strong as that of Germany, and will be supported by a vastly superior force of torpedo-vessels and submarines. If Russia joins the alliance of these Powers, that would signify another addition to the forces of our opponents which must not be underestimated, since the Baltic Fleet in the spring of 1911 contained two large battleships, and the Baltic fleet of cruisers is always in a position to threaten our coasts and to check the free access to the Baltic. In one way or the other we must get even with that fleet. The auxiliary cruiser fleet of the allies, to which England can send a large contingent, would also be superior to us.

As regards matériel and training, it may be assumed that our fleet is distinctly superior to the French and Russian, but that England is our equal in that respect. Our ships' cannons will probably show a superiority over the English, and our torpedo fleet, by its reckless energy, excellent training, and daring spirit of adventure, will make up some of the numerical disadvantage. It remains to be seen whether these advantages will have much weight against the overwhelming superiority of an experienced and celebrated fleet like the English.

Reflection shows that the superiority by sea, with which we must under certain circumstances reckon, is very great, and that our position in this respect is growing worse, since the States of the Triple Entente can build and man far more ships than we can in the same time.

If we consider from the political standpoint the probable attitude of the separate States which may take part in the next war against Germany, we may assume that the intensity of the struggle will not be the same in every case, since the political objects of our possible antagonists are very different.

If we look at France first, we are entitled to assume that single-handed she is not a match for us, but can only be dangerous to us as a member of a coalition. The tactical value of the French troops is, of course, very high; numerically the army of our neighbour on the west is almost equal, and in some directions there may be a superiority in organization and equipment; in other directions we have a distinct advantage. The French army lacks the subordination under a single commander, the united spirit which characterizes the German army, the tenacious strength of the German race, and the esprit de corps of the officers. France, too, has not those national reserves available which would allow us almost to double our forces. These are the conditions now existing. But if the French succeed in making a large African army available for a European theatre, the estimate of strength of the French army as compared with ours will be quite different. This possibility must be borne in mind, for, according to the whole previous development of affairs, we may safely assume that France will leave no stone unturned to acquire, if only for a time, a military superiority over Germany. She knows well that she cannot reach her political goal except by a complete defeat of her eastern neighbour, and that such a result can only be obtained by the exercise of extraordinary efforts.

It is certain that France will not only try to develop her own military power with the utmost energy, but that she will defend herself desperately if attacked by Germany; on the other hand, she will probably not act on the offensive against Germany unless she has increased her own efficiency to the utmost limit, and believes that she has secured the military supremacy by the help of active allies. The stakes are too high to play under unfavourable conditions. But if France thinks she has all the trumps in her hands, she will not shrink from an offensive war, and will stake even thing in order to strike us a mortal blow. We must expect the most bitter hostility from this antagonist. Should the Triple Alliance break up—as seems probable now—this hour will soon have struck.[B] If the war then declared be waged against us in combination with England, it may be assumed that the allied Great Powers would attempt to turn our strategical right flank through Belgium and Holland, and penetrate into the heart of Germany through the great gap in the fortresses between Wesel and Flushing. This operation would have the considerable advantage of avoiding the strong line of the Rhine and threatening our naval bases from the land side. From the superiority of the combined Anglo-French fleet, the army of invasion could without difficulty have its base on our coasts. Such an operation would enormously facilitate the frontal attack on our west frontier, and would enable the French to push a victorious advance onward to the Rhine, after investing Metz and Diedenhofen.

[Footnote B: Written in October, 1911.]

England, with whose hostility, as well with that of the French, we must reckon, could only undertake a land war against us with the support of an ally who would lead the main attack. England's troops would only serve as reinforcements; they are too weak for an independent campaign. English interests also lie in a quite different field, and are not coincident with those of France.

The main issue for England is to annihilate our navy and oversea commerce, in order to prevent, from reasons already explained, any further expansion of our power. But it is not her interest to destroy our position as a Continental Power, or to help France to attain the supremacy in Europe. English interests demand a certain equilibrium between the Continental States. England only wishes to use France in order, with her help, to attain her own special ends, but she will never impose on herself sacrifices which are not absolutely necessary, for the private advantage of her ally. These principles will characterize her plan of campaign, if she sees herself compelled by the political position and the interests of her naval supremacy to take part in a war against us.

If England, as must be regarded probable, determines sooner or later on this step, it is clearly to her advantage to win a rapid victory. In the first place, her own trade will not be injured longer than necessary by the war; in the second place, the centrifugal forces of her loosely compacted World Empire might be set in movement, and the Colonies might consult their own separate interests, should England have her hands tied by a great war. It is not unlikely that revolutions might break out in India and Egypt, if England's forces were long occupied with a European war. Again, the States not originally taking part in the war might interfere in our favour, if the decision were much delayed. It was important for us in 1870-71 to take Paris quickly, in order to forestall any interference of neutrals. Similar conditions might arise in the case of England. We must therefore make up our minds that the attack by sea will be made with the greatest and most persistent vigour, with the firm resolve to destroy completely our fleet and our great commercial centres. It is also not only possible, but probable, that England will throw troops on the Continent, in order to secure the co-operation of her allies, who might demand this guarantee of the sincerity of English policy, and also to support the naval attack on the coast. On the other hand, the land war will display the same kind of desperate energy only so far as it pursues the object of conquering and destroying our naval bases. The English would be the less disposed to do more than this because the German auxiliaries, who have so often fought England's battles, would not be forthcoming. The greatest exertions of the nation will be limited to the naval war. The land war will be waged with a definitely restricted object, on which its character will depend. It is very questionable whether the English army is capable of effectively acting on the offensive against Continental European troops. In South Africa the English regiments for the most part fought very bravely and stood great losses; on the other hand, they completely failed in the offensive, in tactics as in operations, and with few exceptions the generalship was equally deficient. The last manoeuvres on a large scale, held in Ireland, under the direction of General French, did not, according to available information, show the English army in a favourable light so far as strategical ability went.

If we now turn our attention to the East, in order to forecast Russia's probable behaviour, we must begin by admitting that, from a Russian standpoint, a war in the West holds out better prospects of success than a renewed war with Japan, and possibly with China. The Empire of the Czar finds in the West powerful allies, who are impatiently waiting to join in an attack on Germany. The geographical conditions and means of communication there allow a far more rapid and systematic development of power than in Manchuria. Public opinion, in which hatred of Germany is as persistent as ever, would be in favour of such a war, and a victory over Germany and Austria would not only open the road to Constantinople, but would greatly improve the political and economic influence of Russia in Western Europe. Such a success would afford a splendid compensation for the defeats in Asia, and would offer advantages such as never could be expected on the far-distant Eastern frontiers of the Empire.

Should Russia, then, after weighing these chances launch out into an offensive war in the West, the struggle would probably assume a quite different character from that, for example, of a Franco-German war. Russia, owing to her vast extent, is in the first place secure against complete subjugation. In case of defeat her centre of gravity is not shifted. A Russian war can hardly ever, therefore, become a struggle for political existence, and cause that straining of every nerve which such a struggle entails. The inhabitants will hardly ever show self-devotion in wars whose objects cannot be clear to them. Throughout the vast Empire the social and also political education, especially among the peasants, is so poor, that any grasp of the problems of a foreign policy seems quite out of the question. The sections of the people who have acquired a little superficial learning in the defective Russian schools have sworn to the revolutionary colours, or follow a blind anti-progressive policy which seems to them best to meet their interests. The former, at least, would only make use of a war to promote their own revolutionary schemes, as they did in the crisis of the Russo-Japanese War. Under the circumstances, there can be little idea of a united outburst of the national spirit which would enable an offensive war to be carried on with persistent vigour. There has been an extraordinary change in the conditions since 1812, when the people showed some unanimity in repelling the invasion. Should Russia to-day be involved in a Western war with Germany and Austria, she could never bring her whole forces into play. In the first place, the revolutionary elements in the heart of the State would avail themselves of every weakening of the national sources of power to effect a revolution in internal politics, without any regard for the interests of the community. Secondly, in the Far East, Japan or China would seize the moment when Russia's forces in the West were fully occupied to carry out their political intentions towards the Empire of the Czar by force of arms. Forces must always be kept in reserve for this eventuality, as we have already mentioned.

Although Russia, under the present conditions, cannot bring her whole power to bear against Germany and Austria, and must also always leave a certain force on her European Southern frontier, she is less affected by defeats than other States. Neither the Crimean War nor the greater exertions and sacrifices exacted by her hard-won victory over the Turks, nor the heavy defeats by the Japanese, have seriously shaken Russia's political prestige. Beaten in the East or South, she turns to another sphere of enterprise, and endeavours to recoup herself there for her losses on another frontier.

Such conditions must obviously affect the character of the war. Russia will certainly put huge armies into the field against us. In the wars against Turkey and Japan the internal affairs of the Empire prevented the employment of its full strength; in the latter campaign revolutionary agitation in the army itself influenced the operations and battles, and in a European war the same conditions would, in all probability, make themselves emphatically felt, especially if defeats favoured or encouraged revolutionary propaganda. In a war against Russia, more than in any other war, c'est le premier pas qui coûte.

If the first operations are unsuccessful, their effect on the whole position will be wider than in any other war, since they will excite in the country itself not sympathetic feelings only, but also hostile forces which would cripple the conduct of the war.

So far as the efficiency of the Russian army goes, the Russo-Japanese War proved that the troops fight with great stubbornness. The struggle showed numerous instances of heroic self-devotion, and the heaviest losses were often borne with courage. On the other hand, the Russian army quite failed on the offensive, in a certain sense tactically, but essentially owing to the inadequacy of the commanders and the failure of the individuals. The method of conducting the war was quite wrong; indecision and irresolution characterized the Russian officers of every grade, and no personality came forward who ever attempted to rise above mediocrity. It can hardly be presumed that the spirit of Russian generalship has completely changed since the defeats in Manchuria, and that striking personalities have come on the stage. This army must therefore always be met with a bold policy of attack.

When we contrast these conditions with the position of Germany, we cannot blink the fact that we have to deal with immense military difficulties, if we are to attain our own political ends or repel successfully the attack of our opponents.

In the first place, the geographical configuration and position of our country are very unfavourable. Our open eastern frontier offers no opportunity for continued defence, and Berlin, the centre of the government and administration, lies in dangerous proximity to it. Our western frontier, in itself strong, can be easily turned on the north through Belgium and Holland. No natural obstacle, no strong fortress, is there to oppose a hostile invasion and neutrality is only a paper bulwark. So in the south, the barrier of the Rhine can easily be turned through Switzerland. There, of course, the character of the country offers considerable difficulties, and if the Swiss defend themselves resolutely, it might not be easy to break down their resistance. Their army is no despicable factor of strength, and if they were attacked in their mountains they would fight as they did at Sempach and Murten.

The natural approaches from the North Sea to the Baltic, the Sound and the Great Belt, are commanded by foreign guns, and can easily fall a prey to our enemies.

The narrow coast with which we face to the North Sea forms in itself a strong front, but can easily be taken in the rear through Holland. England is planted before our coasts in such a manner that our entire oversea commerce can be easily blocked. In the south and south-east alone are we secured by Austria from direct invasion. Otherwise we are encircled by our enemies. We may have to face attacks on three sides. This circumstance compels us to fight on the inner lines, and so presents certain advantages; but it is also fraught with dangers, if our opponents understand how to act on a correct and consistent plan.

If we look at our general political position, we cannot conceal the fact that we stand isolated, and cannot expect support from anyone in carrying out our positive political plans. England, France, and Russia have a common interest in breaking down our power. This interest will sooner or later be asserted by arms. It is not therefore the interest of any nation to increase Germany's power. If we wish to attain an extension of our power, as is natural in our position, we must win it by the sword against vastly superior foes. Our alliances are defensive, not merely in form, but essentially so. I have already shown that this is a cause of their weakness. Neither Austria nor Italy are in any way bound to support by armed force a German policy directed towards an increase of power. We are not even sure of their diplomatic help, as the conduct of Italy at the conference of Algeçiras sufficiently demonstrated. It even seems questionable at the present moment whether we can always reckon on the support of the members of the Triple Alliance in a defensive war. The recent rapprochement of Italy with France and England goes far beyond the idea of an "extra turn." If we consider how difficult Italy would find it to make her forces fit to cope with France, and to protect her coasts against hostile attacks, and if we think how the annexation of Tripoli has created a new possession, which is not easily defended against France and England, we may fairly doubt whether Italy would take part in a war in which England and France were allied against us. Austria is undoubtedly a loyal ally. Her interests are closely connected with our own, and her policy is dominated by the same spirit of loyalty and integrity as ours towards Austria. Nevertheless, there is cause for anxiety, because in a conglomerate State like Austria, which contains numerous Slavonic elements, patriotism may not be strong enough to allow the Government to fight to the death with Russia, were the latter to defeat us. The occurrence of such an event is not improbable. When enumerating the possibilities that might affect our policy, we cannot leave this one out of consideration.

We shall therefore some day, perhaps, be faced with the necessity of standing isolated in a great war of the nations, as once Frederick the Great stood, when he was basely deserted by England in the middle of the struggle, and shall have to trust to our own strength and our own resolution for victory.

Such a war—for us more than for any other nation—must be a war for our political and national existence. This must be so, for our opponents can only attain their political aims by almost annihilating us by land and by sea. If the victory is only half won, they would have to expect continuous renewals of the contest, which would be contrary to their interests. They know that well enough, and therefore avoid the contest, since we shall certainly defend ourselves with the utmost bitterness and obstinacy. If, notwithstanding, circumstances make the war inevitable, then the intention of our enemies to crush us to the ground, and our own resolve to maintain our position victoriously, will make it a war of desperation. A war fought and lost under such circumstances would destroy our laboriously gained political importance, would jeopardize the whole future of our nation, would throw us back for centuries, would shake the influence of German thought in the civilized world, and thus check the general progress of mankind in its healthy development, for which a flourishing Germany is the essential condition. Our next war will be fought for the highest interests of our country and of mankind. This will invest it with importance in the world's history. "World power or downfall!" will be our rallying cry.

Keeping this idea before us, we must prepare for war with the confident intention of conquering, and with the iron resolve to persevere to the end, come what may.

We must therefore prepare not only for a short war, but for a protracted campaign. We must be armed in order to complete the overthrow of our enemies, should the victory be ours; and, if worsted, to continue to defend ourselves in the very heart of our country until success at last is won.

It is therefore by no means enough to maintain a certain numerical equality with our opponents. On the contrary, we must strive to call up the entire forces of the nation, and prepare and arm for the great decision which impends. We must try also to gain a certain superiority over our opponents in the crucial points, so that we may hold some winning trumps in our hand in a contest unequal from the very first. We must bear these two points in mind when preparing for war. Only by continually realizing the duties thus laid on us can we carry out our preparations to the fullest, and satisfy the demands which the future makes on us. A nation of 65,000,000 which stakes all her forces on winning herself a position, and on keeping that position, cannot be conquered. But it is an evil day for her if she relies on the semblance of power, or, miscalculating her enemies' strength, is content with half-measures, and looks to luck or chance for that which can only be attained by the exertion and development of all her powers.

CHAPTER VIII.THE NEXT NAVAL WAR

In the next European land war we shall probably face our foes with Austria at our side, and thus will be in a position to win the day against any opposing forces. In a naval war we shall be thrown on our own resources, and must protect ourselves single-handed against the superior forces which will certainly press us hard.

There can be no doubt that this war will be waged with England, for, although we cannot contemplate attacking England, as such an attack would be hopeless, that country itself has a lively interest in checking our political power. It will therefore, under certain conditions, attack us, in order to annihilate our fleet and aid France. The English have, besides, taken good care that the prospect of a war with them should always be held before our eyes. They talk so much of a possible German attack that it cannot surprise them if the light thrown on the question is from the opposite point of view. Again, the preparations which they are making in the North Sea show clearly that they certainly have contemplated an attack on Germany. These preparations are like a strategic march, and the natural extension of their naval bases leaves no doubt as to their meaning. The great military harbour of Rosyth is admittedly built for the eventuality of a war with Germany, and can mean nothing else. Harwich has also been recently made into an especially strong naval base, and, further, the roadstead of Scapa Flow in the Orkney Isles has been enlarged into a cruiser station. These are measures so directly and obviously directed against us that they demand an inquiry into the military position thus created.

The English have only considered the possibility of a German war since 1902. Before that year there was no idea of any such contingency, and it is therefore not unnatural that they are eager to make up for lost time. This fact does not alter the hostile character of the measures and the circumstance that the English preparations for war are exclusively directed against Germany. We must therefore—as the general position of the world leads us to believe—reckon on the probability of a naval war with England, and shall then have to fight against an overwhelming superiority. It will be so great that we cannot hope for a long time to be able to take the offensive against the English fleet. But we must contemplate the possibility of becoming its master in one way or another, and of winning the freedom of the seas, if England attacks us. We shall now discuss this possibility. On this matter I am expressing my personal views only, which are not confused by any technical naval knowledge, and rest exclusively on general military considerations, in which our presupposed antagonists can, and will, indulge quite as well as myself. I shall not betray any secrets of the Admiralty, since I do not know any. But I consider it expedient that the German people should clearly understand what dangers threaten from England, and how they can be met.

In the view of these dangers and the circumstance that we are not strong enough to entertain any idea of provoking a battle, the question remains, What are the means of defensive naval strategy to secure protection from a superior and well-prepared enemy, and gradually to become its master?

The plan might be formed of anticipating the enemy by a sudden attack, instead of waiting passively for him to attack first, and of opening the war as the Japanese did before Port Arthur. In this way the English fleet might be badly damaged at the outset of the real hostilities, its superiority might be lessened, and the beginning of the effective blockade delayed at least for a short time. It is not unthinkable that such an attempt will be made. Such an undertaking, however, does not seem to me to promise any great success.

The English have secured themselves against such attacks by comprehensive works of defence in their exposed harbours. It seems dangerous to risk our torpedo-boats and submarines, which we shall urgently need in the later course of the war, in such bold undertakings. Even the war against the English commerce holds out less prospects than formerly. As soon as a state of political tension sets in, the English merchantmen will be convoyed by their numerous cruisers. Under such circumstances our auxiliary cruisers could do little; while our foreign service ships would soon have to set about attacking the enemy's warships, before coal ran short, for to fill up the coal-bunkers of these ships will certainly be a difficult task.

The war against the English commerce must none the less be boldly and energetically prosecuted, and should start unexpectedly. The prizes which fall into our hands must be remorselessly destroyed, since it will usually be impossible, owing to the great English superiority and the few bases we have abroad, to bring them back in safety without exposing our vessels to great risks. The sharpest measures must be taken against neutral ships laden with contraband. Nevertheless, no very valuable results can be expected from a war against England's trade. On the contrary, England, with the numerous cruisers and auxiliary cruisers at her disposal, would be able to cripple our oversea commerce. We must be ready for a sudden attack, even in peace-time. It is not England's custom to let ideal considerations fetter her action if her interests are at stake.

Under these circumstances, nothing would be left for us but to retire with our war-fleet under the guns of the coast fortifications, and by the use of mines to protect our own shores and make them dangerous to English vessels. Mines are only an effective hindrance to attack if they can be defended. But they can cause considerable damage if the enemy has no knowledge of their existence.

It would be necessary to take further steps to secure the importation from abroad of supplies necessary to us, since our own communications will be completely cut off by the English. The simplest and cheapest way would be if we obtained foreign goods through Holland or perhaps neutral Belgium; and could export some part of our own products through the great Dutch and Flemish harbours. New commercial routes might be discovered through Denmark. Our own oversea commerce would remain suspended, but such measures would prevent an absolute stagnation of trade.

It is, however, very unlikely that England would tolerate such communications through neutral territory, since in that way the effect of her war on our trade would be much reduced. The attempt to block these trade routes would approximate to a breach of neutrality, and the States in question would have to face the momentous question, whether they would conform to England's will, and thus incur Germany's enmity, or would prefer that adhesion to the German Empire which geography dictates. They would have the choice between a naval war with England and a Continental war with their German neighbours—two possibilities, each of which contains great dangers. That England would pay much attention to the neutrality of weaker neighbours when such a stake was at issue is hardly credible.

The ultimate decision of the individual neutral States cannot be foreseen. It would probably depend on the general political position and the attitude of the other World Powers to the Anglo-German contest. The policy adopted by France and Russia would be an important factor. One can easily understand under these circumstances that the Dutch are seriously proposing to fortify strongly the most important points on their coast, in order to be able to maintain their neutrality on the sea side. They are also anxious about their eastern frontier, which obviously would be threatened by a German attack so soon as they sided with our enemies.

I shall not enter further into the political and military possibilities which might arise if Holland, Belgium, and Denmark were driven to a sympathetic understanding by the war. I will only point out how widespread an effect the naval war can, or rather must, exercise on the Continental war and on the political relations generally. The attitude of Denmark would be very important, since the passage to and from the Baltic must mainly depend on her. It is vital to us that these communications be kept open, and measures must be taken to insure this. The open door through the Belt and the Sound can become highly important for the conduct of the war. Free commerce with Sweden is essential for us, since our industries will depend more and more on the Swedish iron-ore as imports from other countries become interrupted.

It will rest with the general state of affairs and the policy of the interested nations whether this sea route can be safeguarded by diplomatic negotiations, or must be kept open by military action. We cannot allow a hostile power to occupy the Danish islands.

Complicated and grave questions, military as well as political, are thus raised by an Anglo-German war. Our trade would in any case suffer greatly, for sea communications could be cut off on every side. Let us assume that France and Russia seal our land frontiers, then the only trade route left open to us is through Switzerland and Austria—a condition of affairs which would aggravate difficulties at home, and should stimulate us to carry on the war with increased vigour. In any case, when war threatens we must lose no time in preparing a road on which we can import the most essential foodstuffs and raw materials, and also export, if only in small quantities, the surplus of our industrial products. Such measures cannot be made on the spur of the moment. They must be elaborated in peace-time, and a definite department of the Government must be responsible for these preparations. The Ministry of Commerce would obviously be the appropriate department, and should, in collaboration with the great commercial houses, prepare the routes which our commerce must follow in case of war. There must be a sort of commercial mobilization.

These suggestions indicate the preliminary measures to be adopted by us in the eventuality of a war with England. We should at first carry on a defensive war, and would therefore have to reckon on a blockade of our coasts, if we succeed in repelling the probable English attack.

Such a blockade can be carried out in two ways. England can blockade closely our North Sea coast, and at the same time bar the Danish straits, so as to cut off communications with our Baltic ports; or she can seal up on the one side the Channel between England and the Continent, on the other side the open sea between the North of Scotland and Norway, on the Peterhead-Ekersund line, and thus cripple our oversea commerce and also control the Belgo-Dutch, Danish, and Swedish shipping.

A close blockade in the first case would greatly tax the resources of the English fleet. According to the view of English experts, if a blockade is to be maintained permanently, the distance between the base and the blockading line must not exceed 200 nautical miles. Since all the English naval ports are considerably farther than this from our coast, the difficulties of carrying on the blockade will be enormously increased. That appears to be the reason why the estuary at Harwich has recently been transformed into a strong naval harbour. It is considered the best harbourage on the English coast, and is hardly 300 nautical miles from the German coast. It offers good possibilities of fortification, and safe ingress and egress in time of war. The distance from the German ports is not, however, very material for purposes of blockade. The English, if they planned such a blockade, would doubtless count on acquiring bases on our own coast, perhaps also on the Dutch coast. Our task therefore is to prevent such attempts by every means. Not only must every point which is suitable for a base, such as Heligoland, Borkum, and Sylt, be fortified in time of peace, but all attempts at landing must be hindered and complicated by our fleet. This task can only be fulfilled by the fleet in daytime by submarines; by night torpedo-boats may co-operate, if the landing forces are still on board.

Such close blockade offers various possibilities of damaging the enemy, if the coast fortifications are so constructed with a view to the offensive that the fleet may rally under their protection, and thus gain an opportunity of advancing from their stations for offensive operations. Such possibilities exist on our north coast, and our efforts must be turned towards making the most varied use of them. We must endeavour by renewed and unexpected attacks, especially by night, partly with submarines and torpedo-boats, partly with battleships, to give the blockading fleet no breathing-time, and to cause it as much loss as possible. We must not engage in a battle with superior hostile forces, for it is hardly possible at sea to discontinue a fight, because there is no place whither the loser can withdraw from the effect of the enemy's guns. An engagement, once begun must be fought out to the end. And appreciable damage can be inflicted on the enemy only if a bold attack on him is made. It is only possible under exceptionally favourable circumstances—such, for example, as the proximity of the fortified base—to abandon a fight once begun without very heavy losses. It might certainly be practicable, by successful reconnoitring, to attack the enemy repeatedly at times when he is weakened in one place or another. Blockade demands naturally a certain division of forces, and the battle-fleet of the attacking party, which is supposed to lie behind the farthest lines of blockade and observation, cannot always hold the high seas in full strength. The forces of the defending party, however, lie in safe anchorages, ready to sally out and fight.

Such a blockade might, after all, be very costly to the attacking party. We may therefore fairly assume that the English would decide in favour of the second kind. At all events, the harbour constructions, partly building, partly projected, at Rosyth and Scapa Flow, were chosen with an eye to this line of blockade. It would entail in the north the barring of a line about 300 nautical miles long, a scheme quite feasible from the military aspect. Only a small force is required to seal up the Channel, as the navigation route is very narrow. In addition to all this, the great English naval depots—Dover, Portsmouth, Portland, and Plymouth—are situated either on the line of blockade or immediately behind it. Besides, every advance against this line from the north is flanked by Sheerness and Harwich, so that a retreat to the German coast might be barred. The conditions for the northern line of blockade will be no less favourable when the projected harbour works are finished. The blockading fleet finds, therefore, a base in the great harbour of Rosyth, while a cruiser squadron might lie in support off the Orkney Isles. Every attacking fleet from the German north coast will be unhesitatingly attacked on the flank from Rosyth and Sheerness, and cut off from its line of retreat. It is thus almost impossible, owing to the English superiority, to inflict any serious damage on the blockading fleet on this line, and the only course left is to advance from the Baltic against the north-eastern part of the blockading line. Here we should have a tolerably secure retreat. This accentuates once more the supreme importance to us of keeping open, at all costs, the passage through the Sound and the Great Belt. The command of these straits will not only secure the Baltic basin for us, but also keep open the sally-ports for our offensive operations against the English blockading fleet.

In spite of all the advantages which the extended system of blockade offers to the English, there are two objections against it which are well worth considering from the English point of view. Firstly, it prejudices the interests of a number of nations whose coasts are washed by the North Sea and the Baltic, since they are included in the blockade; secondly, it compels England to break up her fleet into two or three divisions.

As to the first objection, we have hinted that England will scarcely let herself be hindered in the pursuit of her own advantage by the interests of weaker third parties. It is also conceivable that some satisfactory arrangement as to the blockade can be made with the States affected. As regards the splitting up of the fleet, no especially disadvantageous conditions are thereby produced. It is easy to reunite the temporarily divided parts, and the strength of the combined fleet guarantees the superiority of the separate divisions over the German forces at sea. Nevertheless, this division of the attacking fleet gives the defending party the chance of attacking some detached portions before junction with the main body, and of inflicting loss on them, if the enemy can be deceived and surprised by prompt action. The demonstrations which are the ordinary tactics in war on land under such conditions cannot be employed, owing to the facility with which the sea can be patrolled.

This blockade would ultimately weaken and weary the attacking party. But it must be recognized that it is a far easier plan to carry out than the close blockade, and that it would tax the offensive powers of our fleet more severely. We should not only have to venture on attacks in far-distant waters, but must be strong enough to protect efficiently the threatened flank of our attacking fleet.

After all, it is improbable that the English would have recourse to a mere blockade. The reasons which would prompt them to a rapid decision of the war have been already explained. It was shown that, in the event of their fighting in alliance with France, they would probably attempt to land troops in order to support their fleet from the land side. They could not obtain a decisive result unless they attempted to capture our naval bases—Wilhelmshaven, Heligoland, the mouth of the Elbe, and Kiel—and to annihilate our fleet in its attempt to protect these places, and thus render it impossible for us to continue the war by sea.

It is equally certain that our land forces would actively operate against the English attempts at landing, and that they would afford extraordinarily important assistance to the defence of the coast, by protecting it against attacks from the rear, and by keeping open the communications with the hinterland. The success of the English attack will much depend on the strength and armament of the coast fortifications. Such a war will clearly show their value both as purely defensive and as offensive works. Our whole future history may turn upon the impregnability of the fortifications which, in combination with the fleet, are intended to guard our coasts and naval bases, and should inflict such heavy losses on the enemy that the difference of strength between the two fleets would be gradually equalized. Our ships, it must be remembered, can only act effectively so long as our coast fortifications hold out.

No proof is required that a good Intelligence system is essential to a defensive which is based on the policy of striking unexpected blows. Such a system alone can guarantee the right choice of favourable moments for attack, and can give us such early information of the operative movements of the hostile fleet that we can take the requisite measures for defence, and always retreat before an attack in superior numbers. The numerical superiority of the English cruisers is so great that we shall probably only be able to guarantee rapid and trustworthy "scouting" by the help of the air-fleet. The importance of the air-fleet must not therefore be under-valued; and steps must be taken to repel the enemy's airships, either by employing specially contrived cannons, or by attacking them directly.

If it is possible to employ airships for offensive purposes also, they would support our own fleet in their contest with the superior English force by dropping explosives on the enemy's ships, and might thus contribute towards gradually restoring the equilibrium of the opposing forces. These possibilities are, however, vague. The ships are protected to some extent by their armour against such explosives as could be dropped from airships, and it is not easy to aim correctly from a balloon. But the possibility of such methods of attack must be kept in mind.

So far as aviation goes, the defending party has the advantage, for, starting from the German coast, our airships and flying-machines would be able to operate against the English attacking fleet more successfully than the English airships against our forts and vessels, since they would have as a base either the fleet itself or the distant English coast.

Such possibilities of superiority must be carefully watched for, and nothing must be neglected which could injure the enemy; while the boldest spirit of attack and the most reckless audacity must go hand in hand with the employment of every means which, mechanical skill and the science of naval construction and fortification can supply. This is the only way by which we may hope so to weaken our proud opponent, that we may in the end challenge him to a decisive engagement on the open sea.

In this war we must conquer, or, at any rate, not allow ourselves to be defeated, for it will decide whether we can attain a position as a World Power by the side of, and in spite of, England.

This victory will not be gained merely in the exclusive interests of Germany. We shall in this struggle, as so often before, represent the common interests of the world, for it will be fought not only to win recognition for ourselves, but for the freedom of the seas. "This was the great aim of Russia under the Empress Catherine II., of France under Napoleon I., and spasmodically down to 1904 in the last pages of her history; and the great Republic of the United States of North America strives for it with intense energy. It is the development of the right of nations for which every people craves." [A]

[Footnote A: Schiemann.]

In such a contest we should not stand spiritually alone, but all on this vast globe whose feelings and thoughts are proud and free will join us in this campaign against the overweening ambitions of one nation, which, in spite of all her pretence of a liberal and a philanthropic policy, has never sought any other object than personal advantage and the unscrupulous suppression of her rivals.

If the French fleet—as we may expect—combines with the English and takes part in the war, it will be much more difficult for us to wage than a war with England alone. France's blue-water fleet would hold our allies in the Mediterranean in check, and England could bring all her forces to bear upon us. It would be possible that combined fleets of the two Powers might appear both in the Mediterranean and in the North Sea, since England could hardly leave the protection of her Mediterranean interests to France alone. The prospect of any ultimately successful issue would thus shrink into the background. But we need not even then despair. On the contrary, we must fight the French fleet, so to speak, on land—i.e., we must defeat France so decisively that she would be compelled to renounce her alliance with England and withdraw her fleet to save herself from total destruction. Just as in 1870-71 we marched to the shores of the Atlantic, so this time again we must resolve on an absolute conquest, in order to capture the French naval ports and destroy the French naval depots. It would be a war to the knife with France, one which would, if victorious, annihilate once for all the French position as a Great Power. If France, with her falling birth-rate, determines on such a war, it is at the risk of losing her place in the first rank of European nations, and sinking into permanent political subservience. Those are the stakes.

The participation of Russia in the naval war must also be contemplated. That is the less dangerous, since the Russian Baltic fleet is at present still weak, and cannot combine so easily as the English with the French. We could operate against it on the inner line—i.e., we could use the opportunity of uniting rapidly our vessels in the Baltic by means of the Kaiser-Wilhelm Canal; we could attack the Russian ships in vastly superior force, and, having struck our blow, we could return to the North Sea. For these operations it is of the first importance that the Danish straits should not be occupied by the enemy. If they fell into the hands of the English, all free operations in the Baltic would be almost impossible, and our Baltic coast would then be abandoned to the passive protection of our coast batteries.

CHAPTER IX. THE CRUCIAL QUESTION

I have examined the probable conditions of the next naval war in some detail, because I thought that our general political and military position can only be properly estimated by considering the various phases of the war by sea and by land, and by realizing the possibilities and dangers arising from the combined action of the hostile forces on our coasts and land frontiers. In this way only can the direction be decided in which our preparations for war ought to move.

The considerations, then, to which the discussion about the naval war with England and her probable allies gave rise have shown that we shall need to make very great exertions to protect ourselves successfully from a hostile attack by sea. They also proved that we cannot count on an ultimate victory at sea unless we are victorious on land. If an Anglo-French army invaded North Germany through Holland, and threatened our coast defences in the rear, it would soon paralyze our defence by sea. The same argument applies to the eastern theatre. If Russian armies advance victoriously along the Baltic and co-operate with a combined fleet of our opponents, any continuation of the naval war would be rendered futile by the operations of the enemy on land. We know also that it is of primary importance to organize our forces on land so thoroughly that they guarantee the possibility, under all circumstances, of our victoriously maintaining our position on the Continent of Europe. This position must be made absolutely safe before we can successfully carry on a war by sea, and follow an imperial policy based on naval power. So long as Rome was threatened by Hannibal in Italy there could be no possible idea of empire. She did not begin her triumphal progress in history until she was thoroughly secure in her own country. But our discussion shows also that success on land can be influenced by the naval war. If the enemy succeeds in destroying our fleet and landing with strong detachments on the North Sea coast, large forces of the land army would be required to repel them, a circumstance widely affecting the progress of the war on the land frontiers. It is therefore vitally necessary to prepare the defence of our own coasts so well that every attack, even by superior numbers, may be victoriously repelled.

At the same time the consideration of the political position presses the conviction home that in our preparations for war there must be no talk of a gradual development of our forces by sea and land such as may lay the lightest possible burden on the national finances, and leave ample scope for activity in the sphere of culture. The crucial point is to put aside all other considerations, and to prepare ourselves with the utmost energy for a war which appears to be imminent, and will decide the whole future of our politics and our civilization. The consideration of the broad lines of the world policy and of the political aspirations of the individual States showed that the position of affairs everywhere is critical for us, that we live at an epoch which will decide our place as a World Power or our downfall. The internal disruption of the Triple Alliance, as shown clearly by the action of Italy towards Turkey, threatens to bring the crisis quickly to a head. The period which destiny has allotted us for concentrating our forces and preparing ourselves for the deadly struggle may soon be passed. We must use it, if we wish to be mindful of the warning of the Great Elector, that we are Germans. This is the point of view from which we must carry out our preparations for war by sea and land. Thus only can we be true to our national duty.

I do not mean that we should adopt precipitately measures calculated merely for the exigencies of the moment. All that we undertake in the cause of military efficiency must meet two requirements: it must answer the pressing questions of the present, and aid the development of the future. But we must find the danger of our position a stimulus to desperate exertions, so that we may regain at the eleventh hour something of what we have lost in the last years.

Since the crucial point is to safeguard our much-threatened position on the continent of Europe, we must first of all face the serious problem of the land war—by what means we can hope to overcome the great numerical superiority of our enemies. Such superiority will certainly exist if Italy ceases to be an active member of the Triple Alliance, whether nominally belonging to it, or politically going over to Irredentism. The preparations for the naval war are of secondary importance.

The first essential requirement, in case of a war by land, is to make the total fighting strength of the nation available for war, to educate the entire youth of the country in the use of arms, and to make universal service an existing fact.

The system of universal service, born in the hour of need, has by a splendid development of strength liberated us from a foreign yoke, has in long years of peace educated a powerful and well-armed people, and has brought us victory upon victory in the German wars of unification. Its importance for the social evolution of the nation has been discussed in a separate chapter. The German Empire would to-day have a mighty political importance if we had been loyal to the principle on which our greatness was founded.

France has at the present day a population of some 40,000,000; Russia in Europe, with Poland and the Caucasus, has a population of 140,000,000. Contrasted with this, Germany has only 65,000,000 inhabitants. But since the Russian military forces are, to a great extent, hampered by very various causes and cannot be employed at any one time or place, and are also deficient in military value, a German army which corresponded to the population would be certainly in a position to defend itself successfully against its two enemies, if it operated resolutely on the inner line, even though England took part in the war.

Disastrously for ourselves, we have become disloyal to the idea of universal military service, and have apparently definitely discontinued to carry it out effectively. The country where universal service exists is now France. With us, indeed, it is still talked about, but it is only kept up in pretence, for in reality 50 per cent., perhaps, of the able-bodied are called up for training. In particular, very little use has been made of the larger towns as recruiting-grounds for the army. In this direction some reorganization is required which will energetically combine the forces of the nation and create a real army, such as we have not at the present time. Unless we satisfy this demand, we shall not long be able to hold our own against the hostile Powers.

Although we recognize this necessity as a national duty, we must not shut our eyes to the fact that it is impossible in a short time to make up our deficiencies. Our peace army cannot be suddenly increased by 150,000 men. The necessary training staff and equipment would not be forthcoming, and on the financial side the required expenditure could not all at once be incurred.

The full effectiveness of an increased army only begins to be gradually felt when the number of reservists and Landwehr is correspondingly raised. We can therefore only slowly recur to the reinforcement of universal service. The note struck by the new Five Years Act cannot be justified on any grounds. But although we wish to increase our army on a more extensive scale, we must admit that, even if we strain our resources, the process can only work slowly, and that we cannot hope for a long time to equalize even approximately the superior forces of our opponents.

We must not, therefore, be content merely to strengthen our army; we must devise other means of gaining the upper hand of our enemies. These means can only be found in the spiritual domain.

History teaches us by countless examples that numbers in themselves have only been the decisive factor in war when the opponents have been equally matched otherwise, or when the superiority of the one party exceeds the proportion required by the numerical law.[A] In most cases it was a special advantage possessed by the one party—better equipment, greater efficiency of troops, brilliant leadership, or more able strategy—which led to victory over the numerically superior. Rome conquered the world with inferior forces; Frederick the Great with inferior forces withstood the allied armies of Europe. Recent history shows us the victory of the numerically weaker Japanese army over a crushingly superior opponent. We cannot count on seeing a great commander at our head; a second Frederick the Great will hardly appear. Nor can we know beforehand whether our troops will prove superior to the hostile forces. But we can try to learn what will be the decisive factors in the future war which will turn the scale in favour of victory or defeat. If we know this, and prepare for war with a set purpose, and keep the essential points of view always before us, we might create a real source of superiority, and gain a start on our opponents which would be hard for them to make up in the course of the war. Should we then in the war itself follow one dominating principle of the policy which results from the special nature of present-day war, it must be possible to gain a positive advantage which may even equalize a considerable numerical superiority.

[Footnote A: Cf. v. Bernhardi, "Vom heutigen Kriege," vol. i., chap. ii.]

The essential point is not to match battalion with battalion, battery with battery, or to command a number of cannons, machine guns, airships, and other mechanical contrivances equal to that of the probable opponent; it is foolish initiative to strain every nerve to be abreast with the enemy in all material domains. This idea leads to a certain spiritual servility and inferiority.

Rather must an effort be made to win superiority in the factors on which the ultimate decision turns. The duty of our War Department is to prepare these decisive elements of strength while still at peace, and to apply them in war according to a clearly recognized principle of superiority. This must secure for us the spiritual and so the material advantage over our enemies. Otherwise we run the danger of being crushed by their weight of numbers.

We cannot reach this goal on the beaten roads of tradition and habit by uninspired rivalry in arming. We must trace out with clear insight the probable course of the future war, and must not be afraid to tread new paths, if needs be, which are not consecrated by experience and use. New goals can only be reached by new roads, and our military history teaches us by numerous instances how the source of superiority lies in progress, in conscious innovations based on convincing arguments. The spiritual capacity to know where, under altered conditions, the decision must be sought, and the spiritual courage to resolve on this new line of action, are the soil in which great successes ripen.

It would be too long a task in this place to examine more closely the nature of the future war, in order to develop systematically the ideas which will prove decisive in it. These questions have been thoroughly ventilated in a book recently published by me, "Vom heutigen Kriege" ("The War of To-day"). In this place I will only condense the results of my inquiry, in order to form a foundation for the further consideration of the essential questions of the future.

In a future European war "masses" will be employed to an extent unprecedented in any previous one. Weapons will be used whose deadliness will exceed all previous experience. More effective and varied means of communication will be available than were known in earlier wars. These three momentous factors will mark the war of the future.

"Masses" signify in themselves an increase of strength, but they contain elements of weakness as well. The larger they are and the less they can be commanded by professional soldiers, the more their tactical efficiency diminishes. The less they are able to live on the country during war-time, especially when concentrated, and the more they are therefore dependent on the daily renewal of food-supplies, the slower and less mobile they become. Owing to the great space which they require for their deployment, it is extraordinarily difficult to bring them into effective action simultaneously. They are also far more accessible to morally depressing influences than compacter bodies of troops, and may prove dangerous to the strategy of their own leaders, if supplies run short, if discipline breaks down, and the commander loses his authority over the masses which he can only rule under regulated conditions.

The increased effectiveness of weapons does not merely imply a longer range, but a greater deadliness, and therefore makes more exacting claims on the moral of the soldier. The danger zone begins sooner than formerly; the space which must be crossed in an attack has become far wider; it must be passed by the attacking party creeping or running. The soldier must often use the spade in defensive operations, during which he is exposed to a far hotter fire than formerly; while under all circumstances he must shoot more than in bygone days. The quick firing which the troop encounters increases the losses at every incautious movement. All branches of arms have to suffer under these circumstances. Shelter and supplies will be more scanty than ever before. In short, while the troops on the average have diminished in value, the demands made on them have become considerably greater.

Improved means of communication, finally, facilitate the handling and feeding of large masses, but tie them down to railway systems and main roads, and must, if they fail or break down in the course of a campaign, aggravate the difficulties, because the troops were accustomed to their use, and the commanders counted upon them.

The direct conclusion to be drawn from these reflections is that a great superiority must rest with the troops whose fighting capabilities and tactical efficiency are greater than those of their antagonists.

The commander who can carry out all operations quicker than the enemy, and can concentrate and employ greater masses in a narrow space than they can, will always be in a position to collect a numerically superior force in the decisive direction; if he controls the more effective troops, he will gain decisive successes against one part of the hostile army, and will be able to exploit them against other divisions of it before the enemy can gain equivalent advantages in other parts of the field.

Since the tactical efficiency and the moral of the troops are chiefly shown in the offensive, and are then most needful, the necessary conclusion is that safety only lies in offensive warfare.

In an attack, the advantage, apart from the elements of moral strength which it brings into play, depends chiefly on rapidity of action. Inasmuch as the attacking party determines the direction of the attack to suit his own plans, he is able at the selected spot to collect a superior force against his surprised opponent. The initiative, which is the privilege of the attacking party, gives a start in time and place which is very profitable in operations and tactics. The attacked party can only equalize this advantage if he has early intimation of the intentions of the assailant, and has time to take measures which hold out promise of success. The more rapidly, therefore, the attacking General strikes his blow and gains his success, and the more capable his troops, the greater is the superiority which the attack in its nature guarantees.

This superiority increases with the size of the masses. If the advancing armies are large and unwieldy, and the distances to be covered great, it will be a difficult and tedious task for the defending commander to take proper measures against a surprise attack. On the other hand, the prospects of success of the attacking General will be very favourable, especially if he is in the fortunate position of having better troops at his disposal.

Finally, the initiative secures to the numerically weaker a possibility of gaining the victory, even when other conditions are equal, and all the more so the greater the masses engaged. In most cases it is impossible to bring the entire mass of a modern army simultaneously and completely into action. A victory, therefore, in the decisive direction—the direction, that is, which directly cuts the arteries of the opponent—is usually conclusive for the whole course of the war, and its effect is felt in the most distant parts of the field of operations. If the assailant, therefore, can advance in this direction with superior numbers, and can win the day, because the enemy cannot utilize his numerical superiority, there is a possibility of an ultimate victory over the arithmetically stronger army. In conformity to this law, Frederick the Great, through superior tactical capability and striking strength, had always the upper hand of an enemy far more powerful in mere numbers.

No further proof is required that the superiority of the attack increases in proportion to the rapidity with which it is delivered, and to the lack of mobility of the hostile forces. Hence the possibility of concealing one's own movements and damaging the effective tactics of the enemy secures an advantage which, though indirect, is yet very appreciable.

We arrive, then, at the conclusion that, in order to secure the superiority in a war of the future under otherwise equal conditions, it is incumbent on us: First, during the period of preparation to raise the tactical value and capabilities of the troops as much as possible, and especially to develop the means of concealing the attacking movements and damaging the enemy's tactical powers; secondly, in the war itself to act on the offensive and strike the first blow, and to exploit the manoeuvring capacity of the troops as much as possible, in order to be superior in the decisive directions. Above all, a State which has objects to attain that cannot be relinquished, and is exposed to attacks by enemies more powerful than itself, is bound to act in this sense. It must, before all things, develop the attacking powers of its army, since a strategic defensive must often adopt offensive methods.

This principle holds good pre-eminently for Germany. The points which I have tried to emphasize must never be lost sight of, if we wish to face the future with confidence. All our measures must be calculated to raise the efficiency of the army, especially in attack; to this end all else must give way. We shall thus have a central point on which all our measures can be focussed. We can make them all serve one purpose, and thus we shall be kept from going astray on the bypaths which we all too easily take if we regard matters separately, and not as forming parts of a collective whole. Much of our previous omissions and commissions would have borne a quite different complexion had we observed this unifying principle.

The requirements which I have described as the most essential are somewhat opposed to the trend of our present efforts, and necessitate a resolute resistance to the controlling forces of our age.

The larger the armies by which one State tries to outbid another, the smaller will be the efficiency and tactical worth of the troops; and not merely the average worth, but the worth of each separate detachment as such. Huge armies are even a danger to their own cause. "They will be suffocated by their own fat," said General v. Brandenstein, the great organizer of the advance of 1870, when speaking of the mass-formation of the French. The complete neglect of cavalry in their proportion to the whole bulk of the army has deprived the commander of the means to injure the tactical capabilities of the enemy, and to screen effectually his own movements. The necessary attention has never been paid in the course of military training to this latter duty. Finally, the tactical efficiency of troops has never been regarded as so essential as it certainly will prove in the wars of the future.

A mechanical notion of warfare and weak concessions to the pressure of public opinion, and often a defective grasp of the actual needs, have conduced to measures which inevitably result in an essential contradiction between the needs of the army and the actual end attained, and cannot be justified from the purely military point of view. It would be illogical and irrelevant to continue in these paths so soon as it is recognized that the desired superiority over the enemy cannot be reached on them.

This essential contradiction between what is necessary and what is attained appears in the enforcement of the law of universal military service. Opinion oscillates between the wish to enforce it more or less, and the disinclination to make the required outlay, and recourse is had to all sorts of subterfuges which may save appearances without giving a good trial to the system. One of these methods is the Ersatzreserve, which is once more being frequently proposed. But the situation is by no means helped by the very brief training which these units at best receive. This system only creates a military mob, which has no capacity for serious military operations. Such an institution would be a heavy strain on the existing teaching personnel in the army, and would be indirectly detrimental to it as well. Nor would any strengthening of the field army be possible under this scheme, since the cadres to contain the mass of these special reservists are not ready to hand. This mass would therefore only fill up the recruiting depots, and facilitate to some degree the task of making good the losses.

A similar contradiction is often shown in the employment of the troops. Every army at the present time is divided into regular troops, who are already organized in time of peace and are merely brought to full strength in war-time, and new formations, which are only organized on mobilization. The tactical value of these latter varies much according to their composition and the age of the units, but is always much inferior to that of the regular troops. The Landwehr formations, which were employed in the field in 1870-71, were an example of this, notwithstanding the excellent services which they rendered, and the new French formations in that campaign were totally ineffective. The sphere of activity of such troops is the second line. In an offensive war their duty is to secure the railroads and bases, to garrison the conquered territory, and partly also to besiege the enemies' fortresses. In fact, they must discharge all the duties which would otherwise weaken the field army. In a defensive war they will have to undertake the local and mainly passive defence, and the support of the national war. By acting at first in this limited sphere, such new formations will gradually become fitted for the duties of the war, and will acquire a degree of offensive strength which certainly cannot be reckoned upon at the outset of the war; and the less adequately such bodies of troops are supplied with columns, trains, and cavalry, the less their value will be.

Nevertheless, it appears to be assumed by us that, in event of war, such troops will be partly available in the first line, and that decisive operations may be entrusted to them. Reserves and regulars are treated as equivalent pieces on the board, and no one seems to suppose that some are less effective than others. A great danger lies in this mechanical conception.

For operations in the field we must employ, wherever possible, regulars only, and rather limit our numbers than assign to inferior troops tasks for which they are inadequate. We must have the courage to attack, if necessary, with troops numerically inferior but tactically superior and more efficient; we must attack in the consciousness that tactical striking power and efficiency outweigh the advantages of greater numbers, and that with the immense modern armies a victory in the decisive direction has more bearing on the ultimate issue than ever before.

The decision depends on the regular troops, not on the masses which are placed at their side on mobilization. The commander who acts on this principle, and so far restricts himself in the employment of masses that he preserves the complete mobility of the armies, will win a strong advantage over the one whose leader is burdened with inferior troops and therefore is handicapped generally, and has paid for the size of his army by want of efficiency. The mass of reserves must, therefore, be employed as subsidiary to the regular troops, whom they must relieve as much as possible from all minor duties. Thus used, a superiority in the numbers of national reserves will secure an undoubted superiority in the actual war.

It follows directly from this argument that we must do our best to render the regular army strong and efficient, and that it would be a mistake to weaken them unnecessarily by excessive drafts upon their personnel with the object of making the reserves tactically equal to them. This aim may sometimes be realized; but the general level of efficiency throughout the troops would be lowered.

Our one object must therefore be to strengthen our regular army. An increase of the peace footing of the standing army is worth far more than a far greater number of badly trained special reservists. It is supremely important to increase the strength of the officers on the establishment. The stronger each unit is in peace, the more efficient will it become for war, hence the vital importance of aiming at quality, not quantity. Concentration, not dilution, will be our safeguard. If we wish to encourage the enforcement of universal service by strengthening the army, we must organize new peace formations, since the number of professional officers and sub-officers will be thus increased. This step is the more necessary because the present available cadres are insufficient to receive the mass of able-bodied recruits and to provide for their thorough training. The gradual enforcement of universal military service hand in hand with an increase of the regular army is the first practical requirement. We shall now consider how far the tactical value of the troops, the efficiency of the army, the cavalry, and the screening service can be improved by organization, equipment, and training.

I must first point out a factor which lies in a different sphere to the questions already discussed, but has great importance in every branch of military activity, especially in the offensive, which requires prompt original action—I mean the importance of personality.

From the Commander-in-Chief, who puts into execution the conceptions of his own brain under the pressure of responsibility and shifting fortune, and the Brigadier, who must act independently according to a given general scheme; to the dispatch rider, surrounded with dangers, and left to his own resources in the enemy's country, and the youngest private in the field fighting for his own hand, and striving for victory in the face of death; everywhere in the wars of to-day, more than in any other age, personality dominates all else. The effect of mass tactics has abolished all close formations of infantry, and the individual is left to himself. The direct influence of the superior has lessened. In the strategic duties of the cavalry, which represent the chief activity of that arm, the patrol riders and orderlies are separated more than before from their troop and are left to their own responsibility. Even in the artillery the importance of independent action will be more clearly emphasized than previously. The battlefields and area of operations have increased with the masses employed. The Commander-in-Chief is far less able than ever before to superintend operations in various parts of the field; he is forced to allow a greater latitude to his subordinates. These conditions are very prominent in attacking operations.

When on the defensive the duty of the individual is mainly to hold his ground, while the commander's principal business is to utilize the reserves. On the offensive, however, the conditions change from moment to moment, according to the counter-movements of the enemy, which cannot be anticipated, and the success or failure of the attacking troops. Even the individual soldier, as the fight fluctuates, must now push on, now wait patiently until the reinforcements have come up; he will often have to choose for himself the objects at which to fire, while never losing touch with the main body. The offensive makes very varied calls on the commander's qualities. Ruse and strategy, boldness and unsparing energy, deliberate judgment and rapid decision, are alternately demanded from him. He must be competent to perform the most opposite duties. All this puts a heavy strain on personality.

It is evident, then, that the army which contains the greatest number of self-reliant and independent personalities must have a distinct advantage. This object, therefore, we must strive with every nerve to attain: to be superior in this respect to all our enemies. And this object can be attained. Personality can be developed, especially in the sphere of spiritual activity. The reflective and critical powers can be improved by continuous exercise; but the man who can estimate the conditions under which he has to act, who is master of the element in which he has to work, will certainly make up his mind more rapidly and more easily than a man who faces a situation which he does not grasp. Self-reliance, boldness, and imperturbability in the hour of misfortune are produced by knowledge. This is shown everywhere. We see the awkward and shy recruit ripen into a clear-headed smart sergeant; and the same process is often traced among the higher commands. But where the mental development is insufficient for the problems which are to be solved, the personality fails at the moment of action. The elegant guardsman Bourbaki collapsed when he saw himself confronted with the task of leading an army whose conditions he did not thoroughly grasp. General Chanzy, on the other hand, retained his clear judgment and resolute determination in the midst of defeat. Thus one of the essential tasks of the preparations for war is to raise the spiritual level of the army and thus indirectly to mould and elevate character. Especially is it essential to develop the self-reliance and resourcefulness of those in high command. In a long military life ideas all too early grow stereotyped and the old soldier follows traditional trains of thought and can no longer form an unprejudiced opinion. The danger of such development cannot be shut out. The stiff and uniform composition of the army which doubles its moral powers has this defect: it often leads to a one-sided development, quite at variance with the many-sidedness of actual realities, and arrests the growth of personality. Something akin to this was seen in Germany in the tentative scheme of an attack en masse. United will and action are essential to give force its greatest value. They must go hand in hand with the greatest spiritual independence and resourcefulness, capable of meeting any emergency and solving new problems by original methods.

It has often been said that one man is as good as another; that personality is nothing, the type is everything; but this assertion is erroneous. In time of peace, when sham reputations flourish and no real struggle winnows the chaff from the coin, mediocrity in performance is enough. But in war, personality turns the scale. Responsibility and danger bring out personality, and show its real worth, as surely as a chemical test separates the pure metal from the dross.

That army is fortunate which has placed men of this kind in the important posts during peace-time and has kept them there. This is the only way to avoid the dangers which a one-sided routine produces, and to break down that red-tapism which is so prejudicial to progress and success. It redounds to the lasting credit of William I. that for the highest and most responsible posts, at any rate, he had already in time of peace made his selection from among all the apparently great men around him; and that he chose and upheld in the teeth of all opposition those who showed themselves heroes and men of action in the hour of need, and had the courage to keep to their own self-selected paths. This is no slight title to fame, for, as a rule, the unusual rouses envy and distrust, but the cheap, average wisdom, which never prompted action, appears as a refined superiority, and it is only under the pressure of the stern reality of war that the truth of Goethe's lines is proved:

"Folk and thrall and victor can
Witness bear in every zone:
Fortune's greatest gift to man
Is personality alone."

CHAPTER X. ARMY ORGANIZATION

I now turn to the discussion of some questions of organization, but it is not my intention to ventilate all the needs and aims connected with this subject that occupy our military circles at the present time. I shall rather endeavour to work out the general considerations which, in my opinion, must determine the further development of our army, if we wish, by consistent energy, to attain a superiority in the directions which will certainly prove to be all-important in the next war. It will be necessary to go into details only on points which are especially noteworthy or require some explanation. I shall obviously come into opposition with the existing state of things, but nothing is further from my purpose than to criticize them. My views are based on theoretical requirements, while our army, from certain definitely presented beginnings, and under the influence of most different men and of changing views, in the midst of financial difficulties and political disputes, has, by fits and starts, grown up into what it now is. It is, in a certain sense, outside criticism; it must be taken as something already existing, whose origin is only a subject for a subsequent historical verdict. But the further expansion of our army belongs to the future, and its course can be directed. It can follow well-defined lines, in order to become efficient, and it is politically most important that this object should be realized. Therefore I shall not look back critically on the past, but shall try to serve the future.

The guiding principle of our preparations for war must be, as I have already said, the development of the greatest fighting strength and the greatest tactical efficiency, in order through them to be in a position to carry on an offensive war successfully. What follows will, therefore, fall naturally under these two heads. Fighting strength rests partly, as already said, on the training (which will be discussed later), the arming, and the personnel, partly on the composition of the troops, and, therefore, in the case of line regiments, with which we chiefly have to deal, since they are the real field troops, on the strength of their peace establishment. It was shown in the previous chapter how essential it is to have in the standing army not only the necessary cadres ready for the new formations, but to make the separate branches so strong that they can easily be brought up to full strength in war-time.

The efficiency and character of the superiors, the officers and the non-commissioned officers, are equally weighty factors in the value of the troops. They are the professional supporters of discipline, decision, and initiative, and, since they are the teachers of the troops, they determine their intellectual standard. The number of permanent officers on the establishment in peace is exceedingly small in proportion to their duties in the training of the troops and to the demands made of them on mobilization. If we reflect how many officers and non-commissioned officers from the standing army must be transferred to the new formations in order to vitalize them, and how the modern tactical forms make it difficult for the superior officer to assert his influence in battle, the numerical inadequacy of the existing personnel is clearly demonstrated. This applies mainly to the infantry, and in their case, since they are the decisive arm, a sufficient number of efficient officers is essential. All the more important is it, on the one hand, to keep the establishment of officers and non-commissioned officers in the infantry at full strength, and, on the other hand, to raise the efficiency of the officers and non-commissioned officers on leave or in the reserve. This latter is a question of training, and does not come into the present discussion. The task of keeping the establishments at adequate strength is, in a sense, a financial question. The amount of the pay and the prospects which the profession holds out for subsequent civil posts greatly affect the body of non-commissioned officers, and therefore it is important to keep step with the general increase in prices by improved pecuniary advantages. Even for the building up of the corps of officers, the financial question is all-important. The career of the officer offers to-day so little prospect of success and exacts such efficiency and self-devotion from the individual, that he will not long remain in the service, attractive as it is, if the financial sacrifices are so high as they now are. The infantry officer especially must have a better position. Granted that the cavalry and mounted artillery officers incur greater expenses for the keep of their horses than the infantry officer has to pay, the military duties of the latter are by far the most strenuous and require a very considerable outlay on clothing. It would be, in my opinion, expedient to give the infantry officer more pay than the cavalry and artillery officers, in order to make service in that arm more attractive. There is a rush nowadays into the mounted arm, for which there is a plethora of candidates. These arms will always be well supplied with officers. Their greater attractiveness must be counterbalanced by special advantages offered by the infantry service. By no other means can we be sure of having sufficient officers in the chief arm.

If the fighting strength in each detachment depends on its composition and training, there are other elements besides the tactical value of the troops which determine the effectiveness of their combined efforts in action; these are first the leadership, which, however, depends on conditions which are beyond calculation, and secondly the numerical proportion of the arms to each other. Disregarding provisionally the cavalry, who play a special role in battle, we must define the proportion which artillery must bear to infantry.

With regard to machine guns, the idea that they can to some extent replace infantry is quite erroneous. Machine guns are primarily weapons of defence. In attack they can only be employed under very favourable conditions, and then strengthen only one factor of a successful attack—the fire-strength—while they may sometimes hinder that impetuous forward rush which is the soul of every attack. Hence, this auxiliary weapon should be given to the infantry in limited numbers, and employed mainly on the defensive fronts, and should be often massed into large units. Machine-gun detachments should not overburden the marching columns.

The relation of infantry to artillery is of more importance.

Infantry is the decisive arm. Other arms are exclusively there to smooth their road to victory, and support their action directly or indirectly. This relation must not be merely theoretical; the needs of the infantry must ultimately determine the importance of all other fighting instruments in the whole army.

If we make this idea the basis of our argument, the following is the result. Infantry has gained enormously in defensive power owing to modern weapons. The attack requires, therefore, a far greater superiority than ever before. In addition to this, the breadth of front in action has greatly increased in consequence of the former close tactical formations having been broken up through the increase of fire. This refers only to the separate detachment, and does not justify the conclusion that in the future fewer troops will cover the same spaces as before. This assumption applies at the most to defence, and then only in a limited sense. In attack the opposite will probably be the case. The troops must therefore be placed more deeply _en échelon _than in the last wars. Now, the average breadth of the front in attack must regulate the allotment of artillery to infantry. No definite proportion can be settled; but if the theoretical calculation be compared with the experiences of the last wars, conclusions may be obtained which will most probably prove appropriate. No more than this can be expected in the domain of military science.

If we agree to the above-mentioned proportion of breadth and depth in an infantry attack, we shall be driven to insist on a reduction of artillery as compared with the past; but should we think that modern artillery helps the attack, especially by indirect fire, we must advocate, from the standpoint of offensive warfare, an increase of the artillery. Actual war experiences alone can find the true middle path between these two extremes.

If the frontal development of the artillery of a modern army corps, or, better still, two divisions, be regarded from the point of view that the guns cannot advance in connected line, but that only the specially adapted parts of the field can be used for artillery development, the conclusion is certain that by such frontal extension the infantry is reduced to a covering line for the artillery. In forming this opinion we must not assume the normal strength of the infantry, but take into account that the strength of the infantry in war rapidly melts away. If we estimate the companies on the average at two-thirds of their proper strength, we shall be above rather than below the real figures. Such infantry strength will, of course, be sufficient to defend the position taken up by the artillery, but it is hardly enough to carry out, in that section of the field, a decisive attack, which, under present conditions, requires greater numbers and depth than before.

In this connection it is very instructive to study the second part of the Franco-German War, and the Boer War, as well as the Manchurian campaign.

Some of the German infantry had in the first-named period extraordinarily diminished in numbers; companies of 120 men were not rare. The artillery, on the contrary, had remained at its original strength. The consequences naturally was that the powers of the Germans on the offensive grew less and the battles and skirmishes were not so decisive as in the first part of the war. This condition would have shown up more distinctly against an enemy of equal class than in the contest with the loosely-compacted, raw French levies. In the former case the offensive would have been impracticable. The strong artillery, under the existing conditions, no doubt gave great support to the weak infantry; but an unbiassed opinion leads to the conclusion that, under the then existing proportion of the arms to each other, the infantry was too weak to adopt energetic offensive tactics against a well-matched enemy. This is irresistibly proved if we consider what masses of infantry were needed at Wörth and St. Privat, for instance, in spite of the support of very superior artillery, in order to defeat a weaker enemy of equal class.

Again, in South Africa, the overwhelming superiority of the English in artillery was never able to force a victory. In Manchuria the state of things was very instructive. Numerically the Russian artillery was extraordinarily superior to the enemy's, and the range of the Russian field guns was longer than that of the Japanese; nevertheless, the Japanese succeeded in beating an enemy stronger in infantry also, because, in the decisive directions of attack, they were able to unite superior forces of infantry and artillery, while the Russian artillery was scattered along the whole of their broad front.

The lesson of this war is that, apart from the close relation of the arms to each other in the separate units, the co-operation of these units must be looked at, if the strength of the two sister arms is to be appropriately determined.

The requirement that each separate tactical unit should he made equal or superior in artillery to the corresponding hostile unit is thoroughly mechanical, as if in war division always fought against division and corps against corps! Superiority at the decisive point is the crucial test. This superiority is attained by means of an unexpected concentration of forces for attack, and there is no reason why the superiority in artillery should not also be brought about in this way. If by superior tactical skill two army corps, each with 96 guns, combine against a hostile army which brings 144 guns into action, that signifies a superiority of 48 guns and a double superiority in infantry. If it is assumed that on both sides the army corps is armed with 144 guns, and that in consequence of this the tactical superiority has become so slight that neither side can claim a superiority in one direction, then equal forces meet, and chance decides the day. Since the Japanese were tactically more efficient than their enemy and took the offensive, they were enabled to unite the superior forces in the most decisive directions, and this advantage proved far greater than the numerical superiority of the Russian army as a whole.

If we look at the whole matter we shall come to the conclusion that the artillery, if it is not a question of pure defence, need never occupy within a line of battle so much ground that the concentration of a considerably superior force of infantry for attack is rendered doubtful. In this respect we have, in our present organization already exceeded the expedient proportion between the two arms in favour of the artillery. The conclusion is that this latter arm never need, within the separate divisions, be made so strong that the attacking capacities of the army are thereby prejudiced. This is the decisive point. Any excess in artillery can be kept on the battlefield in reserve when space is restricted; if the attacking efficiency of the troops is reduced, then artillery becomes a dead weight on the army instead of an aid to victory. It is far more important to be able to unite superior forces for a decisive attack than to meet the enemy with equally matched forces along the whole front. If we observe this principle, we shall often be weaker than the enemy on the less important fronts; this disadvantage may be partly counterbalanced by remaining on the defensive in such a position. It becomes a positive advantage, if, owing to an overpowering concentration of forces, victory is won at the decisive point. This victory cancels all the failures which may have been recorded elsewhere.

The operative superiority of an enemy is determined by the greater marching capacity of the troops, by the rapid and systematic working of the communications with the rear, and, above all, by the length of the columns of the operating troops. Under the modern system of colossal armaments, an army, especially if in close formation, cannot possibly live on the country; it is driven to trust to daily food-supplies from the rear. Railways are used as far as possible to bring up the supplies; but from the railhead the communication with the troops must be maintained by columns of traction waggons and draught animals, which go to and fro between the troops, the rearward magazines, and the railhead. Since traction waggons are restricted to made roads, the direct communication with the troops must be kept up by columns of draught animals, which can move independently of the roads. The waggons of provisions, therefore, which follow the troops, and are filled daily, must come up with them the same day, or there will be a shortage of food. This is only possible if the troop column does not exceed a certain length and starts at early morning, so that the transport waggons, which, at the end of the march, must be driven from the rear to the head of the column, can reach this before the beginning of the night's rest. The fitness of an army for attack can only be maintained if these supplies are uninterrupted; there must also be a sufficient quantity of tinned rations and provisions which the soldiers can carry with them. If the length of the columns exceeds the limit here laid down, the marches must be proportionately shortened. If unusually lengthy marches are made, so that the provision carts cannot reach the troops, days of rest must be interposed, to regulate the supply. Thus the capacity of an army to march and to carry out operations is directly dependent on the possibility of being fed from the rear. A careful calculation, based on practical experiences, shows that, in order to average 20 to 22 kilometres a day—the minimum distance required from an army—no column on a road ought to exceed a length of about 25 kilometres This consideration determines the depth of the army corps on the march, since in an important campaign and when massing for battle troops seldom march in smaller bodies than a corps.

This calculation, by which the conditions of modern war are compulsorily affected, makes it highly necessary that the system of supplies and rations should be carefully organized. The restoration of any destroyed railways, the construction of light railways, the organization of columns of motor transport waggons and draught animals, must be prepared by every conceivable means in time of peace, in order that in war-time the railroads may follow as closely as possible on the track of the troops, and that the columns may maintain without interruption continuous communications between the troops and the railhead. In order to keep this machinery permanently in working order, and to surmount any crisis in bringing up supplies, it is highly advisable to have an ample stock of tinned rations. This stock should, in consideration of the necessary mass-concentration, be as large as possible. Care must be taken, by the organization of trains and columns, that the stock of tinned provisions can be quickly renewed. This would be best done by special light columns, which are attached to the army corps outside the organization of provision and transport columns, and follow it at such a distance, that, if necessary, they could be soon pushed to the front by forced or night marches. There is naturally some reluctance to increase the trains of the army corps, but this necessity is unavoidable. It is further to be observed that the columns in question would not be very long, since they would mainly convey condensed foods and other provisions compressed into the smallest space.

An immense apparatus of train formations, railway and telegraph corps, and workmen must be got ready to secure the efficiency of a modern army with its millions. This is absolutely necessary, since without it the troops in modern warfare would be practically unable to move. It is far more important to be ahead of the enemy in this respect than in any other, for there lies the possibility of massing a superior force at the decisive point, and of thus defeating a stronger opponent.

However careful the preparations, these advantages can only be attained if the troop columns do not exceed the maximum strength which can be fed from the rear, if the necessary forward movement is carried out. Everything which an army corps requires for the war must be kept within these limits.

Our modern army corps without the heavy artillery of the field army corresponds roughly to this requirement. But should it be lengthened by a heavy howitzer battalion, with the necessary ammunition columns, it will considerably exceed the safe marching depth—if, that is, the necessary advance-guard distance be included. Since, also, the infantry is too weak in proportion to the space required by the artillery to deploy, it becomes advisable in the interests both of powerful attack and of operative efficiency, within the separate troop organizations to strengthen the numbers of the infantry and reduce those of the artillery.

In addition to the length of the column, the arrangement of the division is very important for its tactical efficiency. This must be such as to permit the most varied employment of the troops and the formation of reserves without the preliminary necessity of breaking up all the units. This requirement does not at all correspond to our traditional organization, and the man to insist upon it vigorously has not yet appeared, although there can be no doubt as to the inadequacy of the existing tactical organization, and suitable schemes have already been drawn up by competent officers.

The army corps is divided into two divisions, the division into two infantry brigades. All the brigades consist of two regiments. The formation of a reserve makes it very difficult for the commander to fix the centre of gravity of the battle according to circumstances and his own judgment. It is always necessary to break up some body when a reserve has to be formed, and in most cases to reduce the officers of some detachment to inactivity. Of course, a certain centre of gravity for the battle may be obtained by assigning to one part of the troops a wider and to the other a narrower space for deployment. But this procedure in no way replaces a reserve, for it is not always possible, even in the first dispositions for the engagement, to judge where the brunt of the battle will be. That depends largely on the measures taken by the enemy and the course of the battle.

Napoleon's saying, "Je m'engage et puis je vois," finds its application, though to a lessened extent, even to-day. The division of cavalry brigades into two regiments is simply a traditional institution which has been thoughtlessly perpetuated. It has not been realized that the duties of the cavalry have completely changed, and that brigades of two regiments are, in addition to other disadvantages, too weak to carry these duties out.

This bisecting system, by restricting the freedom of action, contradicts the most generally accepted military principles.

The most natural formation is certainly a tripartition of the units, as is found in an infantry regiment. This system permits the separate divisions to fight near each other, and leaves room for the withdrawal of a reserve, the formation of a detachment, or the employment of the subdivisions in lines (Treffen), for the principle of the wing attack must not be allowed to remain merely a scheme. Finally, it is the best formation for the offensive, since it allows the main body of the troops to be employed at a single point in order to obtain a decisive result there.

A special difficulty in the free handling of the troops is produced by the quite mechanical division of the artillery, who bring into action two kinds of ordnance—cannons and howitzers. These latter can, of course, be used as cannons, but have special functions which are not always required. Their place in the organization, however, is precisely the same as that of the cannons, and it is thus very difficult to employ them as their particular character demands.

The object in the whole of this organization has been to make corps and divisions equal, and if possible superior, to the corresponding formations of the enemy by distributing the batteries proportionately according to numbers among the divisions. This secured, besides, the undeniable advantage of placing the artillery directly under the orders of the commanders of the troops. But, in return, it robbed the commanding General of the last means secured by the organization of enforcing his tactical aims. He is now forced to form a reserve for himself out of the artillery of the division, and thus to deprive one division at least of half its artillery. If he has the natural desire to withdraw for himself the howitzer section, which is found in one division only, the same division must always be subjected to this reduction of its strength, and it is more than problematical whether this result always fits in with the tactical position. It seems at least worth while considering whether, under these circumstances, it would not be a more appropriate arrangement to attach a howitzer section to each division.

The distribution of the heavy field howitzers is another momentous question. It would be in accordance with the principles that guide the whole army to divide them equally among the army corps. This arrangement would have much in its favour, for every corps may find itself in a position where heavy howitzer batteries can be profitably employed. They can also, however, be combined under the command of the General-in-Chief, and attached to the second line of the army. The first arrangement offers, as has been said, many advantages, but entails the great disadvantage that the line of march of the army corps is dangerously lengthened by several kilometres, so that no course is left but either to weaken the other troops of the corps or to sacrifice the indispensable property of tactical efficiency. Both alternatives are inadmissible. On the other hand, since the employment of heavy howitzers is by no means necessary in every engagement, but only when an attack is planned against a strongly-posted enemy, it may be safely assumed that the heavy howitzers could be brought up in time out of the second line by a night march. Besides, their mobility renders it possible to detach single batteries or sections, and on emergency to attach them to an army corps temporarily.

There is a prevalent notion that the heavy howitzers are principally used to fight the enemy's field artillery, and therefore must be on the spot in every engagement. They have even been known to stray into the advance guard. I do not approve of this idea. The enemy's field artillery will fire indirectly from previously masked positions, and in such case they cannot be very successfully attacked by heavy howitzers. It seems to me quite unjustifiable, with the view of attaining this problematic object, to burden the marching columns permanently with long unwieldy trains of artillery and ammunition, and thus to render their effectiveness doubtful.

No doubt the Japanese, who throughout the war continually increased their heavy field howitzers, ultimately attached artillery of that sort to every division. The experiences of that war must not, however, be overestimated or generalized. The conditions were quite sui generis. The Japanese fought on their whole front against fortified positions strengthened by heavy artillery, and as they attacked the enemy's line in its whole extension, they required on their side equally heavy guns. It should be noticed that they did not distribute their very effective 12-centimetre field howitzers along the whole front, but, so far as I can gather, assigned them all to the army of General Nogi, whose duty was to carry out the decisive enveloping movement at Mukden. The Japanese thus felt the need of concentrating the effect of their howitzers, and as we hope we shall not imitate their frontal attack, but break through the enemy's front, though in a different way from theirs, the question of concentration seems to me very important for us.

Under these circumstances it will be most advantageous to unite the heavy batteries in the hand of the Commander-in-Chief. They thus best serve his scheme of offence. He can mass them at the place which he wishes to make the decisive point in the battle, and will thus attain that end most completely, whereas the distribution of them among the army corps only dissipates their effectiveness. His heavy batteries will be for him what the artillery reserves are for the divisional General. There, where their mighty voice roars over the battlefield, will be the deciding struggle of the day. Every man, down to the last private, knows that.

I will only mention incidentally that the present organization of the heavy artillery on a peace footing is unsatisfactory. The batteries which in war are assigned to the field army must in peace also be placed under the orders of the corps commanders (Truppenführer) if they are to become an organic part of the whole. At present the heavy artillery of the field army is placed under the general-inspection of the foot artillery, and attached to the troops only for purposes of manoeuvres. It thus remains an isolated organism so far as the army goes, and does not feel itself an integral part of the whole. A clear distinction between field artillery and fortress artillery would be more practical.

This view seems at first sight to contradict the requirement that the heavy batteries should form a reserve in the hands of the Commander-in-Chief. As the armies do not exist in peace-time, and manoeuvres are seldom carried out in army formation, the result of the present organization is that the tactical relations of the heavy artillery and the other troops are not sufficiently understood. This disadvantage would be removed if heavy artillery were assigned permanently to each army corps. This would not prevent it being united in war-time in the hands of the army leaders. On the contrary, they would be used in manoeuvres in relation to the army corps in precisely the same sense as they would be in war-time in relation to the armies.

The operations of the army in the enemy's countries will be far more effective if it has control of the railways and roads. That implies not merely the restoration of railroads that may have been destroyed, but the rapid capture of the barrier forts and fortresses which impede the advance of the army by cutting off the railway communications. We were taught the lesson in 1870-71 in France how far defective railway communications hindered all operations. It is, therefore, of vital importance that a corps should be available, whose main duty is the discharge of these necessary functions.

Until recently we had only one united corps of pioneers, which was organized alike for operations in the field and for siege operations, but these latter have recently been so much developed that that system can no longer supply an adequate technical training for them.

The demands made by this department of warfare, on the one hand, and by the duties of pioneering in the field on the other, are so extensive and so essentially different that it seems quite impracticable to train adequately one and the same corps in both branches during two years' service. The chief functions of the field pioneer are bridge-building, fortifying positions, and supporting the infantry in the attack on fortified places. The most important part of the fortress pioneer's duties consists in sapping, and, above all, in mining, in preparing for the storming of permanent works, and in supporting the infantry in the actual storm. The army cannot be satisfied with a superficial training for such service; it demands a most thorough going previous preparation.

Starting from this point of view, General v. Beseler, the late Inspector-General of Fortresses and Pioneers, who has done inestimable service to his country, laid the foundations of a new organization. This follows the idea of the field pioneers and the fortress pioneers—a rudimentary training in common, followed by separate special training for their special duties. We must continue on these lines, and develop more particularly the fortress pioneer branch of the service in better proportion to its value.

In connection with the requirements already discussed, which are directly concerned with securing and maintaining an increase of tactical efficiency, we must finally mention two organizations which indirectly serve the same purpose. These diminish the tactical efficiency of the enemy, and so increase our own; while, by reconnoitring and by screening movements, they help the attack and make it possible to take the enemy unawares—an important condition of successful offensive warfare. I refer to the cavalry and the air-fleet.

The cavalry's duties are twofold. On the one hand, they must carry out reconnaissances and screening movements, on the other hand they must operate against the enemy's communications, continually interrupt the regular renewal of his supplies, and thus cripple his mobility.

Every military expert will admit that our cavalry, in proportion to the war-footing of the army, and in view of the responsible duties assigned them in war, is lamentably weak. This disproportion is clearly seen if we look at the probable wastage on the march and in action, and realize that it is virtually impossible to replace these losses adequately, and that formations of cavalry reserves can only possess a very limited efficiency. Popular opinion considers cavalry more or less superfluous, because in our last wars they certainly achieved comparatively little from the tactical point of view, and because they cost a great deal. There is a general tendency to judge cavalry by the standard of 1866 and 1870-71. It cannot be emphasized too strongly that this standard is misleading. On the one hand, the equipment was then so defective that it crippled the powers of the mounted man in the most important points; on the other hand, the employment of the cavalry was conducted on a wholly antiquated system. It was, consequently, not armed for independent movements. What they then did must not be compared with what will be required from them in the future. In wars in which mounted forces were really effective, and not hampered in their movements by preconceived notions (as in the American War of Secession and the Boer War), their employment has been continuously extended, since the great value of their operative mobility was convincingly shown, especially in Africa, notwithstanding all modern weapons. These are the wars which must be studied in order to form a fair opinion. They will convince us that an increase of our cavalry is absolutely imperative. It will, of course, only be valuable when the divisions of the army cavalry are equipped with columns and trains in such a way that they can operate independently. The effectiveness of the cavalry depends entirely on the fulfilment of this condition. It is also imperatively necessary, when the measures of our opponents are considered, to strengthen the fighting force of the cavalry by an adequate addition of cyclist sections. This is the more requisite, as, on the one hand, the attack on the enemy's communications must expect vigorous opposition, and, on the other hand, the screening duties, which are even more important for the offensive than the reconnaissances, are likely to be specially successful if cavalry and cyclists combine. Again, an increased strength of cavalry is undeniably required to meet the reconnoitring and screening troops of the enemy.

Besides the strengthening of this arm and the addition of cyclists, another organization is required if the cavalry are to do useful service. Brigades of two regiments and divisions of six regiments are in war-time, where all depends on decisive action, far too small, as I have repeatedly demonstrated without being refuted.

The brigades must in war be three regiments strong. The strength of the divisions and corps may vary according to the requirements of the time being. Just because our cavalry is so weak, the organization must be in a high degree elastic. There can, besides, be no doubt on the point that the side which commands the services of the stronger cavalry, led on modern lines, will have at the outset quite inestimable advantage over the enemy, which must make itself felt in the ultimate issue.

I might remark incidentally that the mounted batteries which are attached to the army cavalry must be formed with four guns each, so that the division with its three parts would have the control of three batteries, and, if necessary, a battery could be assigned to each brigade. That is an old suggestion which the Emperor William I. once made, but it has never yet been considered. It is not with cavalry usually a question of protracted artillery engagements, but of utilizing momentary opportunities; the greatest mobility is required together with the most many-sided efficiency and adaptability. There can obviously, therefore, be no question of a systematic combination with the artillery. Such a thing can only be of value in the case of cavalry when it is important to make a decisive attack.

The reconnaissance and screening duties of the cavalry must be completed by the air-fleet. Here we are dealing with something which does not yet exist, but we can foresee clearly the great part which this branch of military science will play in future wars.[A] It is therefore necessary to point out in good time those aspects of it which are of special weight in a military sense, and therefore deserve peculiar consideration from the technical side.

[Footnote A: The efficiency and success of the Italian aviators in Tripoli are noteworthy, but must not be overvalued. There were no opponents in the air.]

The first requirement is that airships, in addition to simplicity of handling and independence of weather, should possess a superior fighting strength, for it is impossible effectively to screen the movements of the army and to open the road for reconnaissances without attacking successfully the hostile flying-machines and air cruisers.

The power to fight and destroy the hostile airships must be the leading idea in all constructions, and the tactics to be pursued must be at once thought out in order that the airships may be built accordingly, since tactics will be essentially dependent on the construction and the technical effectiveness. These reciprocal relations must be borne in mind from the first, so as to gain a distinct advantage over our opponents.

If the preceding remarks are epitomized, we have, apart from the necessity of enforcing universal service, quite a long list of proposed changes in organization, the adoption of which will considerably improve the efficiency of our army.

The whole organization must be such that the column length of the army corps does not exceed the size which allows a rapid advance, though the supplies are exclusively drawn from magazine depots.

In case of the larger formations, and especially of the army corps as being the tactical and operative unit, the principle of tripartition must be observed.

The infantry must be, in proportion to the artillery, substantially strengthened.

The artillery must be organized in such a way that it is possible to concentrate the fire of the howitzers where required without breaking up the units.

The cavalry must be increased, strengthened by cyclist sections, and so organized as to insure their efficiency in war.

The formation of reinforcements, especially for supplies, must be so elaborated that, on a rapid advance, an efficient system of feeding the troops entirely from magazine depots can be maintained.

The air-fleet must be energetically developed with the object of making it a better fighting machine than that of the enemy.

Finally, and this is the most important thing, we must strain every nerve to render our infantry tactically the best in the world, and to take care that none but thoroughly efficient formations are employed in the decisive field war.

The fulfilment of all these requirements on the basis of our present organization offers naturally great difficulties and can hardly be carried out. It is impossible to imagine a German Reichstag which, without the most extreme pressure of circumstances, could resolve to make for the army the sacrifices called for by our political condition. The temptation to shut the eyes to existing dangers and to limit political aims in order to repudiate the need of great sacrifices is so strong that men are sure to succumb to it, especially at a period when all political wisdom seems summed up in the maintenance of peace. They comfort themselves with the hope that the worst will not happen, although history shows that the misery produced by weakness has often surpassed all expectations.

But even if the nation can hardly be expected to understand what is necessary, yet the War Department must be asked to do their utmost to achieve what is possible, and not to stop short out of deference to public opinion. When the future of a great and noble nation is at stake there is no room for cowardice or inaction. Nothing must be done, as unhappily has too often been the case, which runs counter to the principles of a sound military organization.

The threefold division of the larger formations could be effected in various ways. Very divergent ideas may be entertained on this subject, and the difficulties of carrying out the scheme need extensive consideration. I will make a few proposals just by way of illustration.

One way would be to split up the army corps into three divisions of three infantry regiments each, and to abolish the superfluous intermediate system of brigades. Another proposal would be to form in every corps one of the present divisions of three brigades, so that the extra brigade combined with the light field howitzers and the Jäger battalion would constitute in event of war a separate detachment in the hands of the commanding General. This last arrangement could be carried out comparatively easily under our present system, but entails the drawback that the system of twofold division is still in force within the brigades and divisions. The most sweeping reform, that of dividing the corps into three divisions, would have the advantage of being thorough and would allow the separate groups to be employed in war in many more ways.

The relations between the infantry and the artillery can naturally only be improved gradually by the strengthening of the infantry through the enforcement of universal service. The assignment of a fifth brigade to each army corps would produce better conditions than exist at present. But so soon as the strengthening of the infantry has gone so far that new army corps must be created, the artillery required for them can be taken from existing formations, and these can be diminished by this means. It will conduce to the general efficiency of the army if the artillery destined for each army corps is to some degree limited, without, however, reducing their total. Care must be taken that only the quantity of ammunition necessary for the first stages of the battle should be habitually carried by the columns of the troops engaged. All that exceeds this must be kept in the rear behind the commissariat waggons, and brought forward only on necessity—that is to say, when a battle is in prospect. The certainty of being able to feed the troops and thus maintain the rapidity of the advance is far more important than the more or less theoretical advantage of having a large quantity of ammunition close at hand during the advance. The soldiers will be inclined to be sparing of ammunition in the critical stages of the fight, and will not be disposed to engage with an unseen enemy, who can only be attacked by scattered fire; the full fire strength will be reserved for the deciding moments of the engagement. Then, however, the required ammunition will be on the spot, in any event, if it is brought forward by stages in good time.

A suitable organization of the artillery would insure that each division had an equal number of batteries at its disposal. The light field howitzers, however, must be attached to a division in such a way that they may form an artillery corps, without necessarily breaking up the formations of the division. The strength of the artillery must be regulated according to that of the infantry, in such a way that the entire marching depth does not exceed some 25 kilometres. The heavy field howitzers, on the other hand, must in peace be placed under the orders of the General commanding, and in event of war be combined as "army" artillery.

It would, perhaps, be advisable if the cavalry were completely detached from the corps formation, since the main body is absolutely independent in war as "army" cavalry. The regiments necessary for service with the infantry could be called out in turn during peace-time for manoeuvres with mixed arms, in order to be trained in the work of divisional cavalry, for which purpose garrison training can also be utilized. On the other hand, it is, I know, often alleged that the Truppenführer are better trained and learn much if the cavalry are under their orders; but this objection does not seem very pertinent.

Another way to adapt the organization better to the efficiency of the arm than at present would be that the four cavalry regiments belonging to each army corps should be combined into a brigade and placed under the commanding General. In event of mobilization, one regiment would be withdrawn for the two divisions, while the brigade, now three regiments strong, would pass over to the "army" cavalry. The regiment intended for divisional cavalry would, on mobilization, form itself into six squadrons and place three of them at the service of each division. If the army corps was formed into three divisions, each division would only be able to receive two squadrons.

In this way, of course, a very weak and inferior divisional cavalry would be formed; the service in the field would suffer heavily under it; but since it is still more important to have at hand a sufficient army cavalry than a divisional cavalry, quite competent for their difficult task, there is, for the time being, no course left than to raise the one to its indispensable strength at the cost of the other. The blame for such a makeshift, which seriously injures the army, falls upon those who did not advocate an increase of the cavalry at the proper moment. The whole discussion shows how absolutely necessary such an increase is. If it were effected, it would naturally react upon the organization of the arm. This would have to be adapted to the new conditions. There are various ways in which a sound and suitable development of the cavalry can be guaranteed.

The absolutely necessary cyclist sections must in any case be attached to the cavalry in peace, in order that the two arms may be drilled in co-operation, and that the cavalry commander may learn to make appropriate use of this important arm. Since the cyclists are restricted to fairly good roads, the co-operation presents difficulties which require to be surmounted.

The views which I have here tried to sketch as aspects of the organization of the army can be combated from several standpoints. In military questions, particularly, different estimates of the individual factors lead to very different results. I believe, however, that my opinions result with a certain logical necessity from the whole aspect of affairs. It is most essential, in preparing for war, to keep the main leading idea fixed and firm, and not to allow it to be shaken by question of detail. Each special requirement must be regarded as part of that general combination of things which only really comes into view in actual warfare. The special standpoint of a particular arm must be rejected as unjustified, and the departmental spirit must be silenced. Care must be taken not to overestimate the technical and material means of power in spite of their undoubted importance, and to take sufficient account of the spiritual and moral factors. Our age, which has made such progress in the conquest of nature, is inclined to attach too much importance to this dominion over natural forces; but in the last resort, the forces that give victory are in the men and not in the means which they employ.

A profound knowledge of generalship and a self-reliant personality are essential to enable the war preparations to be suitably carried out; under the shifting influence of different aims and ideas the "organizer of victory" will often feel doubtful whether he ought to decide this way or that. The only satisfactory solution of such doubts is to deduce from a view of warfare in its entirety and its varied phases and demands the importance of the separate co-operating factors.

"For he who grasps the problem as a whole
Has calmed the storm that rages in his soul"

CHAPTER XI.TRAINING AND EDUCATION

Our first object, then, must be to organize and transform the German army into the most effective tool of German policy, and into a school of health and strength for our nation. We must also try to get ahead of our rivals by superiority of training, and at the same time to do full justice to the social requirements of the army by exerting all our efforts towards raising the spiritual and moral level of the units and strengthening their loyal German feelings.

Diligence and devotion to military education are no longer at the present day sufficient to make our troops superior to the enemy's, for there are men working no less devotedly in the hostile armies. If we wish to gain a start there is only one way to do it: the training must break with all that is antiquated and proceed in the spirit of the war of the future, which will impose fresh requirements on the troops as well as on the officers.

It is unnecessary to go into the details about the training in the use of modern arms and technical contrivances: this follows necessarily from the introduction of these means of war. But if we survey the sphere of training as a whole, two phenomena of modern warfare will strike us as peculiarly important with regard to it: the heightened demands which will be made on individual character and the employment of "masses" to an extent hitherto unknown.

The necessity for increased individualization in the case of infantry and artillery results directly from the character of the modern battle; in the case of cavalry it is due to the nature of their strategical duties and the need of sometimes fighting on foot like infantry; in the case of leaders of every grade, from the immensity of the armies, the vast extent of the spheres of operation and fields of battle, and the difficulty, inseparable from all these conditions, of giving direct orders. Wherever we turn our eyes to the wide sphere of modern warfare, we encounter the necessity of independent action—by the private soldier in the thick of the battle, or the lonely patrol in the midst of the enemy's country, as much as by the leader of an army, who handles huge hosts. In battle, as well as in operations, the requisite uniformity of action can only be attained at the present time by independent co-operation of all in accordance with a fixed general scheme.

The employment of "masses" requires an entirely altered method of moving and feeding the troops. It is one thing to lead 100,000 or perhaps 200,000 men in a rich country seamed with roads, and concentrate them for a battle—it is another to manoeuvre 800,000 men on a scene of war stripped bare by the enemy, where all railroads and bridges have been destroyed by modern explosives. In the first case the military empiric may be equal to the occasion; the second case demands imperatively a scientifically educated General and a staff who have also studied and mastered for themselves the nature of modern warfare. The problems of the future must be solved in advance if a commander wishes to be able to operate in a modern theatre of war with certainty and rapid decision.

The necessity of far-reaching individualization then is universally recognized. To be sure, the old traditions die slowly. Here and there an undeserved importance is still attached to the march past as a method of education, and drilling in close formation is sometimes practised more than is justified by its value. The cavalry is not yet completely awakened from its slumbers, and performs the time-honoured exercises on the parade-grounds with great strain on the horses' strength, oblivious of the existence of long-range quick-firing guns, and as if they were still the old arm which Napoleon or Frederick the Great commanded. Even the artillery is still haunted by some more or less antiquated notions; technical and stereotyped ideas still sometimes restrict the freedom of operations; in the practice of manoeuvres, artillery duels are still in vogue, while sufficient attention is not given to concentration of fire with a definite purpose, and to co-operation with the infantry. Even in theory the necessity of the artillery duel is still asserted. Many conservative notions linger on in the heavy artillery. Obsolete ideas have not yet wholly disappeared even from the new regulations and ordinances where they block the path of true progress; but, on the whole, it has been realized that greater individual responsibility and self-reliance must be encouraged. In this respect the army is on the right road, and if it continues on it and continually resists the temptation of restricting the independence of the subordinate for the sake of outward appearance, there is room for hope that gradually the highest results will be attained, provided that competent military criticism has been equally encouraged.

In this direction a healthy development has started, but insufficient attention has been given to the fact that the main features of war have completely changed. Although in the next war men will have to be handled by millions, the training of our officers is still being conducted on lines which belong to a past era, and virtually ignore modern conditions. Our manoeuvres more especially follow these lines. Most of the practical training is carried out in manoeuvres of brigades and divisions—i.e., in formations which could never occur in the great decisive campaigns of the future. From time to time—financial grounds unfortunately prevent it being an annual affair—a corps manoeuvre is held, which also cannot be regarded as training for the command of "masses." Sometimes, but rarely, several army corps are assembled for combined training under veteran Generals, who soon afterwards leave the service, and so cannot give the army the benefit of any experience which they may have gained.

It cannot, of course, be denied that present-day manoeuvres are extraordinarily instructive and useful, especially for the troops themselves', but they are not a direct training for the command of armies in modern warfare. Even the so-called "Imperial Manoeuvres" only correspond, to a very slight extent, to the requirements of modern war, since they never take account of the commissariat arrangements, and seldom of the arrangements for sheltering, etc., the troops which would be essential in real warfare. A glance at the Imperial Manoeuvres of 1909 is sufficient to show that many of the operations could never have been carried out had it been a question of the troops being fed under the conditions of war. It is an absolute necessity that our officers should learn to pay adequate attention to these points, which are the rule in warfare and appreciably cramp the power of operations. In theory, of course, the commissariat waggons are always taken into account; they are conscientiously mentioned in all orders, and in theory are posted as a commissariat reserve between the corps and the divisions. That they would in reality all have to circulate with a pendulum-like frequency between the troops and the magazines, that the magazines would have to be almost daily brought forward or sent farther back, that the position of the field bakeries is of extreme importance—these are all points which are inconvenient and troublesome, and so are very seldom considered.

In great strategic war-games, too, even in a theatre of war selected in Russia which excludes all living upon the country, the commissariat arrangements are rarely worked out in detail; I should almost doubt whether on such occasions the possibility of exclusive "magazine feeding" has ever been entertained. Even smaller opportunities of being acquainted with these conditions are given to the officer in ordinary manoeuvres, and yet it is extremely difficult on purely theoretical lines to become familiar with the machinery for moving and feeding a large army and to master the subject efficiently.

The friction and the obstacles which occur in reality cannot be brought home to the student in theory, and the routine in managing such things cannot be learnt from books.

These conditions, then, are a great check on the freedom of operations, but, quite apart from the commissariat question, the movements of an army present considerable difficulties in themselves, which it is obviously very hard for the inexperienced to surmount. When, in 1870, some rather complicated army movements were contemplated, as on the advance to Sedan, it was at once seen that the chief commanders were not masters of the situation, that only the fertility of the theatre of war and the deficient attacking powers of the French allowed the operations to succeed, although a man like Moltke was at the head of the army. All these matters have since been thoroughly worked out by our General Staff, but the theoretical labours of the General Staff are by no means the common property of the army.

On all these grounds I believe that first and foremost our manoeuvres must be placed on a new footing corresponding to the completely altered conditions, and that we must leave the beaten paths of tradition. The troops must be trained—as formerly—to the highest tactical efficiency, and the army must be developed into the most effective machine for carrying out operations; success in modern war turns on these two pivots. But the leaders must be definitely educated for that war on the great scale which some day will have to be fought to a finish. The paths we have hitherto followed do not lead to this goal.

All methods of training and education must be in accordance with these views.

I do not propose to go further into the battle training of infantry and cavalry in this place, since I have already discussed the question at length in special treatises.[A] In the case of the artillery alone, some remarks on the principles guiding the technical training of this arm seem necessary.

[Footnote A: v. Bernhardi: "Taktik und Ausbildung der Infanterie," 1910

"Unsere Kavallerie im nächsten Krieg," 1899; "Reiterdienst," 1910.]

The demands on the fighting-efficiency of this arm—as is partly expressed in the regulations—may be summed up as follows: all preconceived ideas and theories as to its employment must be put on one side, and its one guiding principle must be to support the cavalry or infantry at the decisive point. This principle is universally acknowledged in theory, but it ought to be more enforced in practice. The artillery, therefore, must try more than ever to bring their tactical duties into the foreground and to make their special technical requirements subservient to this idea. The ever-recurring tendency to fight chiefly the enemy's artillery must be emphatically checked. On the defensive it will, of course, often be necessary to engage the attacking artillery, if there is any prospect of success, since this is the most dreaded enemy of the infantry on the defensive; but, on the attack, its chief duty always is to fire upon the enemy's infantry, where possible, from masked positions. The principle of keeping the artillery divisions close together on the battlefield and combining the fire in one direction, must not be carried to an extreme. The artillery certainly must be employed on a large plan, and the chief in command must see that there is a concentration of effort at the decisive points; but in particular cases, and among the varying incidents of a battle, this idea will be carried out less effectively by uniformity of orders than by explaining the general scheme to the subordinate officers, and leaving to them the duty of carrying it out. Accordingly, it is important that the personal initiative of the subordinate officer should be recognized more fully than before; for in a crisis such independent action is indispensable. The great extent of the battlefields and the natural endeavour to select wooded and irregular ground for the attack will often force the artillery to advance in groups or in lines one behind the other, and to attempt, notwithstanding, united action against the tactically most important objective. This result is hard to attain by a centralization of command, and is best realized by the independent action of tactically trained subordinates.

This is not the place to enter into technical details, and I will only mention some points which appear especially important.

The Bz shell (Granatschuss) should be withdrawn as unsuitable, and its use should not form part of the training. It requires, in order to attain its specific effect against rifle-pits, such accurate aiming as is very seldom possible in actual warfare.

No very great value should be attached to firing with shrapnel. It seems to be retained in France and to have shown satisfactory results with us; but care must be taken not to apply the experiences of the shooting-range directly to serious warfare. No doubt its use, if successful, promises rapid results, but it may easily lead, especially in the "mass" battle, to great errors in calculation. In any case, practice with Az shot is more trustworthy, and is of the first importance. The Az fire must be reserved principally for the last stages of an offensive engagement, as was lately laid down in the regulations.

Care must be taken generally not to go too far in refinements and complications of strategy and devices. Only the simplest methods can be successfully applied in battle; this fact must never be forgotten.

The important point in the general training of the artillery is that text-book pedantries—for example, in the reports on shooting—should be relegated more than hitherto to the background, and that tactics should be given a more prominent position. In this way only can the artillery do really good service in action; but the technique of shooting must not be neglected in the reports. That would mean rejecting the good and the evil together, and the tendency to abolish such reports as inconvenient must be distinctly opposed.

Under this head, attention must be called to the independent manoeuvres of artillery regiments and brigades in the country, which entail large expenditure, and, in fact, do more harm than good. They must, in my opinion, be abandoned or at least considerably modified, since their possible use is not in proportion to their cost and their drawbacks. They lead to pronounced tactics of position (Stellungstaktik) which are impracticable in war; and the most important lesson in actual war—the timely employment of artillery within a defined space and for a definite object without any previous reconnoitring of the country in search of suitable positions for the batteries—can never be learnt on these manoeuvres. They could be made more instructive if the tactical limits were marked by troops; but the chief defect in these manoeuvres—viz., that the artillery is regarded as the decisive arm—cannot be thus remedied. The usual result is that favourable artillery positions are searched for, and that they are then adhered to under some tactical pretence.

After all, only a slight shifting of the existing centre of gravity may be necessary, so far as the development of the fighting tactics of the various branches of the service is concerned, in order to bring them into line with modern conditions. If, however, the troops are to be educated to a higher efficiency in operations, completely new ground must be broken, on which, I am convinced, great results and an undoubted superiority over our opponents can be attained. Considerable difficulties will have to be surmounted, for the crucial point is to amass immense armies on a genuine war footing; but these difficulties are not, in my opinion, insurmountable. There are two chief points: first, the practice of marching and operations in formations at war strength, fully equipped with well-stocked magazines as on active service; and, secondly, a reorganization of the manoeuvres, which must be combined with a more thorough education of the chief commanders.

As regards the first point, practice on this scale, so far as I know, has never yet been attempted. But if we consider, firstly, how valuable more rapid and accurate movements of great masses will be for the war of the future, and, secondly, what serious difficulties they involve, we shall be rewarded for the attempt to prepare the army systematically for the discharge of such duties, and thus to win an unquestioned advantage over our supposed antagonist.

The preparation for the larger manoeuvres of this sort can naturally also be carried out in smaller formation. It is, moreover, very important to train large masses of troops—brigades and divisions—in long marches across country by night and day with pioneer sections in the vanguard, in order to gain experience for the technique of such movements, and to acquire by practice a certain security in them.

Training marches with full military stores, etc., in columns of 20 to 25 kilometres depth would be still more valuable, since they correspond to the daily needs of real warfare. Should it not be possible to assemble two army corps in such manoeuvres, then the necessary depth of march can be obtained by letting the separate detachments march with suitable intervals, in which case the intervals must be very strictly observed. This does not ever really reproduce the conditions of actual warfare, but it is useful as a makeshift. The waggons for the troops would have to be hired, as On manoeuvres, though only partly, in order to save expense. The supplies could be brought on army transport trains, which would represent the pioneer convoys (Verpflegungsstaffel), and would regulate their pace accordingly.

Marching merely for training purposes in large formations, with food supplied from the field-kitchens during the march, would also be of considerable value provided that care is taken to execute the march in the shortest possible time, and to replace the provisions consumed by bringing fresh supplies forward from the rear; this process is only properly seen when the march, with supplies as if in war, is continued for several days. It is naturally not enough to undertake these manoeuvres once in a way; they must be a permanent institution if they are intended to develop a sound knowledge of marching in the army. Finally, flank marches must be practised, sometimes in separate columns, sometimes in army formation. The flank marches of separate columns will, of course, be useful only when they are combined with practice in feeding an army as if in war, so that the commissariat columns march on the side away from the enemy, in a parallel line, and are thence brought up to the troops at the close of the march. Flank marches in army formation will have some value, even apart from any training in the commissariat system, since the simultaneous crossing of several marching columns on parallel by-roads is not an easy manoeuvre in itself. But this exercise will have its full value only when the regulation commissariat waggons are attached, which would have to move with them and furnish the supplies.

I also consider that operative movements in army formation extending over several days are desirable. Practice must be given in moving backwards and forwards in the most various combinations, in flank movements, and in doubling back, the lines of communication in the rear being blocked when necessary. Then only can all the difficulties which occur on such movements be shown one by one, and it can be seen where the lever must be applied in order to remove them. In this way alone can the higher commanders gain the necessary certainty in conducting such operations, so as to be able to employ them under the pressure of a hostile attack. An army so disciplined would, I imagine, acquire a pronounced superiority over any opponent who made his first experiments in such operations in actual war. The major strategic movements on both sides in the Franco-German War of 1870-71 sufficiently showed that.

I recognize naturally that all exercises on this scale would cost a great deal of money and could never all be carried out systematically one after the other. I wished, however, to ventilate the subject, firstly, in order to recommend all officers in high command to study the points of view under consideration—a thing they much neglect to do; secondly, because it might be sometimes profitable and possible to carry out in practice one or other of them—at the Imperial Manoeuvres, for example, or on some other occasion. How much could be saved in money alone and applied usefully to this purpose were the above-mentioned country manoeuvres of the artillery suspended? From reasons of economy all the commissariat waggons and columns need not actually be employed on such manoeuvres. It would be useful, however, if, in addition to one detachment equipped on a war footing, the head waggons of the other groups were present and were moved along at the proper distance from each other and from the detachment, which could mainly be fed from the kitchen waggon. It would thus be possible to get a sort of presentation of the whole course of the commissariat business and to acquire valuable experience. It is, indeed, extraordinarily difficult to arrange such manoeuvres properly, and it must be admitted that much friction and many obstacles are got rid of if only the heads of the groups are marked out, and that false ideas thus arise which may lead to erroneous conclusions; but under careful direction such manoeuvres would certainly not be wholly useless, especially if attention is mainly paid to the matters which are really essential. They would, at any rate, be far more valuable than many small manoeuvres, which can frequently be replaced by exercises on the large drill-grounds, than many expensive trainings in the country, which are of no real utility, or than many other military institutions which are only remotely connected with the object of training under active service conditions. All that does not directly promote this object must be erased from our system of education at a time when the highest values are at stake.

Even then exercise in operations on a large scale cannot often be carried out, primarily because of the probable cost, and next because it is not advisable to interrupt too often the tactical training of the troops.

It must be repeated in a definite cycle in each large formation, so that eventually all superior officers may have the opportunity of becoming practically acquainted with these operations, and also that the troops may become familiarized with the modern commissariat system; but since such practical exercises must always be somewhat incomplete, they must also be worked out beforehand theoretically. It is not at all sufficient that the officers on the General Staff and the Intendants have a mastery of these subjects. The rank and file must be well up in them; but especially the officers who will be employed on the supply service—that is to say, the transport officers of the standing army and those officers on the furlough establishment, who would be employed as column commanders.

The practical service in the transport battalions and the duties performed by the officers of the last-mentioned category who are assigned to these battalions are insufficient to attain this object. They learn from these mainly practical duties next to nothing of the system as a whole. It would therefore be advisable that all these officers should go through a special preliminary course for this service, in which the whole machinery of the army movements would be explained to them by the officers of the General Staff and the higher transport service officers, and they would then learn by practical examples to calculate the whole movement of the columns in the most varied positions with precise regard to distances and time. This would be far more valuable for war than the many and often excessive trainings in driving, etc., on which so much time is wasted. The technical driver's duty is very simple in all columns and trains, but it is not easy to know in each position what is the crucial point, in order to be able, when occasion arises, to act independently. While, therefore, on the one hand, driving instruction must be thoroughly carried out, on the other hand, the institution of a scientific transport service course, in which, by practical examples out of military history, the importance of these matters can be explained, is under present circumstances an absolute necessity. I have shown elsewhere how necessary it is to proceed absolutely systematically in the arrangements for relays of supplies, since the operative capabilities of the army depend on this system. Its nature, however, cannot be realized by the officers concerned like a sudden inspiration when mobilization takes place; knowledge of its principles must be gained by study, and a proof of the complete misapprehension of the importance which this service has attained under modern conditions is that officers are supposed to be able to manage it successfully without having made in peace-time a profound scientific study of the matter.

The transport service has advanced to a place of extraordinary importance in the general system of modern warfare. It should be appreciated accordingly. Every active transport service officer ought, after some years' service, to attend a scientific course; all the senior officers on the furlough establishment intended for transport service ought, as their first duty, to be summoned to attend such a course. If these educational courses were held in the autumn in the training camps of the troops, they would entail little extra cost, and an inestimable advantage would be gained with a very trifling outlay.

The results of such a measure can only be fully realized in war, when the superior officers also thoroughly grasp these matters and do not make demands contrary to the nature of the case, and therefore impossible to be met. They should therefore be obliged to undergo a thorough education in the practical duties of the General Staff, and not merely in leading troops in action. This reflection leads to the discussion of the momentous question how, generally, the training of the superior officers for the great war should be managed, and how the manoeuvres ought to be reorganized with a view to the training. The essential contradiction between our obsolete method of training and the completely altered demands of a new era appears here with peculiar distinctness.

A large part of our superior commanders pass through the General Staff, while part have attended at least the military academy; but when these men reach the higher positions what they learnt in their youth has long become out of date. The continuation school is missing. It can be replaced only by personal study; but there is generally insufficient time for this, and often a lack of interest. The daily duties of training troops claim all the officer's energy, and he needs great determination and love of hard work to continue vigorously his own scientific education. The result is, that comparatively few of our superior officers have a fairly thorough knowledge, much less an independently thought out view, of the conditions of war on the great scale. This would cost dearly in real war. Experience shows that it is not enough that the officers of the General Staff attached to the leader are competent to fill up this gap. The leader, if he cannot himself grasp the conditions, becomes the tool of his subordinates; he believes he is directing and is himself being directed. This is a far from healthy condition. Our present manoeuvres are, as already mentioned, only occasionally a school for officers in a strategical sense, and from the tactical point of view they do not meet modern requirements. The minor manoeuvres especially do not represent what is the most important feature in present-day warfare—i.e., the sudden concentration of larger forces on the one side and the impossibility, from space considerations, of timely counter-movements on the other. The minor manoeuvres are certainly useful in many respects. The commanders learn to form decisions and to give orders, and these are two important matters; but the same result would follow from manoeuvres on the grand scale, which would also to some extent reproduce the modern conditions of warfare.

Brigade manoeuvres especially belong to a past generation, and merely encourage wrong ideas. All that the soldiers learn from them—that is, fighting in the country—can be taught on the army drill-grounds. Divisional manoeuvres are still of some value even to the commanders. The principles of tactical leadership in detail can be exemplified in them; but the first instructive manoeuvres in the modern sense are those of the army corps; still more valuable are the manoeuvres on a larger scale, in which several army corps are combined, especially when the operating divisions are considered part of one whole, and are compelled to act in connection with one grand general scheme of operation. The great art in organizing manoeuvres is to reproduce such conditions, for only in this way can the strain of the general situation and the collective mass of individual responsibility, such as exist in actual warfare, be distinctly brought home.

This is a most weighty consideration. The superior officers must have clearly brought before their eyes the limits of the possible and the impossible in modern warfare, in order to be trained to deal with great situations.

The requirements which these reflections suggest are the restriction of small-scale manoeuvres in favour of the large and predominantly strategical manoeuvres, and next the abolition of some less important military exercises in order to apply the money thus saved in this direction. We must subject all our resources to a single test—that they conduce to the perfecting of a modern army. We must subject all our resources to a single test—that they conduce to the perfecting of a modern army. If the military drill-grounds are suitably enlarged (a rather difficult but necessary process, since, in view of the range of the artillery and the mass tactics, they have generally become too small) a considerable part of the work which is done in the divisional manoeuvres could be carried out on them. The money saved by this change could be devoted to the large army manoeuvres. One thing is certain: a great impulse must be given to the development of our manoeuvre system if it is to fulfil its purpose as formerly; in organization and execution these manoeuvres must be modern in the best sense of the word.

It seems, however, quite impossible to carry out this sort of training on so comprehensive a scale that it will by itself be sufficient to educate serviceable commanders for the great war. The manoeuvres can only show their full value if the officers of every rank who take part in them have already had a competent training in theory.

To encourage this preliminary training of the superior officers is thus one of the most serious tasks of an efficient preparation for war. These must not regard their duty as lying exclusively in the training of the troops, but must also be ever striving further to educate themselves and their subordinates for leadership in the great war. Strategic war games on a large scale, which in the army corps can be conducted by the commanding Generals, and in the army-inspections by the Inspectors, seem to me to be the only means by which this end can be attained. All superior officers must be criticized by the standard of their efficiency in superior commands. The threads of all this training will meet in the hands of the Chief of the General Army Staff as the strategically responsible authority.

It seems undesirable in any case to leave it more or less to chance to decide whether those who hold high commands will be competent or not for their posts. The circumstances that a man is an energetic commander of a division, or as General in command maintains discipline in his army corps, affords no conclusive proof that he is fitted to be the leader of an army. Military history supplies many instances of this.

No proof is required to show that under the conditions of modern warfare the reconnoitring and screening units require special training. The possibility and the success of all operations are in the highest degree dependent on their activity. I have for years pointed out the absolute necessity of preparing our cavalry officers scientifically for their profession, and I can only repeat the demand that our cavalry riding-schools should be organized also as places of scientific education. I will also once more declare that it is wrong that the bulk of the training of the army cavalry should consist in the divisional cavalry exercises on the military drill-grounds. These exercises do not correspond at all to actual conditions, and inculcate quite wrong notions in the officers, as every cavalry officer in high command finds out who, having been taught on the drill-ground, has to lead a cavalry division on manoeuvres.

The centre of gravity of effectiveness in war rests on the directing of operations and on the skilful transition from strategical independence to combination in attack; the great difficulty of leading cavalry lies in these conditions, and this can no more be learnt on the drill-grounds than systematic screening and reconnaissance duties. The perpetual subject of practice on the drill-grounds, a cavalry engagement between two divisions in close formation, will hardly ever occur in war. Any unprejudiced examination of the present conditions must lead to this result, and counsels the cavalry arm to adopt a course which may be regarded as a serious preparation for war.

It is a truly remarkable fact that the artillery, which in fact, always acts only in combination with the other arms, carries out annually extensive independent manoeuvres, as if it had by itself a definite effect on the course of the campaign, while the army cavalry, which always takes the field independently, hardly ever trains by itself, but carefully practises that combination with infantry which is only rarely necessary in war. This clearly demonstrates the unsystematic and antiquated methods of all our training.

Practice in reconnoitring and screening tactics, as well as raids on a large scale, are what is wanted for the training of the cavalry. Co-operation with the air-fleet will be a further development, so soon as aviation has attained such successes that it may be reckoned as an integral factor of army organization. The airship division and the cavalry have kindred duties, and must co-operate under the same command, especially for screening purposes, which are all-important.

The methods for the training of pioneers which correspond fully to modern requirements have been pointed out by General v. Beseler. This arm need only be developed further in the direction which this distinguished officer has indicated in order to satisfy the needs of the next war.

In the field war its chief importance will be found to be in the support of the infantry in attacks on fortified positions, and in the construction of similar positions. Tactical requirements must, however, be insisted upon in this connection. The whole training must be guided by considerations of tactics. This is the main point. As regards sieges, especial attention must be devoted to training the miners, since the object is to capture rapidly the outlying forts and to take the fortresses which can resist the attack of the artillery.

The duties of the Army Service Corps[B] are clear. They must, on the one hand, be efficiently trained for the intelligence department, especially for the various duties of the telegraph branch, and be ready to give every kind of assistance to the airships; on the other hand, they must look after and maintain the strategical capacities of the army. The rapid construction of railroads, especially light railways, the speedy repair of destroyed lines, the protection of traffic on military railways, and the utilization of motors for various purposes, are the duties for which these troops must be trained. A thorough knowledge and mastery of the essential principles of operations are indispensable qualifications in their case also. They can only meet their many-sided and all-important duties by a competent acquaintance with the methods and system of army movements on every scale. It is highly important, therefore, that the officers of the Army Service Corps should be thoroughly trained in military science.

[Footnote B: Verkehrstruppen.]

Thus in every direction we see the necessity to improve the intellectual development of the army, and to educate it to an appreciation of the close connection of the multifarious duties of war. This appreciation is requisite, not merely for the leaders and special branches of the service; it must permeate the whole corps of officers, and to some degree the non-commissioned officers also. It will bear good fruit in the training of the men. The higher the stage on which the teacher stands, and the greater his intellectual grasp of the subject, the more complete will be his influence on the scholars, the more rapidly and successfully will he reach the understanding of his subordinates, and the more thoroughly will he win from them that confidence and respect which are the firmest foundations of discipline. All the means employed to improve the education of our establishment of officers in the science of war and general subjects will be richly repaid in efficient service on every other field of practical activity. Intellectual exercise gives tone to brain and character, and a really deep comprehension of war and its requirements postulates a certain philosophic mental education and bent, which makes it possible to assess the value of phenomena in their reciprocal relations, and to estimate correctly the imponderabilia. The effort to produce this higher intellectual standard in the officers' corps must be felt in their training from the military school onwards, and must find its expression in a school of military education of a higher class than exists at present.

A military academy as such was contemplated by Scharnhorst. To-day it assumed rather the character of a preparatory school for the General Staff. Instruction in history and mathematics is all that remains of its former importance. The instruction in military history was entirely divested of its scientific character by the method of application employed, and became wholly subservient to tactics. In this way the meaning of the study of military history was obscured, and even to-day, so far as I know, the lectures on military history primarily serve purposes of directly professional education. I cannot say how far the language teaching imparts the spirit of foreign tongues. At any rate, it culminates in the examination for interpretships, and thus pursues a directly practical end. This development was in a certain sense necessary. A quite specifically professional education of the officers of the General Staff is essential under present conditions. I will not decide whether it was therefore necessary to limit the broad and truly academical character of the institution. In any case, we need in the army of to-day an institution which gives opportunity for the independent study of military science from the higher standpoint, and provides at the same time a comprehensive general education. I believe that the military academy could be developed into such an institution, without any necessity of abandoning the direct preparation of the officers for service on the General Staff. By the side of the military sciences proper, which might be limited in many directions, lectures on general scientific subjects might be organized, to which admission should be free. In similar lectures the great military problems might be discussed from the standpoint of military philosophy, and the hearers might gain some insight into the legitimacy of war, its relations to politics, the co-operation of material and imponderable forces, the importance of free personality under the pressure of necessary phenomena, sharp contradictions and violent opposition, as well as into the duties of a commander viewed from the higher standpoint.

Limitation and concentration of the compulsory subjects, such as are now arranged on an educational plan in three consecutive annual courses, and the institution of free lectures on subjects of general culture, intended not only to educate officers of the General Staff, but to train men who are competent to discharge the highest military and civic duties—this is what is required for the highest military educational institution of the German army.

CHAPTER XII.PREPARATION FOR THE NAVAL WAR

"Germany's future lies on the sea." A proud saying, which contains a great truth. If the German people wish to attain a distinguished future and fulfil their mission of civilization, they must adopt a world policy and act as a World Power. This task can only be performed if they are supported by an adequate sea power. Our fleet must be so strong at least that a war with us involves such dangers, even to the strongest opponent, that the losses, which might be expected, would endanger his position as a World Power.

Now, as proved in another place, we can only stake our forces safely on a world policy if our political and military superiority on the continent of Europe be immovably established. This goal is not yet reached, and must be our first objective. Nevertheless, we must now take steps to develop by sea also a power which is sufficient for our pretensions. It is, on the one hand, indispensably necessary for the full security of our Continental position that we guard our coasts and repel oversea attacks. On the other hand, it is an absolute economic necessity for us to protect the freedom of the seas—by arms if needs be—since our people depend for livelihood on the export industry, and this, again, requires a large import trade. The political greatness of Germany rests not least on her flourishing economic life and her oversea trade. The maintenance of the freedom of the seas must therefore be always before our eyes as the object of all our naval constructions. Our efforts must not be merely directed towards the necessary repulse of hostile attacks; we must be conscious of the higher ideal, that we wish to follow an effective world policy, and that our naval power is destined ultimately to support this world policy. Unfortunately, we did not adopt this view at the start, when we first ventured on the open sea. Much valuable time was wasted in striving for limited and insufficient objects. The Emperor William II. was destined to be the first to grasp this question in its bearing on the world's history, and to treat it accordingly. All our earlier naval activity must be set down as fruitless.

We have been busied for years in building a fleet. Most varied considerations guided our policy. A clear, definite programme was first drawn up by the great Naval Act of 1900, the supplementary laws of 1906, and the regulations as to the life of the ships in 1908. It is, of course, improbable that the last word has been said on the subject. The needs of the future will decide, since there can be no certain standard for the naval forces which a State may require: that depends on the claims which are put forward, and on the armaments of the other nations. At first the only object was to show our flag on the sea and on the coasts on which we traded. The first duty of the fleet was to safeguard this commerce. Opposition to the great outlay thus necessitated was soon shown by a party which considered a fleet not merely superfluous for Germany, but actually dangerous, and objected to the plans of the Government, which they stigmatized as boundless. Another party was content with a simple scheme of coast-protection only, and thought this object attained if some important points on the coast were defended by artillery and cheap flotillas of gunboats were stationed at various places.

This view was not long maintained. All discerning persons were convinced of the necessity to face and drive back an aggressive rival on the high seas. It was recognized that ironclads were needed for this, since the aggressor would have them at his disposal. But this policy, it was thought, could be satisfied by half-measures. The so-called Ausfallkorvetten were sanctioned, but emphasis was laid on the fact that we were far from wishing to compete with the existing large navies, and that we should naturally be content with a fleet of the second rank. This standpoint was soon recognized to be untenable, and there was a fresh current of feeling, whose adherents supported the view that the costly ironclads could be made superfluous by building in their place a large number of torpedo-boats. These, in spite of their small fighting capacity, would be able to attack the strongest ironclads by well-aimed torpedoes. It was soon realized that this theory rested on a fallacy—that a country like the German Empire, which depends on an extensive foreign trade in order to find work and food for its growing population, and, besides, is hated everywhere because of its political and economic prosperity, could not forego a strong armament at sea and on its coasts. At last a standpoint had been reached which corresponded with actual needs.

The different abortive attempts to solve the navy question in the most inexpensive manner have cost us much money and, above all, as already stated, much time; so that, at the present day, when we stand in the midst of a great crisis in the world's history, we must summon all our strength to make up for lost opportunities, and to build a thoroughly effective ocean-going fleet of warships in addition to an adequate guard for our coasts. We have at last come to see that the protection of our commerce and the defence of our shores cannot possibly be the only object of such a fleet, but that it, like the land army, is an instrument for carrying out the political ends of the State and supporting its justifiable ambitions. There can be no question of such limited objects as protection of commerce and passive coast defence. A few cruisers are enough to protect commerce in times of peace; but in war the only way to safeguard it is to defeat and, where possible, destroy the hostile fleet. A direct protection of all trade lines is obviously impossible. Commerce can only be protected indirectly by the defeat of the enemy. A passive defence of the coast can never count on permanent success. The American War of Secession, amongst others, showed that sufficiently.

The object of our fleet, therefore, is to defeat our possible rivals at sea, and force them to make terms, in order to guarantee unimpeded commerce to our merchantmen and to protect our colonies.

It is therefore an erroneous idea that our fleet exists merely for defence, and must be built with that view. It is intended to meet our political needs, and must therefore be capable of being employed according to the exigencies of the political position; on the offensive, when the political situation demands it, and an attack promises success; on the defensive, when we believe that more advantages can be obtained in this way. At the present day, indeed, the political grouping of the Great Powers makes a strategical offensive by sea an impossibility. We must, however, reckon with the future, and then circumstances may arise which would render possible an offensive war on a large scale.

The strength which we wish to give to our fleet must therefore be calculated with regard to its probable duties in war. It is obvious that we must not merely consider the possible opponents who at the moment are weaker than we are, but rather, and principally, those who are stronger, unless we were in the position to avoid a conflict with them under all circumstances. Our fleet must in any case be so powerful that our strongest antagonist shrinks from attacking us without convincing reasons. If he determines to attack us, we must have at least a chance of victoriously repelling this attack—in other words, of inflicting such heavy loss on the enemy that he will decline in his own interests to carry on the war to the bitter end, and that he will see his own position threatened if he exposes himself to these losses.

This conception of our duty on the sea points directly to the fact that the English fleet must set the standard by which to estimate the necessary size of our naval preparations. A war with England is probably that which we shall first have to fight out by sea; the possibility of victoriously repelling an English attack must be the guiding principle for our naval preparations; and if the English continuously increase their fleet, we must inevitably follow them on the same road, even beyond the limits of our present Naval Estimates.

We must not, however, forget that it will not be possible for us for many years to attack on the open sea the far superior English fleet. We may only hope, by the combination of the fleet with the coast fortifications, the airfleet, and the commercial war, to defend ourselves successfully against this our strongest opponent, as was shown in the chapter on the next naval war. The enemy must be wearied out and exhausted by the enforcement of the blockade, and by fighting against all the expedients which we shall employ for the defence of our coast; our fleet, under the protection of these expedients, will continually inflict partial losses on him, and thus gradually we shall be able to challenge him to a pitched battle on the high seas. These are the lines that our preparation for war must follow. A strong coast fortress as a base for our fleet, from which it can easily and at any moment take the offensive, and on which the waves of the hostile superiority can break harmlessly, is the recognized and necessary preliminary condition for this class of war. Without such a trustworthy coast fortress, built with a view to offensive operations, our fleet could be closely blockaded by the enemy, and prevented from any offensive movements. Mines alone cannot close the navigation so effectively that the enemy cannot break through, nor can they keep it open in such a way that we should be able to adopt the offensive under all circumstances. For this purpose permanent works are necessary which command the navigation and allow mines to be placed.

I cannot decide the question whether our coast defence, which in the North Sea is concentrated in Heligoland and Borkum, corresponds to these requirements. If it is not so, then our first most serious duty must be to fill up the existing gaps, in order to create an assured base for our naval operations. This is a national duty which we dare not evade, although it demands great sacrifices from us. Even the further development of our fleet, important as that is, would sink into the background as compared with the urgency of this duty, because its only action against the English fleet which holds out any prospect of success presupposes the existence of some such fortress.

But the question must be looked at from another aspect.

The Morocco negotiations in the summer of 1911 displayed the unmistakable hostility of England to us. They showed that England is determined to hinder by force any real expansion of Germany's power. Only the fear of the possible intervention of England deterred us from claiming a sphere of interests of our own in Morocco, and, nevertheless, the attempt to assert our unquestionable rights in North Africa provoked menacing utterances from various English statesmen.

If we consider this behaviour in connection with England's military preparations, there can be no doubt that England seriously contemplates attacking Germany should the occasion arise. The concentration of the English naval forces in the North Sea, the feverish haste to increase the English fleet, the construction of new naval stations, undisguisedly intended for action against Germany, of which we have already spoken; the English espionage, lately vigorously practised, on the German coasts, combined with continued attempts to enlist allies against us and to isolate us in Europe—all this can only be reasonably interpreted as a course of preparation for an aggressive war. At any rate, it is quite impossible to regard the English preparations as defensive and protective measures only; for the English Government knows perfectly well that Germany cannot think of attacking England: such an attempt would be objectless from the first. Since the destruction of the German naval power lies in the distinct interests of England and her schemes for world empire, we must reckon at least with the possibility of an English attack. We must make it clear to ourselves that we are not able to postpone this attack as we wish. It has been already mentioned that the recent attitude of Italy may precipitate a European crisis; we must make up our minds, then, that England will attack us on some pretext or other soon, before the existing balance of power, which is very favourable for England, is shifted possibly to her disadvantage. Especially, if the Unionist party comes into power again, must we reckon upon a strong English Imperial policy which may easily bring about war.

Under these circumstances we cannot complete our armament by sea and our coast defences in peaceful leisure, in accordance with theoretical principles. On the contrary, we must strain our financial resources in order to carry on, and if possible to accelerate, the expansion of our fleet, together with the fortification of our coast. It would be justifiable, under the conditions, to meet our financial requirements by loans, if no other means can be found; for here questions of the greatest moment are at stake—questions, it may fairly be said, of existence.

Let us imagine the endless misery which a protracted stoppage or definite destruction of our oversea trade would bring upon the whole nation, and, in particular, on the masses of the industrial classes who live on our export trade. This consideration by itself shows the absolute necessity of strengthening our naval forces in combination with our coast defences so thoroughly that we can look forward to the decisive campaign with equanimity. Even the circumstance that we cannot, perhaps, find crews at once for the ships which we are building need not check the activity of our dockyards; for these ships will be valuable to replace the loss in vessels which must occur in any case.

The rapid completion of the Kaiser-Wilhelm Canal is of great importance, in order that our largest men-of-war may appear unexpectedly in the Baltic or in the North Sea. But it does not meet all military requirements. It is a question whether it is not expedient to obtain secure communication by a canal between the mouth of the Ems, the Bay of Jahde, and the mouth of the Elbe, in order to afford our fleet more possibilities of concentration. All three waters form a sally-port in the North Sea, and it would be certainly a great advantage if our battleships could unexpectedly unite in these three places. I cannot give any opinion as to the feasibility of this scheme. If it is feasible, we ought to shirk no sacrifices to realize it. Such a canal might prove of decisive value, since our main prospect of success depends on our ability to break up the forces of the enemy by continuous unexpected attacks, and on our thus finding an opportunity to inflict heavy losses upon him.

As regards the development of the fleet itself, we must push on the completion of our battle-fleet, which consists of ships of the line and the usual complement of large cruisers. It does not possess in its present condition an effective value in proportion to its numbers. There can be no doubt on this point. Five of the ships of the line, of the Kaiser class, are quite obsolete, and the vessels of the Wittelsbach class carry as heaviest guns only 24-centimetre cannons, which must be considered quite inadequate for a sea-battle of to-day. We are in a worse plight with regard to our large cruisers. The five ships of the Hansa class have no fighting value; the three large cruisers of the Prince class (Adalbert, Friedrich Karl, Heinrich) fulfil their purpose neither in speed, effective range, armament, nor armour-plating. Even the armoured cruisers Fürst Bismarck, Roon, York, Gneisenau, and Scharnhorst do not correspond in any respect to modern requirements. If we wish, therefore, to be really ready for a war, we must shorten the time allowed for building, and replace as rapidly as possible these totally useless vessels—nine large cruisers and five battleships—by new and thoroughly effective ships.

Anyone who regards the lowering thunder-clouds on the political horizon will admit this necessity. The English may storm and protest ever so strongly: care for our country must stand higher than all political and all financial considerations. We must create new types of battleships, which may be superior to the English in speed and fighting qualities. That is no light task, for the most modern English ships of the line have reached a high stage of perfection, and the newest English cruisers are little inferior in fighting value to the battleships proper. But superiority in individual units, together with the greatest possible readiness for war, are the only means by which a few ships can be made to do, at any rate, what is most essential. Since the Krupp guns possess a certain advantage—which is not, in fact, very great—over the English heavy naval guns, it is possible to gain a start in this department, and to equip our ships with superior attacking power. A more powerful artillery is a large factor in success, which becomes more marked the more it is possible to distribute the battery on the ship in such a way that all the guns may be simultaneously trained to either side or straight ahead.

Besides the battle-fleet proper, the torpedo-boats play a prominent part in strategic offence and defence alike. The torpedo-fleet, therefore—especially having regard to the crushing superiority of England—requires vigorous encouragement, and all the more so because, so far, at least, as training goes, we possess a true factor of superiority in them. In torpedo-boats we are, thanks to the high standard of training in the personnel and the excellence of construction, ahead of all other navies. We must endeavour to keep this position, especially as regards the torpedoes, in which, according to the newspaper accounts, other nations are competing with us, by trying to excel us in range of the projectile at high velocity. We must also devote our full attention to submarines, and endeavour to make these vessels more effective in attack. If we succeed in developing this branch of our navy, so that it meets the military requirements in every direction, and combines an increased radius of effectiveness with increased speed and seaworthiness, we shall achieve great results with these vessels in the defence of our coasts and in unexpected attacks on the enemy's squadrons. A superior efficiency in this field would be extraordinarily advantageous to us.

Last, not least, we must devote ourselves more energetically to the development of aviation for naval purposes. If it were possible to make airships and flying-machines thoroughly available for war, so that they could be employed in unfavourable weather and for aggressive purposes, they might render essential services to the fleet. The air-fleet would then, as already explained in Chapter VIII., be able to report successfully, to spy out favourable opportunities for attacks by the battle-fleet or the torpedo-fleet, and to give early notice of the approach of the enemy in superior force. It would also be able to prevent the enemy's airships from reconnoitring, and would thus facilitate the execution of surprise attacks. Again, it could repulse or frustrate attacks on naval depots and great shipping centres. If our airships could only be so largely developed that they, on their side, could undertake an attack and carry fear and destruction to the English coasts, they would lend still more effective aid to our fleet when fighting against the superior force of the enemy. It can hardly be doubted that technical improvements will before long make it possible to perform such services. A pronounced superiority of our air-fleet over the English would contribute largely to equalize the difference in strength of the two navies more and more during the course of the war. It should be the more possible to gain a superiority in this field because our supposed enemies have not any start on us, and we can compete for the palm of victory on equal terms.

Besides the campaign against the enemy's war-fleet, preparations must be carefully made in peace-time for the war on commerce, which would be especially effective in a struggle against England, as that country needs imports more than any other. Consequently great results would follow if we succeeded in disturbing the enemy's commerce and harassing his navigation. The difficulties of such an undertaking have been discussed in a previous chapter. It is all the more imperative to organize our preparations in such a way that the swift ships intended for the commercial war should be able to reach their scene of activity unexpectedly before the enemy has been able to block our harbours. The auxiliary cruisers must be so equipped in peace-time that when on the open sea they may assume the character of warships at a moment's notice, when ordered by wireless telegraphy to do so.

A rapid mobilization is especially important in the navy, since we must be ready for a sudden attack at any time, possibly in time of peace. History tells us what to expect from the English on this head.

In the middle of peace they bombarded Copenhagen from September 2 to September 5, 1807, and carried off the Danish fleet. Four hundred houses were burnt, 2,000 damaged, 3,000 peaceful and innocent inhabitants were killed. If some explanation, though no justification, of the conduct of England is seen in the lawlessness of all conditions then existing, and in the equally ruthless acts of Napoleon, still the occurrence shows distinctly of what measures England is capable if her command of the seas is endangered. And this practice has not been forgotten. On July 11 and 12, 1882, exactly thirty years ago, Alexandria was similarly bombarded in peace-time, and Egypt occupied by the English under the hypocritical pretext that Arabi Pasha had ordered a massacre of the foreigners. The language of such historical facts is clear. It is well not to forget them. The Russo-Japanese War also is a warning how modern wars begin; so also Italy, with her political and military attack on Turkey. Turkish ships, suspecting nothing of war, were attacked and captured by the Italians.

Now, it must not be denied that such a method of opening a campaign as was adopted by Japan and Italy may be justified under certain conditions. The interests of the State may turn the scale. The brutal violence shown to a weak opponent, such as is displayed in the above-described English procedure, has nothing in common with a course of action politically justifiable. A surprise attack, in order to be justified, must be made in the first place only on the armed forces of the hostile State, not on peaceful inhabitants. A further necessary preliminary condition is that the tension of the political situation brings the possibility or probability of a war clearly before the eyes of both parties, so that an expectation of, and preparations for, war can be assumed. Otherwise the attack becomes a treacherous crime. If the required preliminary conditions are granted, then a political coup is as justifiable as a surprise attack in warfare, since it tries to derive advantage from an unwarrantable carelessness of the opponent. A definite principle of right can never be formulated in this question, since everything depends on the views taken of the position, and these may be very divergent among the parties concerned. History alone can pass a final verdict on the conduct of States. But in no case can a formal rule of right in such cases—especially when a question of life or death is depending on it, as was literally the fact in the Manchurian War as regards Japan—limit the undoubted right of the State. If Japan had not obtained from the very first the absolute command of the seas, the war with Russia would have been hopeless. She was justified, therefore, in employing the most extreme measures. No such interests were at stake for England either in 1807 or 1882, and Italy's proceedings in 1911 are certainly doubtful from the standpoint of political morality.

These examples, however, show what we may expect from England, and we must be the more prepared to find her using this right to attack without warning, since we also may be under the necessity of using this right. Our mobilization preparations must therefore be ready for all such eventualities, especially in the period after the dismissal of the reservists.

Public policy forbids any discussion of the steps that must be taken to secure that our fleet is ready for war during this time. Under all circumstances, however, our coast defences must be continuously ready for fighting, and permanently garrisoned in times of political tension. The mines must also be prepared for action without delay. The whole matériel requisite for the purpose must be on the spot ready for instant use. So, too, all measures for the protection of commerce at the mouths of our rivers and in the Kaiser Wilhelm Canal must be put in force directly the situation becomes strained. This is a mere simple precept of self-protection. We must also attach as much importance to the observation and intelligence service on our coasts in peace-time as is done in England.

When we realize in their entirety the mass of preparations which are required for the maintenance of our place among the Great Powers by the navy, we see that extraordinarily exacting demands will be made on the resources of our people. These weigh the heavier for the moment, since the crisis of the hour forces us to quite exceptional exertions, and the expenditure on the fleet must go hand-in-hand, with very energetic preparations on land. If we do not possess the strength or the self-devotion to meet this twofold demand, the increase of the fleet must be delayed, and we must restrict ourselves to bringing our coast defences to such a pitch of completeness as will meet all our requirements. Any acceleration in our ship-building would have to be provisionally dropped.

In opposition to this view, it is urged from one quarter that we should limit our fortification of the coast to what is absolutely necessary, devote all our means to developing the fleet, and lay the greatest stress on the number of the ships and their readiness for war, even in case of the reserve fleet. This view starts from the presupposition that, in face of so strong and well-equipped a fleet as the Naval Act contemplates for Germany, England would never resolve to declare war on us. It is also safe to assume that a fleet built expressly on uniform tactical principles represents a more powerful fighting force than we have to-day in an equal number of heterogeneous battleships.

I cannot myself, however, endorse this view. On the one hand, it is to be feared that the fighting strength of the hostile fleets increases quicker than that of ours; on the other hand, I believe that the general situation makes war with England inevitable, even if our naval force in the shortest time reaches its statutory strength in modern men-of-war. My view, therefore, is that we must first of all lay the solid foundation without which any successful action against the superior forces of the enemy is unthinkable. Should the coast fortifications fail to do what is expected from them, success is quite impossible.

It is, however, all the more our duty to spare no sacrifices to carry out both objects—the enlargement of the fleet, as well as whatever may still be necessary to the perfecting of our coast defences. Though this latter point calls for the first attention, the great necessity for the navy admits of no doubt. If we do not to-day stake everything on strengthening our fleet, to insure at least the possibility of a successful war, and if we once more allow our probable opponent to gain a start which it will be scarcely possible to make up in the future, we must renounce for many years to come any place among the World Powers.

Under these circumstances, no one who cherishes German sentiments and German hopes will advocate a policy of renunciation. On the contrary, we must try not only to prosecute simultaneously the fortification of the coast and the development of the fleet, but we must so accelerate the pace of our ship-building that the requirements of the Naval Act will be met by 1914—a result quite possible according to expert opinion.

The difficult plight in which we are to-day, as regards our readiness for war, is due to two causes in the past. It has been produced in the first place because, from love of the pleasures of peace, we have in the long years since the founding of the German Empire neglected to define and strengthen our place among the Powers of Europe, and to win a free hand in world politics, while around us the other Powers were growing more and more threatening. It was, in my opinion, the most serious mistake in German policy that a final settling of accounts with France was not effected at a time when the state of international affairs was favourable and success might confidently have been expected. There has, indeed, been no lack of opportunities. We have only our policy of peace and renunciation to thank for the fact that we are placed in this difficult position, and are confronted by the momentous choice between resigning all claim to world power or disputing this claim against numerically superior enemies. This policy somewhat resembles the supineness for which England has herself to blame, when she refused her assistance to the Southern States in the American War of Secession, and thus allowed a Power to arise in the form of the United States of North America, which already, although barely fifty years have elapsed, threatens England's own position as a World Power. But the consequences of our peace policy hit us harder than England has suffered under her former American policy. The place of Great Britain as a Great Power is far more secured by her insular position and her command of the seas than ours, which is threatened on all sides by more powerful enemies. It is true that one cannot anticipate success in any war with certainty, and there was always the possibility during the past forty years that we might not succeed in conquering France as effectually as we would have wished. This uncertainty is inseparable from every war. Neither in 1866 nor in 1870 could Bismarck foresee the degree of success which would fall to him, but he dared to fight. The greatness of the statesman is shown when at the most favourable moment he has the courage to undertake what is the necessary and, according to human calculation, the best course. Just Fate decides the issue.

The second cause of our present position is to be seen in the fact that we started to build our fleet too late. The chief mistake which we have made is that, after the year 1889, when we roused ourselves to vote the Brandenburg type of ship, we sank back until 1897 into a period of decadence, while complete lack of system prevailed in all matters concerning the fleet. We have also begun far too late to develop systematically our coast defences, so that the most essential duties which spring out of the political situation are unfulfilled, since we have not foreseen this situation nor prepared for it.

This experience must be a lesson to us in the future. We must never let the petty cares and needs of the moment blind us to the broad views which must determine our world policy. We must always adopt in good time those measures which are seen to be necessary for the future, even though they make heavy financial calls on our resources.

This is the point of view that we must keep in mind with regard to our naval armament. Even at the eleventh hour we may make up a little for lost time. It will be a heinous mistake if we do not perform this duty devotedly.

CHAPTER XIII.THE ARMY AND POPULAR EDUCATION

The policy of peace and restraint has brought us to a position in which we can only assert our place among the Great Powers and secure the conditions of life for the future by the greatest expenditure of treasure and, so far as human conjecture can go, of blood. We shall be compelled, therefore, to adopt, without a moment's delay, special measures which will enable us to be more or less a match for our enemies—I mean accelerated ship-building and rapid increase of the army. We must always bear in mind in the present that we have to provide for the future.

Apart from the requirements of the moment, we must never forget to develop the elements on which not only our military strength, but also the political power of the State ultimately rest. We must maintain the physical and mental health of the nation, and this can only be done if we aim at a progressive development of popular education in the widest sense, corresponding to the external changes in the conditions and demands of existence.

While it is the duty of the State to guide her citizens to the highest moral and mental development, on the other hand the elements of strength, rooted in the people, react upon the efficiency of the State. Only when supported by the strong, unanimous will of the nation can the State achieve really great results; she is therefore doubly interested in promoting the physical and mental growth of the nation. Her duty and her justification consist in this endeavour, for she draws from the fulfilment of this duty the strength and capacity to be in the highest sense true to it.

It is, under present conditions, expedient also from the merely military standpoint to provide not only for the healthy physical development of our growing youth, but also to raise its intellectual level. For while the demands which modern war makes have increased in every direction, the term of service has been shortened in order to make enlistment in very great numbers possible. Thus the full consummation of military training cannot be attained unless recruits enter the army well equipped physically and mentally, and bringing with them patriotic sentiments worthy of the honourable profession of arms.

We have already shown in a previous chapter how important it is to raise the culture of the officers and non-commissioned officers to the best of our power, in order to secure not only a greater and more independent individual efficiency, but also a deeper and more lasting influence on the men; but this influence of the superiors must always remain limited if it cannot count on finding in the men a receptive and intelligent material. This fact is especially clear when we grasp the claims which modern war will make on the individual fighter. In order to meet these demands fully, the people must be properly educated.

Each individual must, in modern warfare, display a large measure of independent judgment, calm grasp of the facts, and bold resolution. In the open methods of fighting, the infantryman, after his appointed duty has been assigned him, is to a great degree thrown on his own resources; he may often have to take over the command of his own section if the losses among his superiors are heavy. The artilleryman will have to work his gun single-handed when the section leaders and gun captains have fallen victims to the shrapnel fire; the patrols and despatch-riders are often left to themselves in the middle of the enemy's country; and the sapper, who is working against a counter-mine, will often find himself unexpectedly face to face with the enemy, and has no resource left beyond his own professional knowledge and determination.

But not only are higher claims made on the independent responsibility of the individual in modern warfare, but the strain on the physique will probably be far greater in the future than in previous wars. This change is due partly to the large size of the armies, partly to the greater efficiency of the firearms. All movements in large masses are more exacting in themselves than similar movements in small detachments, since they are never carried out so smoothly. The shelter and food of great masses can never be so good as with smaller bodies; the depth of the marching columns, which increases with the masses, adds to the difficulties of any movements—abbreviated rest at night, irregular hours for meals, unusual times for marching, etc. The increased range of modern firearms extends the actual fighting zone, and, in combination with the larger fronts, necessitates wide détours whenever the troops attempt enveloping movements or other changes of position on the battlefield.

In the face of these higher demands, the amount of work done in the army has been enormously increased. The State, however, has done little to prepare our young men better for military service, while tendencies are making themselves felt in the life of the people which exercise a very detrimental influence on their education. I specially refer to the ever-growing encroachments of a social-democratic, anti-patriotic feeling, and, hand-in-hand with this, the flocking of the population into the large towns, which is unfavourable to physical development. This result is clearly shown by the enlistment statistics. At the present day, out of all the German-born military units, over 6.14 per cent. come from the large towns, 7.37 per cent, from the medium-sized towns, 22.34 per cent. from the small or country towns, and 64.15 per cent. from the rural districts; while the distribution of the population between town and country is quite different. According to the census of 1905, the rural population amounted to 42.5 per cent., the small or country towns to 25.5 per cent., the medium-sized towns to 12.9 per cent., and the large towns to 19.1 per cent. of the entire number of inhabitants. The proportion has probably changed since that year still more unfavourably for the rural population, while the large towns have increased in population. These figures clearly show the physical deterioration of the town population, and signify a danger to our national life, not merely in respect of physique, but in the intellect and compact unity of the nation. The rural population forms part and parcel of the army. A thousand bonds unite the troops and the families of their members, so far as they come from the country; everyone who studies the inner life of our army is aware of this. The interest felt in the soldier's life is intense. It is the same spirit, transmitted from one to another. The relation of the army to the population of the great cities which send a small and ever-diminishing fraction of their sons into the army is quite different. A certain opposition exists between the population of the great cities and the country-folk, who, from a military point of view, form the backbone of the nation. Similarly, the links between the army and the large towns have loosened, and large sections of the population in the great cities are absolutely hostile to the service.

It is in the direct interests of the State to raise the physical health of the town population by all imaginable means, not only in order to enable more soldiers to be enlisted, but to bring the beneficial effect of military training more extensively to bear on the town population, and so to help to make our social conditions more healthy. Nothing promotes unity of spirit and sentiment like the comradeship of military service.

So far as I can judge, it is not factory work alone in itself which exercises a detrimental effect on the physical development and, owing to its monotony, on the mental development also, but the general conditions of life, inseparable from such work, are prejudicial. Apart from many forms of employment in factories which are directly injurious to health, the factors which stunt physical development may be found in the housing conditions, in the pleasure-seeking town life, and in alcoholism. This latter vice is far more prevalent in the large cities than in the rural districts, and, in combination with the other influences of the great city, produces far more harmful results.

It is therefore the unmistakable duty of the State, first, to fight alcoholism with every weapon, if necessary by relentlessly taxing all kinds of alcoholic drinks, and by strictly limiting the right to sell them; secondly, most emphatic encouragement must be given to all efforts to improve the housing conditions of the working population, and to withdraw the youth of the towns from the ruinous influences of a life of amusements. In Munich, Bavarian officers have recently made a praiseworthy attempt to occupy the leisure time of the young men past the age of attendance at school with health-producing military exercises. The young men's clubs which Field-Marshal v.d. Goltz is trying to establish aim at similar objects. Such undertakings ought to be vigorously carried out in every large town, and supported by the State, from purely physical as well as social considerations. The gymnastic instruction in the schools and gymnastic clubs has an undoubtedly beneficial effect on physical development, and deserves every encouragement; finally, on these grounds, as well as all others, the system of universal service should have been made an effective reality. It is literally amazing to notice the excellent effect of military service on the physical development of the recruits. The authorities in charge of the reserves should have been instructed to make the population of the great cities serve in larger numbers than hitherto.

On the other hand, a warning must, in my opinion, be issued against two tendencies: first, against the continual curtailing of the working hours for factory hands and artisans; and, secondly, against crediting sport with an exaggerated value for the national health. As already pointed out, it is usually not the work itself, but the circumstances attendant on working together in large numbers that are prejudicial.

The wish to shorten the working hours on principle, except to a moderate degree, unless any exceptionally unfavourable conditions of work are present, is, in my opinion, an immoral endeavour, and a complete miscomprehension of the real value of work. It is in itself the greatest blessing which man knows, and ill betide the nation which regards it no longer as a moral duty, but as the necessary means of earning a livelihood and paying for amusements. Strenuous labour alone produces men and characters, and those nations who have been compelled to win their living in a continuous struggle against a rude climate have often achieved the greatest exploits, and shown the greatest vitality.

So long as the Dutch steeled their strength by unremitting conflict with the sea, so long as they fought for religious liberty against the Spanish supremacy, they were a nation of historical importance; now, when they live mainly for money-making and enjoyment, and lead a politically neutral existence, without great ambitions or great wars, their importance has sunk low, and will not rise again until they take a part in the struggle of the civilized nations. In Germany that stock which was destined to bring back our country from degradation to historical importance did not grow up on the fertile banks of the Rhine or the Danube, but on the sterile sands of the March. We must preserve the stern, industrious, old-Prussian feeling, and carry the rest of Germany with us to Kant's conception of life; we must continuously steel our strength by great political and economic endeavours, and must not be content with what we have already attained, or abandon ourselves to the indolent pursuit of pleasure; thus only we shall remain healthy in mind and body, and able to keep our place in the world.

Where Nature herself does not compel hard toil, or where with growing wealth wide sections of the people are inclined to follow a life of pleasure rather than of work, society and the State must vie in taking care that work does not become play, or play work. It is work, regarded as a duty, that forges men, not fanciful play. Sport, which is spreading more and more amongst us too, must always remain a means of recreation, not an end in itself, if it is to be justified at all. We must never forget this. Hard, laborious work has made Germany great; in England, on the contrary, sport has succeeded in maintaining the physical health of the nation; but by becoming exaggerated and by usurping the place of serious work it has greatly injured the English nation. The English nation, under the influence of growing wealth, a lower standard of labour efficiency—which, indeed, is the avowed object of the English trades unions—and of the security of its military position, has more and more become a nation of gentlemen at ease and of sportsmen, and it may well be asked whether, under these conditions, England will show herself competent for the great duties which she has taken on herself in the future. If, further, the political rivalry with the great and ambitious republic in America be removed by an Arbitration Treaty, this circumstance might easily become the boundary-stone where the roads to progress and to decadence divide, in spite of all sports which develop physique.

The physical healthiness of a nation has no permanent value, unless it comes from work and goes hand-in-hand with spiritual development; while, if the latter is subordinated to material and physical considerations, the result must be injurious in the long-run.

We must not therefore be content to educate up for the army a physically healthy set of young men by elevating the social conditions and the whole method of life of our people, but we must also endeavour to promote their spiritual development in every way. The means for doing so is the school. Military education under the present-day conditions, which are continually becoming more severe, can only realize its aims satisfactorily if a groundwork has been laid for it in the schools, and an improved preliminary training has been given to the raw material.

The national school is not sufficient for this requirement. The general regulations which settle the national school system in Prussia date from the year 1872, and are thus forty years old, and do not take account of the modern development which has been so rapid of late years. It is only natural that a fundamental opposition exists between them and the essentials of military education. Present-day military education requires complete individualization and a conscious development of manly feeling; in the national school everything is based on teaching in classes, and there is no distinction between the sexes. This is directly prescribed by the rules.

In the army the recruits are taught under the superintendence of the superiors by specially detached officers and selected experienced non-commissioned officers; and even instruction is given them in quite small sections; while each one receives individual attention from the non-commissioned officers of his section and the higher superior officers. In a school, on the contrary, the master is expected to teach as many as eighty scholars at a time; in a school with two teachers as many as 120 children are divided into two classes. A separation of the sexes is only recommended in a school of several classes. As a rule, therefore, the instruction is given in common. It is certain that, under such conditions, no insight into the personality of the individual is possible. All that is achieved is to impart more or less mechanically and inefficiently a certain amount of information in some branch of knowledge, without any consideration of the special dispositions of boys and girls, still less of individuals.

Such a national school can obviously offer no preparation for a military education. The principles which regulate the teaching in the two places are quite different. That is seen in the whole tendency of the instruction.

The military education aims at training the moral personality to independent thought and action, and at the same time rousing patriotic feelings among the men. Instruction in a sense of duty and in our national history thus takes a foremost place by the side of professional teaching. Great attention is given to educate each individual in logical reasoning and in the clear expression of his thoughts.

In the national school these views are completely relegated to the background—not, of course, as a matter of intention and theory, but as the practical result of the conditions. The chief stress in such a school is laid on formal religious instruction, and on imparting some facility in reading, writing, and ciphering. The so-called Realign (history, geography, natural history, natural science) fall quite into the background. Only six out of thirty hours of instruction weekly are devoted to all the Realien in the middle and upper standards; in the lower standards they are ignored altogether, while four to five hours are assigned to religious instruction in every standard. There is no idea of any deliberate encouragement of patriotism. Not a word in the General Regulations suggests that any weight is to be attached to this; and while over two pages are filled with details of the methods of religious instruction, history, which is especially valuable for the development of patriotic sentiments, is dismissed in ten lines. As for influencing the character and the reasoning faculties of the scholars to any extent worth mentioning, the system of large classes puts it altogether out of the question.

While the allotment of subjects to the hours available for instruction is thus very one-sided, the system on which instruction is given, especially in religious matters, is also unsatisfactory. Beginning with the lower standard onwards (that is to say, the children of six years), stories not only from the New Testament, but also from the Old Testament are drummed into the heads of the scholars. Similarly every Saturday the portions of Scripture appointed for the next Sunday are read out and explained to all the children. Instruction in the Catechism begins also in the lower standard, from the age of six onwards; the children must learn some twenty hymns by heart, besides various prayers. It is a significant fact that it has been found necessary expressly to forbid "the memorizing of the General Confession and other parts of the liturgical service," as "also the learning by heart of the Pericopes." On the other hand, the institution of Public Worship is to be explained to the children. This illustrates the spirit in which this instruction has to be imparted according to the regulations.

It is really amazing to read these regulations. The object of Evangelical religious instruction is to introduce the children "to the comprehension of the Holy Scriptures and to the creed of the congregation," in order that they "may be enabled to read the Scriptures independently and to take an active part both in the life and the religious worship of the congregation." Requirements are laid down which entirely abandon the task of making the subject suitable to the comprehension of children from six to fourteen years of age, and presuppose a range of ideas totally beyond their age. Not a word, however, suggests that the real meaning of religion—its influence, that is, on the moral conduct of man—should be adequately brought into prominence. The teacher is not urged by a single syllable to impress religious ideas on the receptive child-mind; the whole course of instruction, in conformity with regulations, deals with a formal religiosity, which is quite out of touch with practical life, and if not deliberately, at least in result, renounces any attempt at moral influence. A real feeling for religion is seldom the fruit of such instruction; the children, as a rule, are glad after their Confirmation to have done with this unspiritual religious teaching, and so they remain, when their schooling is over, permanently strangers to the religious inner life, which the instruction never awakened in them. Nor does the instruction for Confirmation do much to alter that, for it is usually conceived in the same spirit. All other subjects which might raise heart and spirit and present to the young minds some high ideals—more especially our own country's history—are most shamefully neglected in favour of this sort of instruction; and yet a truly religious and patriotic spirit is of inestimable value for life, and, above all, for the soldier. It is the more regrettable that instruction in the national school, as fixed by the regulations, and as given in practice in a still duller form, is totally unfitted to raise such feelings, and thus to do some real service to the country. It is quite refreshing to read in the new regulations for middle schools of February 10,1910, that by religious instruction the "moral and religious tendencies of the child" should be awakened and strengthened, and that the teaching of history should aim at exciting an "intelligent appreciation of the greatness of the fatherland."

The method of religious instruction which is adopted in the national school is, in my opinion, hopelessly perverted. Religious instruction can only become fruitful and profitable when a certain intellectual growth has started and the child possesses some conscious will. To make it the basis of intellectual growth, as was evidently intended in the national schools, has never been a success; for it ought not to be directed at the understanding and logical faculties, but at the mystical intuitions of the soul, and, if it is begun too early, it has a confusing effect on the development of the mental faculties. Even the missionary who wishes to achieve real results tries to educate his pupils by work and secular instruction before he attempts to impart to them subtle religious ideas. Yet every Saturday the appointed passages of Scripture (the Pericopes) are explained to six-year-old children.

Religious instruction proper ought to begin in the middle standard. Up to that point the teacher should be content, from the religious standpoint, to work on the child's imagination and feelings with the simplest ideas of the Deity, but in other respects to endeavour to awaken and encourage the intellectual life, and make it able to grasp loftier conceptions. The national school stands in total contradiction to this intellectual development. This is in conformity to regulations, for the same children who read the Bible independently are only to be led to "an approximate comprehension of those phenomena which are daily around them." In the course of eight years they learn a smattering of reading, writing, and ciphering.[A] It is significant of the knowledge of our national history which the school imparts that out of sixty-three recruits of one company to whom the question was put who Bismarck was, not a single one could answer. That the scholars acquire even a general idea of their duties to the country and the State is quite out of the question. It is impossible to rouse the affection and fancy of the children by instruction in history, because the two sexes are taught in common. One thing appeals to the heart of boys, another to those of girls; and, although I consider it important that patriotic feelings should be inculcated among girls, since as mothers they will transmit them to the family, still the girls must be influenced in a different way from the boys. When the instruction is common to both, the treatment of the subject by the teacher remains neutral and colourless. It is quite incomprehensible how such great results are expected in the religious field when so little has been achieved in every other field.

This pedantic school has wandered far indeed from the ideal that Frederick the Great set up. He declared that the duty of the State was "to educate the young generation to independent thinking and self-devoted love of country."

[Footnote A: Recently a boy was discharged from a well-known national school as an exceptionally good scholar, and was sent as well qualified to the office of a Head Forester. He showed that he could not copy correctly, to say nothing of writing by himself.]

Our national school of to-day needs, then, searching and thorough reform if it is to be a preparatory school, not only for military education, but for life generally. It sends children out into the world with undeveloped reasoning faculties, and equipped with the barest elements of knowledge, and thus makes them not only void of self-reliance, but easy victims of all the corrupting influences of social life. As a matter of fact, the mind and reasoning faculties of the national schoolboy are developed for the first time by his course of instruction as a recruit.

It is obviously not my business to indicate the paths to such a reform. I will only suggest the points which seem to me the most important from the standpoint of a citizen and a soldier. First and foremost, the instruction must be more individual. The number of teachers, accordingly, must be increased, and that of scholars diminished. It is worth while considering in this connection the feasibility of beginning school instruction at the age of eight years. Then all teaching must be directed, more than at present, to the object of developing the children's minds, and formal religious instruction should only begin in due harmony with intellectual progress. Finally, the Realien, especially the history of our own country, should claim more attention, and patriotic feelings should be encouraged in every way; while in religious instruction the moral influence of religion should be more prominent than the formal contents. The training of the national school teacher must be placed on a new basis. At present it absolutely corresponds to the one-sided and limited standpoint of the school itself, and does not enable the teachers to develop the minds and feelings of their pupils. It must be reckoned a distinct disadvantage for the upgrowing generation that all instruction ends at the age of fourteen, so that, precisely at the period of development in which the reasoning powers are forming, the children are thrown back on themselves and on any chance influences. In the interval between school life and military service the young people not only forget all that they learnt, perhaps with aptitude, in the national school, but they unthinkingly adopt distorted views of life, and in many ways become brutalized from a lack of counteracting ideals.

A compulsory continuation school is therefore an absolute necessity of the age. It is also urgently required from the military standpoint. Such a school, to be fruitful in results, must endeavour, not only to prevent the scholar from forgetting what he once learnt, and to qualify him for a special branch of work, but, above all, to develop his patriotism and sense of citizenship. To do this, it is necessary to explain to him the relation of the State to the individual, and to explain, by reference to our national history, how the individual can only prosper by devotion to the State. The duties of the individual to the State should be placed in the foreground. This instruction must be inspired by the spirit which animated Schleiermacher's sermons in the blackest hour of Prussia, and culminated in the doctrine that all the value of the man lies in the strength and purity of his will, in his free devotion to the great whole; that property and life are only trusts, which must be employed for higher ideals; that the mind, which thinks only of itself, perishes in feeble susceptibility, but that true moral worth grows up only in the love for the fatherland and for the State, which is a haven for every faith, and a home of justice and honourable freedom of purpose. Only if national education works in this sense will it train up men to fill our armies who have been adequately prepared for the school of arms, and bring with them the true soldierly spirit from which great deeds spring. What can be effected by the spirit of a nation we have learnt from the history of the War of Liberation, that never-failing source of patriotic sentiment, which should form the backbone and centre of history-teaching in the national and the continuation schools.

We can study it also by an example from most recent history, in the Russo-Japanese War. "The education of the whole Japanese people, beginning at home and continued at school, was based on a patriotic and warlike spirit. That education, combined with the rapidly acquired successes in culture and warfare, aroused in the Japanese a marvellous confidence in their own strength. They served with pride in the ranks of the army, and dreamed of heroic deeds.... All the thoughts of the nation were turned towards the coming struggle, while in the course of several years they had spent their last farthing in the creation of a powerful army and a strong fleet."[B] This was the spirit that led the Japanese to victory. "The day when the young Japanese enlisted was observed as a festival in his family."[B]

In Russia, on the contrary, the idea was preached and disseminated that "Patriotism was an obsolete notion," "war was a crime and an anachronism," that "warlike deeds deserved no notice, the army was the greatest bar to progress, and military service a dishonourable trade."[B] Thus the Russian army marched to battle without any enthusiasm, or even any comprehension of the momentous importance of the great racial war, "not of free will, but from necessity." Already eaten up by the spirit of revolution and unpatriotic selfishness, without energy or initiative, a mechanical tool in the hand of uninspired leaders, it tamely let itself be beaten by a weaker opponent.

[Footnote B: "The Work of the Russian General Staff," from the Russian by Freiheu v. Tettau.]

I have examined these conditions closely because I attach great importance to the national school and the continuation school as a means to the military education of our people. I am convinced that only the army of a warlike and patriotic people can achieve anything really great. I understand, of course, that the school alone, however high its efficiency, could not develop that spirit in our people which we, in view of our great task in the future, must try to awaken by every means if we wish to accomplish something great. The direct influence of school ends when the young generation begins life, and its effect must at first make itself felt very gradually. Later generations will reap the fruits of its sowing. Its efficiency must be aided by other influences which will not only touch the young men now living, but persist throughout their lives. Now, there are two means available which can work upon public opinion and on the spiritual and moral education of the nation; one is the Press, the other is a policy of action. If the Government wishes to win a proper influence over the people, not in order to secure a narrow-spirited support of its momentary policy, but to further its great political, social, and moral duties, it must control a strong and national Press, through which it must present its views and aims vigorously and openly. The Government will never be able to count upon a well-armed and self-sacrificing people in the hour of danger or necessity, if it calmly looks on while the warlike spirit is being systematically undermined by the Press and a feeble peace policy preached, still less if it allows its own organs to join in with the same note, and continually to emphasize the maintenance of peace as the object of all policy. It must rather do everything to foster a military spirit, and to make the nation comprehend the duties and aims of an imperial policy.

It must continually point to the significance and the necessity of war as an indispensable agent in policy and civilization, together with the duty of self-sacrifice and devotion to State and country. A parliamentary Government, which always represents merely a temporary majority, may leave the party Press to defend and back its views; but a Government like the German, which traces its justification to the fact that it is superior to all parties, cannot act thus. Its point of view does not coincide with that of any party; it adopts a middle course, conscious that it is watching the welfare of the whole community. It must therefore represent its attitude, on general issues as well as on particular points, independently, and must endeavour to make its aims as widely understood as possible. I regard it, therefore, as one of the most important duties of a Government like ours to use the Press freely and wisely for the enlightenment of the people. I do not mean that a few large political journals should, in the interests of the moment, be well supplied with news, but that the views of the Government should find comprehensive expression in the local Press. It would be an advantage, in my opinion, were all newspapers compelled to print certain announcements of the Government, in order that the reader might not have such a one-sided account of public affairs as the party Press supplies. It would be a measure of public moral and intellectual hygiene, as justifiable as compulsory regulations in the interests of public health. Epidemics of ideas and opinions are in our old Europe more dangerous and damaging than bodily illnesses, and it is the duty of the State to preserve the moral healthiness of the nation.

More important, perhaps, than teaching and enlightenment by the Press is the propaganda of action. Nothing controls the spirit of the multitude so effectually as energetic, deliberate, and successful action conceived in a broad-minded, statesmanlike sense. Such education by a powerful policy is an absolute necessity for the German people. This nation possesses an excess of vigour, enterprise, idealism, and spiritual energy, which qualifies it for the highest place; but a malignant fairy laid on its cradle the most petty theoretical dogmatism. In addition to this, an unhappy historical development which shattered the national and religious unity of the nation created in the system of small States and in confessionalism a fertile soil for the natural tendency to particularism, on which it flourished luxuriantly as soon as the nation was no longer inspired with great and unifying thoughts. Yet the heart of this people can always be won for great and noble aims, even though such aims can only be attended by danger. We must not be misled in this respect by the Press, which often represents a most one-sided, self-interested view, and sometimes follows international or even Anti-German lines rather than national. The soul of our nation is not reflected in that part of the Press with its continual dwelling on the necessity of upholding peace, and its denunciation of any bold and comprehensive political measure as a policy of recklessness.

On the contrary, an intense longing for a foremost place among the Powers and for manly action fills our nation. Every vigorous utterance, every bold political step of the Government, finds in the soul of the people a deeply felt echo, and loosens the bonds which fetter all their forces. In a great part of the national Press this feeling has again and again found noble expression. But the statesman who could satisfy this yearning, which slumbers in the heart of our people undisturbed by the clamour of parties and the party Press, would carry all spirits with him.

He is no true statesman who does not reckon with these factors of national psychology; Bismarck possessed this art, and used k with a master-hand. True, he found ready to hand one idea which was common to all—the sincere wish for German unification and the German Empire; but the German nation, in its dissensions, did not know the ways which lead to the realization of this idea. Only under compulsion and after a hard struggle did it enter on the road of success; but the whole nation was fired with high enthusiasm when it finally recognized the goal to which the great statesman was so surely leading it. Success was the foundation on which Bismarck built up the mighty fabric of the German Empire. Even in the years of peace he understood how to rivet the imagination of the people by an ambitious and active policy, and how, in spite of all opposition, to gain over the masses to his views, and make them serve his own great aims. He, too, made mistakes as man and as politician, and the motto Homo sum, humani nihil a me alienum puto holds good of him; but in its broad features his policy was always imperial and of world-wide scope, and he never lost sight of the principle that no statesman can permanently achieve great results unless he commands the soul of his people.

This knowledge he shared with all the great men of our past, with the Great Elector, Frederick the Incomparable, Scharnhorst and Blücher; for even that hoary marshal was a political force, the embodiment of a political idea, which, to be sure, did not come into the foreground at the Congress of Vienna.

The statesman who wishes to learn from history should above all things recognize this one fact— that success is necessary to gain influence over the masses, and that this influence can only be obtained by continually appealing to the national imagination and enlisting its interest in great universal ideas and great national ambitions. Such a policy is also the best school in which to educate a nation to great military achievements. When their spirits are turned towards high aims they feel themselves compelled to contemplate war bravely, and to prepare their minds to it: "The man grows up, with manhood's nobler aims."

We may learn something from Japan on this head. Her eyes were fixed on the loftiest aims; she did not shrink from laying the most onerous duties on the people, but she understood how to fill the soul of the whole people with enthusiasm for her great ideals, and thus a nation of warriors was educated which supplied the best conceivable material for the army, and was ready for the greatest sacrifices.

We Germans have a far greater and more urgent duty towards civilization to perform than the Great Asiatic Power. We, like the Japanese, can only fulfil it by the sword.

Shall we, then, decline to adopt a bold and active policy, the most effective means with which we can prepare our people for its military duty? Such a counsel is only for those who lack all feeling for the strength and honour of the German people.

CHAPTER XIV.FINANCIAL AND POLITICAL PREPARATION FOR WAR

From the discussions in the previous chapter it directly follows that the political conduct of the State, while affecting the mental attitude of the people, exercises an indirect but indispensable influence on the preparation for war, and is to some degree a preparation for war itself.

But, in addition to the twofold task of exercising this intellectual and moral influence, and of placing at the disposal of the military authorities the necessary means for keeping up the armaments, still further demands must be made of those responsible for the guidance of the State. In the first place, financial preparations for war must be made, quite distinct from the current expenditure on the army; the national finances must be so treated that the State can bear the tremendous burdens of a modern war without an economic crash. Further, as already mentioned in another place, there must be a sort of mobilization in the sphere of commercial politics in order to insure under all eventualities the supply of the goods necessary for the material and industrial needs of the country. Finally, preparations for war must also be made politically; that is to say, efforts must be made to bring about a favourable political conjuncture, and, so far as possible, to isolate the first enemy with whom a war is bound to come. If that cannot be effected, an attempt must he made to win allies, in whom confidence can be reposed should war break out.

I am not a sufficient expert to pronounce a definite opinion on the commercial and financial side of the question. In the sphere of commercial policy especially I cannot even suggest the way in which the desired end can be obtained. Joint action on the part of the Government and the great import houses would seem to be indicated. As regards finance, speaking again from a purely unprofessional standpoint, one may go so far as to say that it is not only essential to keep the national household in order, but to maintain the credit of the State, so that, on the outbreak of war, it may be possible to raise the vast sums of money required for carrying it on without too onerous conditions.

The credit of State depends essentially on a regulated financial economy, which insures that the current outgoings are covered by the current incomings. Other factors are the national wealth, the indebtedness of the State, and, lastly, the confidence in its productive and military capabilities. As regards the first point, I have already pointed out that in a great civilized World State the balancing of the accounts must never be brought about in the petty-State fashion by striking out expenditure for necessary requirements, more especially expenditure on the military forces, whose maintenance forms the foundation of a satisfactory general progress. The incomings must, on the contrary, be raised in proportion to the real needs. But, especially in a State which is so wholly based on war as the German Empire, the old manly principle of keeping all our forces on the stretch must never be abandoned out of deference to the effeminate philosophy of the day. Fichte taught us that there is only one virtue—to forget the claims of one's personality; and only one vice—to think of self. Ultimately the State is the transmitter of all culture, and is therefore entitled to claim all the powers of the individual for itself.[A] These ideas, which led us out of the deepest gloom to the sunlit heights of success, must remain our pole-star at an epoch which in many respects can be compared with the opening years of the last century. The peace-loving contentment which then prevailed in Prussia, as if the age of everlasting peace had come, still sways large sections of our people, and exerts an appreciable influence on the Government. Among that peaceful nation "which behind the rampart of its line of demarcation observed with philosophic calm how two mighty nations contested the sole possession of the world," nobody gave any thought to the great change of times. In the same way many Germans to-day look contentedly and philosophically at the partition of the world, and shut their eyes to the rushing stream of world-history and the great duties imposed upon us by it. Even to-day, as then, the same "super-terrestrial pride, the same super-clever irresolution" spreads among us "which in our history follows with uncanny regularity the great epochs of audacity and energy."[B]

[Footnote A: Treitschke.]

[Footnote: B Treitschke, "Deutsche Geschichte."]

Under conditions like the present the State is not only entitled, but is bound to put the utmost strain on the financial powers of her citizens, since it is vital questions that are at stake. It is equally important, however, to foster by every available means the growth of the national property, and thus to improve the financial capabilities.

This property is to a certain extent determined by the natural productiveness of the country and the mineral wealth it contains. But these possessions are utilized and their value is enhanced by the labour of all fellow-countrymen—that immense capital which cannot be replaced. Here, then, the State can profitably step in. It can protect and secure labour against unjustifiable encroachments by regulating the labour conditions; it can create profitable terms for exports and imports by concluding favourable commercial agreements; it can help and facilitate German trade by vigorous political representation of German interests abroad; it can encourage the shipping trade, which gains large profits from international commerce;[C] it can increase agricultural production by energetic home colonization, cultivation of moorland, and suitable protective measures, so as to make us to some extent less dependent on foreign countries for our food. The encouragement of deep-sea fishery would add to this.[D]

[Footnote: C England earns some 70 millions sterling by international commerce, Germany about 15 millions sterling.]

[Footnote D: We buy annually some 2 millions sterling worth of fish from foreign countries.]

From the military standpoint, it is naturally very important to increase permanently the supply of breadstuffs and meat, so that in spite of the annual increase in population the home requirements may for some time be met to the same extent as at present; this seems feasible. Home production now supplies 87 per cent, of the required breadstuffs and 95 per cent, of the meat required. To maintain this proportion, the production in the next ten years must be increased by at most two double-centners per Hectare, which is quite possible if it is considered that the rye harvest alone in the last twenty years has increased by two million tons.

A vigorous colonial policy, too, will certainly improve the national prosperity if directed, on the one hand, to producing in our own colonies the raw materials which our industries derive in immense quantities from foreign countries, and so making us gradually independent of foreign countries; and, on the other hand, to transforming our colonies into an assured market for our goods by effective promotion of settlements, railroads, and cultivation. The less we are tributaries of foreign countries, to whom we pay many milliards, [E] the more our national wealth and the financial capabilities of the State will improve.

[Footnote E: We obtained from abroad in 1907, for instance, 476,400 tons of cotton, 185,300 tons of wool, 8,500,000 tons of iron, 124,000 tons of copper, etc.]

If the State can thus contribute directly to the increase of national productions, it can equally raise its own credit by looking after the reduction of the national debt, and thus improving its financial position. But payment of debts is, in times of high political tension, a two-edged sword, if it is carried out at the cost of necessary outlays. The gain in respect of credit on the one side of the account may very easily be lost again on the other. Even from the financial aspect it is a bad fault to economize in outlay on the army and navy in order to improve the financial position. The experiences of history leave no doubt on that point. Military power is the strongest pillar of a nation's credit. If it is weakened, financial security at once is shaken. A disastrous war involves such pecuniary loss that the State creditors may easily become losers by it. But a State whose army holds out prospects of carrying the war to a victorious conclusion offers its creditors far better security than a weaker military power. If our credit at the present day cannot be termed very good, our threatened political position is chiefly to blame. If we chose to neglect our army and navy our credit would sink still lower, in spite of all possible liquidation of our debt. We have a twofold duty before us: first to improve our armament; secondly, to promote the national industry, and to keep in mind the liquidation of our debts so far as our means go.

The question arises whether it is possible to perform this twofold task.

It is inconceivable that the German people has reached the limits of possible taxation. The taxes of Prussia have indeed, between 1893-94 and 1910-11, increased by 56 per cent, per head of the population—from 20.62 marks to 32.25 marks (taxes and customs together)—and the same proportion may hold in the rest of Germany. On the other hand, there is a huge increase in the national wealth. This amounts, in the German Empire now, to 330 to 360 milliard marks, or 5,000 to 6,000 marks per head of the population. In France the wealth, calculated on the same basis, is no higher, and yet in France annually 20 marks, in Germany only 16 marks, per head of the population are expended on the army and navy. In England, on the contrary, where the average wealth of the individual is some 1,000 marks higher than in Germany and France, the outlay for the army and navy comes to 29 marks per head. Thus our most probable opponents make appreciably greater sacrifices for their armaments than we do, although they are far from being in equal danger politically.

Attention must at the same time be called to the fact that the increase of wealth in Germany continues to be on an ascending scale. Trades and industries have prospered vastly, and although the year 1908 saw a setback, yet the upward tendency has beyond doubt set in again.

The advance in trade and industry, which began with the founding of the Empire, is extraordinary. "The total of imports and exports has increased in quantity from 32 million tons to 106 million tons in the year 1908, or by 232 per cent., and in value from 6 milliards to 14 1/2-16 milliards marks in the last years. Of these, the value of the imports has grown from 3 to 8-9 milliards marks, and the value of the exports from 3 1/2 to 6 1/2-7 milliards.... The value of the import of raw materials for industrial purposes has grown from 1 1/2 milliards in 1879 to 4 1/2 milliards marks lately, and the value of the export of such raw materials from 850 million to 1 1/2 milliard marks. The import of made goods had in 1879 a value of 600 million marks, and in 1908 a value of 1 1/4 milliard marks, while the value of the export of manufactured goods mounted from 1 to 4 milliards. The value of the import of food-stuffs and delicacies has grown from 1 to 2 1/2-2 1/3 milliard marks, while the value of the export of articles of food remained at about the same figure.

The mineral output can also point to an undreamed-of extension in Germany during the last thirty years. The amount of coal raised amounted in 1879 to only 42 million tons; up to 1908 it has increased to 148 1/2 million tons, and in value from 100 million to 1 1/2 milliard marks. The quantity of brown coal raised was only 11 1/2 million tons in 1879; in 1908 it was 66 3/4 million tons, and in value it has risen from 35 million to 170 million marks. The output of iron-ore has increased from 6 million tons to 27 million tons, and in value from 27 million to 119 million marks.... From 1888 to 1908 the amount of coal raised in Germany has increased by 127 per cent.; in England only by about 59 per cent. The raw iron obtained has increased in Germany from 1888 to 1908 by 172 per cent.; in England there is a rise of 27 per cent. only.[F]

[Footnote F: Professor Dr. Wade, Berlin.]

Similar figures can be shown in many other spheres. The financial position of the Empire has considerably improved since the Imperial Finance reform of 1909, so that the hope exists that the Budget may very soon balance without a loan should no new sacrifices be urgent.

It was obvious that with so prodigious a development a continued growth of revenue must take place, and hand-in-hand with it a progressive capitalization. Such a fact has been the case, and to a very marked extent. From the year 1892-1905 in Prussia alone an increase of national wealth of about 2 milliard marks annually has taken place. The number of taxpayers and of property in the Property Tax class of 6,000 to 100,000 marks has in Prussia increased in these fourteen years by 29 per cent., from 1905-1908 by 11 per cent.; in the first period, therefore, by 2 per cent., in the last years by 3 per cent. annually. In these classes, therefore, prosperity is increasing, but this is so in much greater proportion in the large fortunes. In the Property Tax class of 100,000 to 500,000 marks, the increase has been about 48 per cent.—i.e., on an average for the fourteen years about 3 per cent. annually, while in the last three years it has been 4.6 per cent. In the class of 500,000 marks and upwards, the increase for the fourteen years amounts to 54 per cent. in the taxpayers and 67 per cent. in the property; and, while in the fourteen years the increase is on an average 4.5 per cent. annually, it has risen in the three years 1905-1908 to 8.6 per cent. This means per head of the population in the schedule of 6,000 to 100,000 marks an increase of 650 marks, in the schedule of 100,000 to 500,000 marks an increase per head of 6,400 marks, and in the schedule of 500,000 marks and upwards an increase of 70,480 marks per head and per year. We see then, especially in the large estates, a considerable and annually increasing growth, which the Prussian Finance Minister has estimated for Prussia alone at 3 milliards yearly in the next three years, so that it may be assumed to be for the whole Empire 5 milliards yearly in the same period. Wages have risen everywhere. To give some instances, I will mention that among the workmen at Krupp's factory at Essen the daily earnings have increased from 1879-1906 by 77 per cent., the pay per hour for masons from 1885-1905 by 64 per cent., and the annual earnings in the Dortmund district of the chief mining office from 1886 to 1907 by 121 per cent. This increase in earnings is also shown by the fact that the increase of savings bank deposits since 1906 has reached the sum of 4 milliard marks, a proof that in the lower and poorer strata of the population, too, a not inconsiderable improvement in prosperity is perceptible. It can also be regarded as a sign of a healthy, improving condition of things that emigration and unemployment are considerably diminished in Germany. In 1908 only 20,000 emigrants left our country; further, according to the statistics of the workmen's unions, only 4.4 per cent, of their members were unemployed, whereas in the same year 336,000 persons emigrated from Great Britain and 10 per cent. (in France it was as much as 11.4 per cent.) of members of workmen's unions were unemployed.

Against this brilliant prosperity must be placed a very large national debt, both in the Empire and in the separate States. The German Empire in the year 1910 had 5,016,655,500 marks debt, and in addition the national debt of the separate States on April 1, 1910, reached in—

Marks

Prussia 9,421,770,800
Bavaria 2,165,942,900
Saxony 893,042,600
Würtemberg 606,042,800
Baden 557,859,000
Hesse 428,664,400
Alsace-Lorraine 31,758,100
Hamburg 684,891,200
Lübeck 666,888,400
Bremen 263,431,400

Against these debts may be placed a considerable property in domains, forests, mines, and railways. The stock capital of the State railways reached, on March 31, 1908, in millions of marks, in—

Marks,

Prussia (Hesse) 9,888
Bavaria 1,694
Saxony 1,035
Würtemburg 685
Baden 727
Alsace-Lorraine 724

—a grand total, including the smaller State systems, of 15,062 milliard marks. This sum has since risen considerably, and reached at the end of 1911 for Prussia alone 11,050 milliards. Nevertheless, the national debts signify a very heavy burden, which works the more disadvantageously because these debts are almost all contracted in the country, and presses the more heavily because the communes are also often greatly in debt.

The debt of the Prussian towns and country communes of 10,000 inhabitants and upwards alone amounts to 3,000 million marks, in the whole Empire to some 5,000 million marks. This means that interest yearly has to be paid to the value of 150 million marks, so that many communes, especially in the east and in the western industrial regions, are compelled to raise additional taxation to the extent of 200, 300, or even 400 per cent. The taxes also are not at all equally distributed according to capacity to pay them. The main burden rests on the middle class; the large fortunes are much less drawn upon. Some sources of wealth are not touched by taxation, as, for example, the speculative income not obtained by carrying on any business, but by speculations on the Stock Exchange, which cannot be taxed until it is converted into property. Nevertheless, the German nation is quite in a position to pay for the military preparations, which it certainly requires for the protection and the fulfilment of its duties in policy and civilization, so soon as appropriate and comprehensive measures are taken and the opposing parties can resolve to sacrifice scruples as to principles on the altar of patriotism.

The dispute about the so-called Imperial Finance reform has shown how party interests and selfishness rule the national representation; it was not pleasant to see how each tried to shift the burden to his neighbour's shoulders in order to protect himself against financial sacrifices. It must be supposed, therefore, that similar efforts will be made in the future, and that fact must be reckoned with. But a considerable and rapid rise of the Imperial revenue is required if we wish to remain equal to the situation and not to abandon the future of our country without a blow.

Under these conditions I see no other effectual measure but the speedy introduction of the Reichserbrecht (Imperial right of succession), in order to satisfy the urgent necessity. This source of revenue would oppress no class in particular, but would hit all alike, and would furnish the requisite means both to complete our armament and to diminish our burden of debt.

If the collateral relations, with exception of brothers and sisters, depended on mention in the will for any claim—that is to say, if they could only inherit when a testamentary disposition existed in their favour—and if, in absence of such disposition, the State stepped in as heir, a yearly revenue of 500 millions, according to a calculation based on official material, could be counted upon. This is not the place to examine this calculation more closely. Even if it is put at too high a figure, which I doubt, yet the yield of such a tax would be very large under any circumstances. Since this, like every tax on an inheritance, is a tax on capital—that is to say, it is directly derived from invested capital—it is in the nature of things that the proceeds should be devoted in the first instance to the improvement of the financial situation, especially to paying off debts.

Otherwise there would be the danger of acting like a private gentleman who lives on his capital. This idea is also to be recommended because the proceeds of the tax are not constant, but liable to fluctuations. It would be advisable to devote the proceeds principally in this way, and to allow a part to go towards extinguishing the debt of the communes, whose financial soundness is extremely important. This fundamental standpoint does not exclude the possibility that in a national crisis the tax may be exceptionally applied to other important purposes, as for example to the completion of our armaments on land and sea.

There are two objections—one economic, the other ethical—which may be urged against this right of the State or the Empire to inherit. It is argued that the proceeds of the tax were drawn from the national wealth, that the State would grow richer, the people poorer, and that in course of time capital would be united in the hand of the State, that the independent investor would be replaced by the official, and thus the ideal of Socialism would be realized. Secondly, the requirement that relations, in order to inherit, must be specially mentioned in the will, is thought to be a menace to the coherence of the family. "According to our prevailing law, the man who wishes to deprive his family of his fortune must do some positive act. He must make a will, in which he bequeathes the property to third persons, charitable institutions, or to any other object. It is thus brought before his mind that his natural heirs are his relations, his kin, and that he must make a will if he wishes to exclude his legal heirs. It is impressed upon him that he is interfering by testamentary disposition in the natural course of things, that he is wilfully altering it. The Imperial right of succession is based on the idea that the community stands nearer to the individual than his family. This is in its inmost significance a socialistic trait. The socialistic State, which deals with a society made up of atoms, in which every individual is freed from the bonds of family, while all are alike bound by a uniform socialistic tie, might put forward a claim of this sort."[F]

[Footnote F: Bolko v. Katte, in the Kreuzzeitung of November 18, 1910.]

Both objections are unconvincing.

So long as the State uses the proceeds of the inheritances in order to liquidate debts and other outgoings, which would have to be met otherwise, the devolution of such inheritances on the State is directly beneficial to all members of the State, because they have to pay less taxes. Legislation could easily prevent any accumulation of capital in the hands of the State, since, if such results followed, this right of succession might be restricted, or the dreaded socialization of the State be prevented in other ways. The science of finance could unquestionably arrange that. There is no necessity to push the scheme to its extreme logical conclusion.

The so-called ethical objections are still less tenable. If a true sense of family ties exists, the owner of property will not fail to make a will, which is an extremely simple process under the present law. If such ties are weak, they are assuredly not strengthened by the right of certain next of kin to be the heirs of a man from whom they kept aloof in life. Indeed, the Crown's right of inheritance would produce probably the result that more wills were made, and thus the sense of family ties would actually be strengthened. The "primitive German sense of law," which finds expression in the present form of the law of succession, and is summed up in the notion that the family is nearer to the individual than the State, has so far borne the most mischievous results. It is the root from which the disruption of Germany, the particularism and the defective patriotism of our nation, have grown up. It is well that in the coming generation some check on this movement should be found, and that the significance of the State for the individual, no less than for the family, should be thoroughly understood.

These more or less theoretical objections are certainly not weighty enough to negative a proposal like that of introducing this Imperial right of succession if the national danger demands direct and rapid help and the whole future of Germany is at stake.

If, therefore, no other proposals are forthcoming by which an equally large revenue can be obtained; the immediate reintroduction of such a law of succession appears a necessity, and will greatly benefit our sorely-pressed country. Help is urgently needed, and there would be good prospects of such law being passed in the Reichstag if the Government does not disguise the true state of the political position.

Political preparations are not less essential than financial. We see that all the nations of the world are busily securing themselves against the attack of more powerful opponents by alliances or ententes, and are winning allies in order to carry out their own objects. Efforts are also often made to stir up ill-feeling between the other States, so as to have a free hand for private schemes. This is the policy on which England has built up her power in Europe, in order to continue her world policy undisturbed. She cannot be justly blamed for this; for even if she has acted with complete disregard of political morality, she has built up a mighty Empire, which is the object of all policy, and has secured to the English people the possibility of the most ambitious careers. We must not deceive ourselves as to the principles of this English policy. We must realize to ourselves that it is guided exclusively by unscrupulous selfishness, that it shrinks from no means of accomplishing its aims, and thus shows admirable diplomatic skill.

There must be no self-deception on the point that political arrangements have only a qualified value, that they are always concluded with a tacit reservation. Every treaty of alliance presupposes the rebus sic stantibus; for since it must satisfy the interests of each contracting party, it clearly can only hold as long as those interests are really benefited. This is a political principle that cannot be disputed. Nothing can compel a State to act counter to its own interests, on which those of its citizens depend. This consideration, however, imposes on the honest State the obligation of acting with the utmost caution when concluding a political arrangement and defining its limits in time, so as to avoid being forced into a breach of its word. Conditions may arise which are more powerful than the most honourable intentions. The country's own interests—considered, of course, in the highest ethical sense—must then turn the scale.

"Frederick the Great was all his life long charged with treachery, because no treaty or alliance could ever induce him to renounce the right of free self-determination."[A]

The great statesman, therefore, will conclude political ententes or alliances, on whose continuance he wishes to be able to reckon, only if he is convinced that each of the contracting parties will find such an arrangement to his true and unqualified advantage. Such an alliance is, as I have shown in another place, the Austro-German. The two States, from the military no less than from the political aspect, are in the happiest way complements of each other. The German theatre of war in the east will be protected by Austria from any attempt to turn our flank on the south, while we can guard the northern frontier of Austria and outflank any Russian attack on Galicia.

Alliances in which each contracting party has different interests will never hold good under all conditions, and therefore cannot represent a permanent political system.

"There is no alliance or agreement in the world that can be regarded as effective if it is not fastened by the bond of the common and reciprocal interests; if in any treaty the advantage is all on one side and the other gets nothing, this disproportion destroys the obligation." These are the words of Frederick the Great, our foremost political teacher pace Bismarck.

We must not be blinded in politics by personal wishes and hopes, but must look things calmly in the face, and try to forecast the probable attitude of the other States by reference to their own interests. Bismarck tells us that "Illusions are the greatest danger to the diplomatist. He must take for granted that the other, like himself, seeks nothing but his own advantage." It will prove waste labour to attempt to force a great State by diplomatic arrangements to actions or an attitude which oppose its real interests. When a crisis arises, the weight of these interests will irresistibly turn the scale.

When Napoleon III. planned war against Prussia, he tried to effect an alliance with Austria and Italy, and Archduke Albert was actually in Paris to conclude the military negotiations.[B] These probably were going on, as the French General Lebrun was in Vienna on the same errand. Both countries left France in the lurch so soon as the first Prussian flag flew victoriously on the heights of the Geisberg. A statesman less biassed than Napoleon would have foreseen this, since neither Austria nor Italy had sufficient interests at stake to meddle in such a war under unfavourable conditions.

[Footnote B: When Colonel Stoffel, the well-known French Military Attaché in Berlin, returned to Paris, and was received by the Emperor, and pointed out the danger of the position and the probable perfection of Prussia's war preparations, the Emperor declared that he was better informed. He proceeded to take from his desk a memoir on the conditions of the Prussian army apparently sent to him by Archduke Albert, which came to quite different conclusions. The Emperor had made the facts therein stated the basis of his political and military calculations. (Communications of Colonel Stoffel to the former Minister of War, v. Verdy, who put them at the service of the author.)]

France, in a similar spirit of selfish national interests, unscrupulously brushed aside the Conventions of Algeciras, which did not satisfy her. She will equally disregard all further diplomatic arrangements intended to safeguard Germany's commercial interests in Morocco so soon as she feels strong enough, since it is clearly her interest to be undisputed master in Morocco and to exploit that country for herself. France, when she no longer fears the German arms, will not allow any official document in the world to guarantee German commerce and German enterprise any scope in Morocco; and from the French standpoint she is right.

The political behaviour of a State is governed only by its own interests, and the natural antagonism and grouping of the different Great Powers must be judged by that standard. There is no doubt, however, that it is extraordinarily difficult to influence the political grouping with purely selfish purposes; such influence becomes possible only by the genuine endeavour to further the interests of the State with which closer relations are desirable and to cause actual injury to its opponents. A policy whose aim is to avoid quarrel with all, but to further the interests of none, runs the danger of displeasing everyone and of being left isolated in the hour of danger.

A successful policy, therefore, cannot be followed without taking chances and facing risks. It must be conscious of its goal, and keep this goal steadily in view. It must press every change of circumstances and all unforeseen occurrences into the service of its own ideas. Above all things, it must he ready to seize the psychological moment, and take bold action if the general position of affairs indicates the possibility of realizing political ambitions or of waging a necessary war under favourable conditions. "The great art of policy," writes Frederick the Great, "is not to swim against the stream, but to turn all events to one's own profit. It consists rather in deriving advantage from favourable conjunctures than in preparing such conjunctures." Even in his Rheinsberg days he acknowledged the principle to which he adhered all his life: "Wisdom is well qualified to keep what one possesses; but boldness alone can acquire." "I give you a problem to solve," he said to his councillors when the death of Emperor Charles VI. was announced. "When you have the advantage, are you to use it or not?"

Definite, clearly thought out political goals, wise foresight, correct summing up alike of one's own and of foreign interests, accurate estimation of the forces of friends and foes, bold advocacy of the interests, not only of the mother-country, but also of allies, and daring courage when the critical hour strikes—these are the great laws of political and military success.

The political preparation for war is included in them. He who is blinded by the semblance of power and cannot resolve to act, will never be able to make political preparations for the inevitable war with any success. "The braggart feebleness which travesties strength, the immoral claim which swaggers in the sanctity of historical right, the timidity which shelters its indecision behind empty and formal excuses, never were more despised than by the great Prussian King," so H. v. Treitschke tells us. "Old Fritz" must be our model in this respect, and must teach us with remorseless realism so to guide our policy that the position of the political world may be favourable for us, and that we do not miss the golden opportunity.

It is an abuse of language if our unenterprising age tries to stigmatize that energetic policy which pursued positive aims as an adventurist policy. That title can only be given to the policy which sets up personal ideals and follows them without just estimation of the real current of events, and so literally embarks on incalculable adventures, as Napoleon did in Mexico, and Italy in Abyssinia.

A policy taking all factors into consideration, and realizing these great duties of the State, which are an historical legacy and are based on the nature of things, is justified when it boldly reckons with the possibility of a war. This is at once apparent if one considers the result to the State when war is forced on it under disadvantageous circumstances. I need only instance 1806, and the terrible catastrophe to which the feeble, unworthy peace policy of Prussia led.

In this respect the Russo-Japanese War speaks a clear language. Japan had made the most judicious preparations possible, political as well as military, for the war, when she concluded the treaty with England and assured herself of the benevolent neutrality of America and China. Her policy, no less circumspect than bold, did not shrink from beginning at the psychological moment the war which was essential for the attainment of her political ends. Russia was not prepared in either respect. She had been forced into a hostile position with Germany from her alliance with France, and therefore dared not denude her west front in order to place sufficient forces in the Far East. Internal conditions, moreover, compelled her to retain large masses of soldiers in the western part of the Empire. A large proportion of the troops put into the field against Japan were therefore only inferior reserves. None of the preparations required by the political position had been made, although the conflict had long been seen to be inevitable. Thus the war began with disastrous retreats, and was never conducted with any real vigour. There is no doubt that things would have run a different course had Russia made resolute preparations for the inevitable struggle and had opened the campaign by the offensive.

England, too, was politically surprised by the Boer War, and consequently had not taken any military precautions at all adequate to her aims or suited to give weight to political demands.

Two points stand out clearly from this consideration.

First of all there is a reciprocal relation between the military and political preparations for war. Proper political preparations for war are only made if the statesman is supported by a military force strong enough to give weight to his demands, and if he ventures on nothing which he cannot carry through by arms. At the same time the army must be developed on a scale which takes account of the political projects. The obligation imposed on the General to stand aloof from politics in peace as well as in war only holds good in a limited sense. The War Minister and the

Head of the General Staff must be kept au courant with the all-fluctuating phases of policy; indeed, they must be allowed a certain influence over policy, in order to adapt their measures to its needs, and are entitled to call upon the statesman to act if the military situation is peculiarly favourable. At the same time the Minister who conducts foreign policy must, on his side, never lose sight of what is in a military sense practicable; he must be constantly kept informed of the precise degree in which army and navy are ready for war, since he must never aim at plans which cannot, if necessary, be carried out by war. A veiled or open threat of war is the only means the statesman has of carrying out his aims; for in the last resort it is always the realization of the possible consequences of a war which induces the opponent to give in. Where this means is renounced, a policy of compromise results, which satisfies neither party and seldom produces a permanent settlement; while if a statesman announces the possibility of recourse to the arbitrament of arms, his threat must be no empty one, but must be based on real power and firm determination if it is not to end in political and moral defeat.

The second point, clearly brought before us, is that a timid and hesitating policy, which leaves the initiative to the opponent and shrinks from ever carrying out its purpose with warlike methods, always creates an unfavourable military position. History, as well as theory, tells us by countless instances that a far-seeing, energetic policy, which holds its own in the face of all antagonism, always reacts favourably on the military situation.

In this respect war and policy obey the same laws; great results can only be expected where political and military foresight and resolution join hands.

If we regard from this standpoint the political preparation for the next war which Germany will have to fight, we must come to this conclusion: the more unfavourable the political conjuncture the greater the necessity for a determined, energetic policy if favourable conditions are to be created for the inevitably threatening war.

So long as we had only to reckon on the possibility of a war on two fronts against France and Russia, and could count on help in this war from all the three parties to the Triple Alliance, the position was comparatively simple. There were, then, of course, a series of various strategical possibilities; but the problem could be reduced to a small compass: strategical attack on the one side, strategical defence on the other, or, if the Austrian army was taken into calculation, offensive action on both sides. To-day the situation is different.

We must consider England, as well as France and Russia. We must expect not only an attack by sea on our North Sea coasts, but a landing of English forces on the continent of Europe and a violation of Belgo-Dutch neutrality by our enemies. It is also not inconceivable that England may land troops in Schleswig or Jutland, and try to force Denmark into war with us. It seems further questionable whether Austria will be in a position to support us with all her forces, whether she will not rather be compelled to safeguard her own particular interests on her south and south-east frontiers. An attack by France through Switzerland is also increasingly probable, if a complete reorganization of the grouping of the European States is effected. Finally, we should be seriously menaced in the Baltic if Russia gains time to reconstruct her fleet.

All these unfavourable conditions will certainly not occur simultaneously, but under certain not impossible political combinations they are more or less probable, and must be taken into account from the military aspect. The military situation thus created is very unfavourable.

If under such uncertain conditions it should be necessary to place the army on a war footing, only one course is left: we must meet the situation by calling out strategic reserves, which must be all the stronger since the political conditions are so complicated and obscure, and those opponents so strong on whose possible share in the war we must count. The strategic reserve will be to some extent a political one also. A series of protective measures, necessary in any case, would have to be at once set on foot, but the mass of the army would not be directed to any definite point until the entire situation was clear and all necessary steps could be considered. Until that moment the troops of the strategic reserve would be left in their garrisons or collected along the railway lines and at railway centres in such a way that, when occasion arose, they could be despatched in any direction. On the same principle the rolling-stock on the lines would have to be kept in readiness, the necessary time-tables for the different transport arrangements drawn up, and stores secured in safe depots on as many different lines of march as possible. Previous arrangements for unloading at the railway stations must be made in accordance with the most various political prospects. We should in any case be forced to adopt a waiting policy, a strategic defensive, which under present conditions is extremely unfavourable; we should not be able to prevent an invasion by one or other of our enemies.

No proof is necessary to show that a war thus begun cannot hold out good prospects of success. The very bravest army must succumb if led against a crushingly superior force under most unfavourable conditions. A military investigation of the situation shows that a plan of campaign, such as would be required here on the inner line, presents, under the modern system of "mass" armies, tremendous difficulties, and has to cope with strategic conditions of the most unfavourable kind.

The disadvantages of such a situation can only be avoided by a policy which makes it feasible to act on the offensive, and, if possible, to overthrow the one antagonist before the other can actively interfere. On this initiative our safety now depends, just as it did in the days of Frederick the Great. We must look this truth boldly in the face. Of course, it can be urged that an attack is just what would produce an unfavourable position for us, since it creates the conditions on which the Franco-Russian alliance would be brought into activity. If we attacked France or Russia, the ally would be compelled to bring help, and we should be in a far worse position than if we had only one enemy to fight. Let it then be the task of our diplomacy so to shuffle the cards that we may be attacked by France, for then there would be reasonable prospect that Russia for a time would remain neutral.

This view undoubtedly deserves attention, but we must not hope to bring about this attack by waiting passively. Neither France nor Russia nor England need to attack in order to further their interests. So long as we shrink from attack, they can force us to submit to their will by diplomacy, as the upshot of the Morocco negotiations shows.

If we wish to bring about an attack by our opponents, we must initiate an active policy which, without attacking France, will so prejudice her interests or those of England, that both these States would feel themselves compelled to attack us. Opportunities for such procedure are offered both in Africa and in Europe, and anyone who has attentively studied prominent political utterances can easily satisfy himself on this point.

In opposition to these ideas the view is frequently put forward that we should wait quietly and let time fight for us, since from the force of circumstances many prizes will fall into our laps which we have now to struggle hard for. Unfortunately such politicians always forget to state clearly and definitely what facts are really working in their own interests and what advantages will accrue to us therefrom. Such political wisdom is not to be taken seriously, for it has no solid foundation. We must reckon with the definitely given conditions, and realize that timidity and laissez-aller have never led to great results.

It is impossible for anyone not close at hand to decide what steps and measures are imposed upon our foreign policy, in order to secure a favourable political situation should the pending questions so momentous to Germany's existence come to be settled by an appeal to arms. This requires a full and accurate knowledge of the political and diplomatic position which I do not possess. One thing only can be justly said: Beyond the confusion and contradictions of the present situation we must keep before us the great issues which will not lose their importance as time goes on.

Italy, which has used a favourable moment in order to acquire settlements for her very rapidly increasing population (487,000 persons emigrated from Italy in 1908), can never combine with France and England to fulfil her political ambition of winning the supremacy in the Mediterranean, since both these States themselves claim this place. The effort to break up the Triple Alliance has momentarily favoured the Italian policy of expansion. But this incident does not alter in the least the fact that the true interest of Italy demands adherence to the Triple Alliance, which alone can procure her Tunis and Biserta. The importance of these considerations will continue to be felt.

Turkey also cannot permanently go hand-in-hand with England, France, and Russia, whose policy must always aim directly at the annihilation of present-day Turkey. Islam has now as ever her most powerful enemies in England and Russia, and will, sooner or later, be forced to join the Central European Alliance, although we committed the undoubted blunder of abandoning her in Morocco.

There is no true community of interests between Russia and England; in Central Asia, in Persia, as in the Mediterranean, their ambitions clash in spite of all conventions, and the state of affairs in Japan and China is forcing on a crisis which is vital to Russian interests and to some degree ties her hands.

All these matters open out a wide vista to German statesmanship, if it is equal to its task, and make the general outlook less gloomy than recent political events seemed to indicate. And, then, our policy can count on a factor of strength such as no other State possesses—on an army whose military efficiency, I am convinced, cannot be sufficiently valued. Not that it is perfect in all its arrangements and details. We have amply shown the contrary. But the spirit which animates the troops, the ardour of attack, the heroism, the loyalty which prevail amongst them, justify the highest expectations. I am certain that if they are soon to be summoned to arms, their exploits will astonish the world, provided only that they are led with skill and determination. The German nation, too—of this I am equally convinced—will rise to the height of its great duty. A mighty force which only awaits the summons sleeps in its soul. Whoever to-day can awaken the slumbering idealism of this people, and rouse the national enthusiasm by placing before its eyes a worthy and comprehensible ambition, will be able to sweep this people on in united strength to the highest efforts and sacrifices, and will achieve a truly magnificent result.

In the consciousness of being able at any time to call up these forces, and in the sure trust that they will not fail in the hour of danger, our Government can firmly tread the path which leads to a splendid future; but it will not be able to liberate all the forces of Germany unless it wins her confidence by successful action and takes for its motto the brave words of Goethe:

"Bid defiance to every power!
Ever valiant, never cower!
To the brave soldier open flies
The golden gate of Paradise."

EPILOGUE

After I had practically finished the preceding pages, the Franco-German convention as to Morocco and the Congo Compensation were published; the Turko-Italian War broke out; the revolution in China assumed dimensions which point to the probability of new disorders in Eastern Asia; and, lastly, it was known that not merely an entente cordiale, but a real offensive and defensive alliance, aimed at us, exists between France and England. Such an alliance does not seem to be concluded permanently between the two States, but clearly every possibility of war has been foreseen and provided for.

I have been able to insert all the needful references to the two first occurrences in my text; but the light which has lately been cast on the Anglo-French conventions compels me to make a few concluding remarks.

The German Government, from important reasons which cannot be discussed, have considered it expedient to avoid, under present conditions, a collision with England or France at any cost. It has accomplished this object by the arrangement with France, and it may be, of course, assumed that no further concessions were attainable, since from the first it was determined not to fight at present. Only from this aspect can the attitude of the Government towards France and England be considered correct. It is quite evident from her whole attitude that Great Britain was resolved to take the chance of a war. Her immediate preparations for war, the movements of her ships, and the attack of English high finance on the foremost German banking establishments, which took place at this crisis, exclude all doubt on the point. We have probably obtained the concessions made by France only because she thought the favourable moment for the long-planned war had not yet come. Probably she will wait until, on the one hand, the Triple Alliance is still more loosened and Russia's efficiency by sea and land is more complete, and until, on the other hand, her own African army has been so far strengthened that it can actively support the Rhine army. This idea may sufficiently explain the Morocco policy of the Government, but there can be no doubt, if the convention with France be examined, that it does not satisfy fully our justifiable wishes.

It will not be disputed that the commercial and political arrangement as regards Morocco creates favourable conditions of competition for our manufacturers, entrepreneurs and merchants; that the acquisition of territory in the French Congo has a certain and perhaps not inconsiderable value in the future, more especially if we succeed in obtaining the Spanish enclave on the coast, which alone will make the possession really valuable. On the other hand, what we obtained can never be regarded as a sufficient compensation for what we were compelled to abandon.

I have emphasized in another place the fact that the commercial concessions which France has made are valuable only so long as our armed force guarantees that they are observed; the acquisitions in the Congo region must, as the Imperial Chancellor announced in his speech of November 9, 1911, be regarded, not only from the point of view of their present, but of their future value; but, unfortunately, they seem from this precise point of view very inferior to Morocco, for there can be no doubt that in the future Morocco will be a far more valuable possession for France than the Congo region for Germany, especially if that Spanish enclave cannot be obtained. The access to the Ubangi and the Congo has at present a more or less theoretical value, and could be barred in case of war with us by a few companies of Senegalese. It would be mere self-deception if we would see in the colonial arrangement which we have effected with France the paving of the way for a better understanding with this State generally. It certainly cannot be assumed that France will abandon the policy of revanche, which she has carried out for decades with energy and unflinching consistency, at a moment when she is sure of being supported by England, merely because she has from opportunist considerations come to terms with us about a desolate corner of Africa. No importance can be attached to this idea, in spite of the views expounded by the Imperial Chancellor, v. Bethmann-Hollweg, in his speech of

November 9, 1911. We need not, therefore, regard this convention as definitive. It is as liable to revision as the Algeciras treaty, and indeed offers, in this respect, the advantage that it creates new opportunities of friction with France.

The acquisition of territory in the Congo region means at first an actual loss of power to Germany; it can only be made useful by the expenditure of large sums of money, and every penny which is withdrawn from our army and navy signifies a weakening of our political position. But, it seems to me, we must, when judging the question as a whole, not merely calculate the concrete value of the objects of the exchange, but primarily its political range and its consequences for our policy in its entirety. From this standpoint it is patent that the whole arrangement means a lowering of our prestige in the world, for we have certainly surrendered our somewhat proudly announced pretensions to uphold the sovereignty of Morocco, and have calmly submitted to the violent infraction of the Algeciras convention by France, although we had weighty interests at stake. If in the text of the Morocco treaty such action was called an explanation of the treaty of 1909, and thus the notion was spread that our policy had followed a consistent line, such explanation is tantamount to a complete change of front.

An additional political disadvantage is that our relations with Islam have changed for the worse by the abandonment of Morocco. I cannot, of course, judge whether our diplomatic relations with Turkey have suffered, but there can be little doubt that we have lost prestige in the whole Mohammedan world, which is a matter of the first importance for us. It is also a reasonable assumption that the Morocco convention precipitated the action of Italy in Tripoli, and thus shook profoundly the solidity of the Triple Alliance. The increase of power which France obtained through the acquisition of Morocco made the Italians realize the importance of no longer delaying to strengthen their position in the Mediterranean.

The worst result of our Morocco policy is, however, undoubtedly the deep rift which has been formed in consequence between the Government and the mass of the nationalist party, the loss of confidence among large sections of the nation, extending even to classes of society which, in spite of their regular opposition to the Government, had heartily supported it as the representative of the Empire abroad. In this weakening of public confidence, which is undisguisedly shown both in the Press and in the Reichstag (although some slight change for the better has followed the latest declarations of the Government), lies the great disadvantage of the Franco-German understanding; for in the critical times which we shall have to face, the Government of the German Empire must be able to rely upon the unanimity of the whole people if it is to ride the storm. The unveiling of the Anglo-French agreement as to war removes all further doubt on this point.

The existence of such relations between England and France confirms the view of the political situation which I have tried to bring out in the various chapters of this book. They show that we are confronted by a firm phalanx of foes who, at the very least, are determined to hinder any further expansion of Germany's power. With this object, they have done their best, not unsuccessfully, to break up the Triple Alliance, and they will not shrink from a war. The English Ministers have left no doubt on this point.[A]

[Footnote A: Cf. speech of Sir E. Grey on November 27, 1911.]

The official statements of the English statesmen have, in spite of all pacific assurances, shown clearly that the paths of English policy lead in the direction which I have indicated. The warning against aggressive intentions issued to Germany, and the assurance that England would support her allies if necessary with the sword, clearly define the limits that Germany may not transgress if she wishes to avoid war with England. The meaning of the English Minister's utterances is not altered by his declaration that England would raise no protest against new acquisitions by Germany in Africa. England knows too well that every new colonial acquisition means primarily a financial loss to Germany, and that we could not long defend our colonies in case of war. They form objects which can be taken from us if we are worsted. Meanwhile a clear commentary on the Minister's speech may be found in the fact that once more the Budget includes a considerable increase in the naval estimates.

In this position of affairs it would be more than ever foolish to count on any change in English policy. Even English attempts at a rapprochement must not blind us as to the real situation. We may at most use them to delay the necessary and inevitable war until we may fairly imagine we have some prospect of success.

If the Imperial Government was of the opinion that it was necessary in the present circumstances to avoid war, still the situation in the world generally shows there can only be a short respite before we once more face the question whether we will draw the sword for our position in the world or renounce such position once and for all. We must not in any case wait until our opponents have completed their arming and decide that the hour of attack has come.

We must use the respite we still enjoy for the most energetic warlike preparation, according to the principles which I have already laid down. All national parties must rally round the Government, which has to represent our dearest interests abroad. The willing devotion of the people must aid it in its bold determination and help to pave the way to military and political success, without carrying still further the disastrous consequences of the Morocco policy by unfruitful and frequently unjustified criticism and by thus widening the gulf between Government and people. We may expect from the Government that it will prosecute the military and political preparation for war with the energy which the situation demands, in clear knowledge of the dangers threatening us, but also, in correct appreciation of our national needs and of the warlike strength of our people, and that it will not let any conventional scruples distract it from this object.

Repeal of the Five Years Act, reconstruction of the army on an enlarged basis, accelerated progress in our naval armaments, preparation of sufficient financial means—these are requirements which the situation calls for. New and creative ideas must fructify our policy, and lead it to the happy goal.

The political situation offers many points on which to rest our lever. England, too, is in a most difficult position. The conflict of her interests with Russia's in Persia and in the newly arisen Dardanelles question, as well as the power of Islam in the most important parts of her colonial Empire, are the subjects of permanent anxiety in Great Britain. Attention has already been called to the significance and difficulty of her relations with North America. France also has considerable obstacles still to surmount in her African Empire, before it can yield its full fruits. The disturbances in the Far East will probably fetter Russia's forces, and England's interests will suffer in sympathy. These are all conditions which an energetic and far-sighted German policy can utilize in order to influence the general political situation in the interests of our Fatherland.

If people and Government stand together, resolved to guard the honour of Germany and make every sacrifice of blood and treasure to insure the future of our country and our State, we can face approaching events with confidence in our rights and in our strength; then we need not fear to fight for our position in the world, but we may, with Ernst Moritz Arndt, raise our hands to heaven and cry to God:

"From the height of the starry sky
May thy ringing sword flash bright;

Let every craven cry
Be silenced by thy might!"

Printed in Great Britain
by Amazon

41907431R00086